GARLAND PUBLICATIONS IN AMERICAN AND ENGLISH LITERATURE

Editor
Stephen Orgel
Stanford University

GARLAND PUBLISHING, INC.

Magazine Editors and Professional Authors in Nineteenth-Century America

The Genteel Tradition and
the American Dream

Carol Klimick Cyganowski

GARLAND PUBLISHING, INC.
NEW YORK & LONDON 1988

Copyright © 1988
Carol Klimick Cyganowski
All Rights Reserved

Library of Congress Cataloging-in-Publication Data

Cyganowski, Carol Klimick.
  Magazine editors and professional authors in nineteenth-century America : the genteel tradition and the American dream / Carol Klimick Cyganowski.
    p. cm. — (Garland publications in American and English literature)
  Originally presented as the author's thesis (doctoral—University of Chicago, 1980)
  Bibliography : p.
  ISBN 0-8240-6384-8
  1. American fiction—19th century—History and criticism. 2. Journalism—United States—Editing—History—19th century. 3. American periodicals—History—19th century. 4. Fiction—Publishing—United States—History—19th century. 5. Authors and publishers—United States—History—19th century. 6. Journalism and literature—United States—History—19th century. I. Title. II. Series
PS374.J68C94 1988
813'.3'09—dc 19   88-16271

Printed on acid-free, 250-year-life paper
Manufactured in the United States of America

CONTENTS

ACKNOWLEDGMENTS iii

FOREWORD v

   I.   AMERICAN MAGAZINES IN THE NINETEENTH CENTURY 1

PART ONE
MAGAZINE EDITORS

   II.   JAMES RUSSELL LOWELL AND JAMES T. FIELDS:
        BEGINNINGS OF THE ATLANTIC MONTHLY 41

   III.   WILLIAM DEAN HOWELLS AND THE ATLANTIC MONTHLY 56

   IV.   THOMAS BAILEY ALDRICH AND THE ATLANTIC MONTHLY 120

   V.   GEORGE WILLIAM CURTIS AND PUTNAM'S,
       HARPER'S MONTHLY AND HARPER'S WEEKLY 156

   VI.   RICHARD WATSON GILDER AND SCRIBNER'S MONTHLY
       AND THE CENTURY ILLUSTRATED MONTHLY MAGAZINE 179

PART TWO
MAGAZINE CONTRIBUTORS

   VII.   HARRIET BEECHER STOWE 229

   VIII.   EDWARD EGGLESTON 248

   IX.   BRET HARTE 272

   X.   CHARLES W. CHESNUTT 295

CONCLUSION 312

SELECTED BIBLIOGRAPHY 318

ACKNOWLEDGMENTS

There are numerous scholarly debts in any dissertation, and for this study which ranges widely through the careers of major and minor figures in nineteenth century American literature and publishing, my indebtedness to literary critics and historians can barely be suggested. Among the scholars to whom I am most grateful for having gone before--finding, organizing, and interpreting large volumes of correspondence--are James C. Austin, whose <u>Fields of the Atlantic Monthly</u> (San Marino: The Huntington Library, 1953) brings together much of the significant correspondence with contributors in the <u>Atlantic Monthly</u>'s early years, and Donald R. Tuttle, whose Western Reserve University dissertation (1939), "Thomas Bailey Aldrich's Editorship of the <u>Atlantic Monthly</u>," is as yet the only thorough compilation of Aldrich's editorial letters.

To the late Frederick Anderson, I am indebted for his generous encouragement to use letters to Samuel Clemens in the Mark Twain Papers of the University of California Libraries, Berkeley. The Houghton Library of Harvard University and the New York Public Library allowed me access to their collections of letters for William Dean Howells and Richard Watson Gilder. The Department of Manuscripts and University Archives of the Cornell University Libraries was more than obliging in searching for and sending to me correspondence between Josiah Holland and Edward Eggleston.

FOREWORD

As we, in the last quarter of the twentieth century, consider the implications of a small number of conglomerates absorbing and reducing the variety of publishing enterprises in the United States, the soaring sales of popular formula romances coincident with a declining market for critically-lauded trade books, and the tenuous fortunes of innovative literary journals unable to share the market of large circulation national magazines with their stables of regular established contributors, it seems time to look again at the history of authorship as a profession in America. It has lately become fashionable to give scholarly attention to the phenomena of popular literature for mass audiences, but we still generally tend to see our first, classic American authors as primarily outside, and opposed by, the dynamics of practical publishing for a profit. The conflict between innovations in art and philosophy and the conservatism associated with a large, general readership has been especially interesting to Americanists because of our tradition of political democracy and our creation of a national literature in the modern world of technological innovation, increased literacy, an expanding middle class audience, and an established British literature. We have, however, tended to assess our literary accomplishment in terms of apexes of national achievement and to look toward failure in our cultural sensibility for explanations of stasis or insufficient recognition of those we have deemed great. Blaming American materialism, provincialism, conservative publishing establishments, etc., we have seldom considered the coalescence of the profit motives of popular publishing and the artistic accomplishment of literary quality-- except for our continual fascination with Mark Twain, the one seeming exception to the opposition of popularity and art, profit and literary accomplishment. With a few exceptions in the search for historical identity of special interest groups, we have also given comparatively little attention to the differing histories of publication and professional authorship in America's regions. Instead, we have created a general concept of American literary opportunities as restricted by a traditional eastern publishing establishment which stymied creative accomplishment, impeded the progress of American literature, and refused recognition to the vanguard by following rather than leading the broad popular audience.

From the beginning of this century, we have expressed this view of literary history in the identification of a "genteel tradition" in American culture and publishing. The "genteel tradition" got its name in George Santayana's 1918 address to the American Philosophical Society, "The Genteel Tradition in American Philosophy." Santayana claimed America was a country with two distinct mentalities: one traditional and feminine, controlling the "higher things of the mind . . . religion . . . literature . . . the moral emotions" and the other contemporary and masculine, dealing in the practical and "real" world of the everyday, "an expression of the instincts, practice, and discoveries of the younger generations." This disjunction had resulted, Santayana felt, in an atrophy of America's intellectual and artistic life:

> that one-half of the American mind, that not occupied intensely in practical affairs, has remained, I will not say high-and-dry, but slightly becalmed; it has floated gently in the back-water, while alongside . . . the other half of the mind was leaping down a sort of Niagara Rapids. . . . The one is the sphere of the American man, the other, at least predominantly, of the American woman. The one is all aggressive enterprise; the other is all genteel tradition.[1]

Though not using the phrase "genteel tradition," Van Wyck Brooks had declared "America's Coming-of-Age" in 1915 with a similar warning about separate "highbrow" and "lowbrow" value systems in America. Working from his theory expressed in the 1909 The Wine of the Puritans that a lingering American Puritan tradition favored materialistic over aesthetic concerns, Brooks described the predicament such oppositions created for a maturing society.

> In everything one finds this frank acceptance of twin values which are not expected to have anything in common: on the one hand, a quite unclouded, quite unhypocritical assumption of transcendent theory ("high ideals"), on the other, a simultaneous acceptance of catchpenny realities. Between university ethics and business ethics, . . . between academic pedantry and pavement slang, there is no community, no genial middle ground.[2]

---

[1] George Santayana, The Genteel Tradition: Nine Essays by George Santayana, ed. Douglas L. Wilson (Cambridge: Harvard University Press, 1967), pp. 29, 39-40.

[2] Van Wyck Brooks, "America's Coming-of-Age," in Three Essays on America (New York: E. P. Dutton, 1934), pp. 17-18.

From Santayana's distinction between feminine and masculine mentalities and Brooks's between the high brow and low brow fast developed a conception of literary relationships in which the masculine artist--presumably free, vital, realistic, and artistic-- is emasculated, repressed, and kept from his highest accomplishment by middle class cultural respectability, by audiences and editors who insist on gentility in literature. This required gentility was taken, most largely and generally, to mean propriety and reticence, unquestioning adherence to traditional cultural values, and separation between what is privately known and publicly discussed. Brooks rendered the deleterious effects wrought by the genteel Olivia Clemens, William Dean Howells, and eastern literary establishment in The Ordeal of Mark Twain (1920). While Brooks's estimate of Twain's failure of accomplishment brought attacks from critics, they accepted the concept of a repressive genteel tradition enforced by wives, editors, and a publishing and cultural climate which denied the "drastic reconstructions of life . . . essence of all masculine fiction," favoring "the moral and social taboos of the time" in a sort of "unconscious conspiracy against the creative life" which in "the cultural domination of this emasculated New England played into the hands of the business regime" (Ordeal, pp. 94-95).

H. L. Mencken joined the castigators of genteel influence and standards about the same time as Brooks, and in Mencken's iconoclasm there was surely no "genial middle ground." Mencken early and consistently attacked genteel pedants by retailing with mock incredulity the judgments of traditionalists, hooting at the professors who finally acknowledge Mark Twain's greatness, "indignant at the stupidity" of their predecessors, but who then attempt "to prove that Mark was really a great moralist, and more a great optimist." No progress was possible, according to Mencken, since "College professors, alas, never learn anything."--a point proven for Mencken in the treatment of Theodore Dreiser which he saw as a continuation of editorial and critical offenses against nineteenth century writers.[1] Mencken's sympathetic treatment of Dreiser in the 1917 A Book of Prefaces remained for some time the most common version of the "suppression" of Sister Carrie.

Santayana, Brooks, and Mencken set the parameters for considering literary history in terms of a genteel tradition which allowed the popular, feminine, and second-rate to override vital new literature. In 1926, Thomas Beer followed his first novel on the conflicting demands of art and commercialism and his biography of Stephen Crane with The Mauve Decade, an anecdotal cultural history which documented and popularized the effects of a genteel tradition in Americans' peculiar attitudes toward and veneration of women. Analyzing our literary development and the "extraordinary deference" paid to American women, Beer connected the restrictions of art and the promotion of popular sentiment in the nineteenth century to the romantic fiction of the 1920s in that both were "fictional flattery

---

[1] H. L. Mencken, "The Dreiser Bugaboo" in The Young Mencken, ed. Carl Bode (New York: Dial Press, 1973), p. 552.

of women." He traced the feminine dominance of American letters to the figure of "The Titaness" who, because of the American male's withdrawal from domestic and cultural concerns in pursuit of business, browbeat both the American husband and the American editor. Beer claimed, "if you were a proper editor, bred in the society of Newark or of Hartford, you did not trifle with the Titaness and for her sake you issued tales of women, by women, for women . . ." He saw the flattery of the countryside in the fiction of the 1840s developing into the feminine provincial's insistence on literature which flattered her sense of values, propriety, justice, and etiquette. Relating the complaints of outraged subscribers which influenced magazine editors, Beer found

> . . . not a trace of intellectual process. They were annoyed; etiquette had been battered or an opinion expressed they didn't like. It is the voice of the porch shaded by dusty maples along Grand Avenue in a hundred towns, a resolute violence of the cheapest kind, without breeding, without taste.
> The main topics of objurgations are three . . . A nice woman has been killed or failed of marrying the right man in some story. Liquor, including beer and claret, has been drunk by otherwise respectable people or has been mentioned without assault in an article. The story teaches nothing.

Beer clinched his case by telling how a manuscript from John Ford Bemis was rejected by editors of the major national magazines until finally H. M. Alden, for Harper's, suggested: "Would it not be possible to mitigate the final scenes: Is it strictly necessary that Mrs. Orme should die with her husband? We have so many ladies on the list of our subscribers . . ."[1]

---

[1] Thomas Beer, The Mauve Decade (New York: A. A. Knopf, 1926), pp. 50-52.

While Beer focused on the obeisance of editors to the taste of Grand Avenue matrons, Sinclair Lewis in his much-quoted 1930 Nobel Prize address redirected national and international attention to the split psyche which devalued the individual artist in favor of simplistic mass culture and business interests. Lewis's address reviled those who objected to him as "a man who had scoffed so much at American institutions" that his selection was "an insult to our country" by calling Dr. Henry Van Dyke, the principal objector and a member of the American Academy of Arts and Letters, a spokesman of the "genteel tradition" which repressed writers and "poisoned" literary accomplishment in America. Lewis explained to the international symposium that

> . . . most of us--not readers alone but even writers--are still afraid of any literature which is not a glorification of everything American . . . we still most revere the writers for the popular magazines who in a hearty and edifying chorus chant that the America of a hundred and twenty million population is still as simple, as pastoral, as it was when it had but forty million . . . that, in fine, America has gone through the revolutionary change from rustic colony to world empire without having in the least altered the bucolic and Puritanic simplicity of Uncle Sam.

The writer was kept from representing and rectifying American realities not only by fear, the popular magazines, and carry-overs of bucolic and Puritanic simplicities, but also by the role assigned to him in the culture, his existence outside its vital and practical life,

> . . . by the feeling that what he creates does not matter, that he is expected by his readers to be only a decorator or a clown, or that he is good-naturedly

>accepted as a scoffer whose bark is probably worse than his bite and who certainly does not count in a land that produces eighty-story buildings . . .

While Sinclair Lewis's total address hardly substantiated his title of "The American Fear of Literature," the force of his statement reflected the usefulness of the genteel tradition construct to progressives and crusaders in a variety of causes.

Literary histories, like Vernon L. Parrington's 1930 <u>The Beginnings of Critical Realism</u>, traced origins in the literary climate of the 1870s. New England magazines' dominance of American literature and gentility's rejection of "all frontier leveling and romantic liberalisms" had made "--a timid and uncreative culture that lays its inhibitions on every generation that is content to live upon the past. It was a penalty for backsliding." Parrington grounded his warning in exemplary lessons from nineteenth century publishing:

>The idea of morality--with its corollary of reticence--and the idea of excellence were well enough in the abstract, but became empty conventions, cut off from reality, they were little more than a refuge for respectability, a barricade against the intrusion of the unpleasant. In compressing literature within the rigid bounds of a genteel morality and a genteel excellence, New England was in a way of falsifying it.

He also intensified the identification of genteel standards and restriction of literature with New England's dominance of American culture and with the major national magazines.

>Boston determined American literary standards, and Boston taste rejected most of the new movements then getting under way. Stoddard and Stedman in New York,

Boker in Philadelphia, and Aldrich in Boston, stoutly upheld the genteel tradition, of which the *Atlantic Monthly* was the authoritative spokesman.[1]

Bernard DeVoto in 1932 targeted his *Mark Twain's America* as a rebuttal of Van Wyck Brooks's estimate of Twain's accomplishment and as an indictment of New England Brahmin society and the *Atlantic Monthly*, generated from DeVoto's rage at the eastern establishment's acceptance of Bret Harte and relative rejection of Mark Twain.

The phrase "genteel tradition" with its negative associations became generally used in viewing the progress of American literature and literary careers in a dialectic of conflict between moribund tradition and individual radical genius. It was a foil for castigating middle class sensibility and the failure of establishments and popular audiences to prefer "good" aesthetically or socially innovative writing over formulaic, ideal, sentimental, optimistic, nationalistic, sensational, or romantic mediocrity. Scholars found in the effects of the genteel tradition explanation for anomalies in the careers of their subjects and the meat of exegesis for studies of audience reception and publishing history. Sharing the delight of hindsight with their readers, critics created scenarios of repression, often aided by the selective reminiscences of repression's victims, like Hamlin Garland's 1930 *Roadside Meetings*. The genteel tradition expanded from a literary application to become a code to attack traditionalists of any stripe. By the 1930s, as Douglas Wilson has observed, even Santayana was "yielding

---

[1] Vernon L. Parrington, *The Beginnings of Critical Realism* (New York: Harcourt, Brace & Co., 1930), p. 54.

to what had become by then a common temptation to use the phrase as nothing more than a stick with which to beat one's adversaries."[1] In the 1931 "The Genteel Tradition at Bay," Santayana expressed his moral rationalist dissent to the Platonic-Christian New Humanism of Paul Elmer More, et. al. by characterizing them as decadent holdovers of genteel tradition values and "poetic self-indulgence."

The more contemporary criticism dealing with the existence and effects of a genteel tradition influencing American literary development has tended either to revision and reaction from the bold generalizations of adversary relationships or to detailed consideration of single figures or issues. Interest in the genteel tradition and editorial/publishing restrictions on American authors peaked in the 1930s through 1950s with dissertations, scholarly articles and books, introductions and editions offering diffuse alternative causes, explanations, and scenarios. The cumulative effect of a half-century of variant characterizations and genealogies is indicated in a 1954 University of Minnesota dissertation by Danforth R. Ross largely devoted to establishing the lack of consensus in uses of the term or concept of a "genteel tradition."

While some criticism has been directed toward arguing sources in Puritanism, middle class morality, eastern dominance of American economic life, the industrial revolution, and women's changing cultural role, others have concentrated on applying the new interest

---

[1] Douglas L. Wilson, "Introduction" to The Genteel Tradition: Nine Essays by George Santayana, p. 18.

in native American humor and language to increase the list of restricted material and approaches. Large historical reference works have drawn the general outlines and supplied details of objective publishing history and quantifiable audience reaction. Frank Luther Mott's work on American magazines stays within the realm of balanced recording, but James D. Hart's The Popular Book, still our general guide to American best sellers and the popular taste, seems to have so absorbed the association of the feminine with the negative that tabulations of the success of female writers are inevitably accompanied by derogatory judgments of the author or volume.

The most critical attention has gone, however, to arguing whether individuals are rightly placed in the circle of genteel belief or can be excluded from the full scope of indictment by associating them with alternative configurations of transcendentalism, neo-romanticism, political or social reform, etc. Analysis of the repressed has often focused around conflicts like the Bernard Duffey/James Koerner debate on whether Hamlin Garland "declined" from realism. Generally the focus on individuals has helped to redefine the strength and range of genteel strictures and the means by which they were enforced. We have learned, writer by writer and editor by editor, of the limitations on individual discretionary power, of aid and friendship between those who had been critically perceived as opponents, of changes in motive and action within lives that had been seen as static, and of multiple, and often prosaic extra-literary, factors involved in publishing incidents that had been taken as emblematic of the limitations of gentility and the popular audience.

Biographical approaches have tended to spotlight individuals' motives and possibilities for personal, political, social, and economic development using the publishing establishment. William Dean Howells and the Howells/Clemens relationship continue to get the most concentrated attention. Howells has been moved from the defender of sunny optimism to the pioneer of and crusader for realism of Edwin H. Cady's series to a deeply split and troubled personality in Kenneth Lynn's 1970 psychological biography, William Dean Howells, An American Life. Lynn sees Howells torn between alienation and driving ambition, balancing loyalty and gratitude to the Atlantic Monthly founders with support of the new realists in his relation to the popular audience and to his friends Clemens and James. Lynn's portrait develops within the original construct of the genteel tradition by its reference to the "woman standard" as criterion of literary judgment and its characterization of Olivia Clemens as "the prudish neurasthenic wife in this miserable censorship."[1] New work on Clemens, like Justin Kaplan's Mr. Clemens and Mark Twain and Hamlin Hill's Mark Twain, God's Fool, has provided a researched picture of Samuel and Olivia Clemens which bears little relation to our mythical conceptions of the restrained and repressed.

---

[1] Kenneth Lynn, William Dean Howells, An American Life (New York: Harcourt, Brace, Jovanovich, 1970), p. 160.

Our various new insights have not amounted yet to any radical reassessment of the genteel tradition's significance or of who ultimately belongs on the rosters of villains, victims, and victors.

Such reassessment as we have follows analyses like Malcolm Cowley's After the Genteel Tradition. When Cowley retraced the causes and connections, he saw "gentility" as an outgrowth of British Victorianism, though he felt

> . . . the Victorian spirit in America was also intermingled with the defiant optimism that grew out of pioneering and land speculation. There were always better farms to the westward. Prices would always go up, and the mortgage would be paid at the last moment . . . With this background of belief, many American books had the same innocently hopeful atmosphere as American real estate developments . . . To fail or simply to be discouraged in the midst of so many opportunities was not only a sign of weakness; it was a sin like adultery, and it could scarcely be mentioned in novels written for decent people.

Somewhat paradoxically in terms of this innocently hopeful optimism, Cowley found another source of the genteel tradition in a "moral reaction" against the wartime atmosphere, Reconstruction, and all the various unpleasantries of urban life: "In part it was an attempt to abolish the evils and vulgarities and sometimes the simple changes in American society by never talking about them." But like Sinclair Lewis, to whose Nobel Address Cowley gives prominent attention, the principal focus is on the opportunities denied to American art by the restrictions of the genteel tradition:

> The pity is that much or most of the reaction was not directed toward the real evils of American life at the time. Instead the chief effort of many reformers tried to keep them both unsullied by ignoring or denying the

brutalities of business life. Every cultural object that entered the home was supposed to express the highest ideals and aspirations. Every book or magazine intended to appear on the center table in the parlor was kept as innocent as milk. American women of all ages, especially the unmarried ones, had suddenly become more than earthly creatures; they were presented as milk-white angels of art and compassion and culture. "It is the 'young girl' and the family center table," Frank Norris complained in the 1890's "that determine the standard of the American short story."

The clear result of such standards, Cowley claimed, could be seen in the Atlantic Monthly under the editorships of William Dean Howells and Thomas Bailey Aldrich and in the other major literary magazines of the era: "Scribner's, Harper's and the Century were principal voices of the genteel era. Their standard of fiction was fairly high . . . but in matters of decorum, the standard was that of a rather strict girls' boarding school."[1] Without estimating the reality of American optimism or female innocence, Cowley's associations of the failure of optimism with "a sin like adultery" and his shift from "the brutalities of business" to the sanctified home are evocative both of the dualities consistently ascribed to the genteel era and of the link of economic imperatives with sexuality evident in comments from writers in the 1850s through scholars of the 1970s.

John Tomsich's 1971 A Genteel Endeavor, American Culture and Politics in the Gilded Age took on Vernon Parrington's characterization of the New York/Philadelphia/Boston literary coterie stoutly

---

[1] Malcolm Cowley, "Foreword: The Revolt Against Gentility" in After the Genteel Tradition, ed. Malcolm Cowley (1937; reprint ed., Carbondale: Southern Illinois University Press, 1964), pp. 5, 9-10, 11-12.

upholding Boston taste and the genteel tradition. Working from the
records of personal correspondence, Tomsich refutes the myth of
homogeneous belief, values, and action, claiming that the portrait
of genteel enforcers has been misdrawn expressly because of the
genteel separations between private life and public demeanor and
utterance. Tomsich shows his eight genteel figures as essentially
alienated atheists, who were aesthetics rather than moralists or
sunny optimists. Tomsich's search behind the public facade reveals
divisions with the group, attitudes toward women and the "Old Saints"
of New England literature which have little to do with respect,
private lives hardly consonant with middle class respectability, and
an essentially commercial motive for dealing with strictures,
conventions, and personalities that would most easily forward popular
success and reward.

Ann Douglas in The Feminization of American Culture (1977)
does not clash as strongly with the stereotypes of genteel figures,
but reinterprets the motive and force of gentility as an alliance
of middle class women and clergymen who took over the values of home
and culture in compensation for their disenfranchisement from active
participation in American economic life. Douglas's analysis sees
historical and poetic sensibility opposed by sentimental popular
literature, polarities which generally coincide with high vs. popular
culture, artistic vs. practical life, and repressive cultural
definitions of femininity vs. vital masculine life. In a chapter on
the periodical press, Douglas focuses on the enforcement of strictures

which react against radical vision and creative genius, producing instead novels like Henry Ward Beecher's Norwood.

Henry Nash Smith's Democracy and the Novel, Popular Resistance to Classic American Writers (1978) joins in Douglas's view of Norwood and uses the insights into popular literature of John G. Cawelti and others to reassess the strategies American writers developed to deal with the restrictions of the popular audience's sensibility and taste and with editorial suggestions and revisions. Smith's analysis follows directly from the early theories of Santayana and Van Wyck Brooks, and he stays with Brooks's 1920 Ordeal concept of William Dean Howells as a contrastive figure who accepted middle class values and enforced them on his friends and contemporaries. Smith does not, however, use Brooks's early insights into the motive power of "the pursuit of prestige" and freedom from financial worry nor Brooks's revised view of Howells's alienation and pessimism in the 1959 Howells, His Life and World. While Smith generally sees America's classic writers as outside and unaware of the formulas of popular literature, in Melville and others he discovers attempts at Shakespearean ploys to appeal simultaneously to the intellectual and popular audience with variously available levels of meaning.

Alongside the theses of art struggling against the reluctant mass mind, we have also linear studies of individual publishers and special regions. Eugene Exman has written a series of books on the Harper's empire which show publisher and writers in a continuum of political and economic change and corporate organization. Ellen

Ballou has written less extensively of Houghton & Mifflin. Publishing firms, at various centennials and anniversaries, have issued volumes of house correspondence showing progress, reaction, change. Both the West and South have had studies into their peculiar histories and dynamics, the myths seemingly necessary to audience, development, and self-image. Strangely enough, since so much of the battle of gentility has been seen as a battle against literary realism, the Midwest has not been separately examined. With all the attention given to Boston taste and New England dominance of American culture, the Midwestern origins of both writers and editors have seldom been part of the consideration. The family literary magazines which provided the largest audiences and fees for the majority of classic American nineteenth century writers--as well as for their popular counterparts--have not had their histories written apart from the publishers with which they were associated or the interests of individual editors.

Since most twentieth century scholars have worked from the original characterizations of a "genteel tradition," our criticism has generally been structured by the basic oppositions between high and popular culture, between feminine convention and masculine creativity, and between art and commerce. Much of the power of this literary history comes from its indictments of a publishing establishment, and specifically of a periodical press, which stultified American writers. If we move away from compiling emblematic instances of editorial repression and move away from positing an ideal world for writers, however, nineteenth century American magazines can be seen as essential, if imperfect, factors in making authorship a viable profession in the United States.

Rather than embodying a genteel culture separated from practical American economic life, the magazines represented attempts to make publishing literature practical and economically profitable. With few non-commercial means of sponsorship and patronage and in the absence of International Copyright, American writers could live by their work only by publishing in periodicals which made literature merchantable to consistent, large audiences. From the beginnings of the nineteenth century, American writers and thinkers found magazines the best way to attract an audience for a position or an author. The financially successful magazines, those which could offer generous compensation to contributors, were the most eclectic magazines. They printed a wide variety of material designed to appeal to all members of the literate American family. Marketing to a family audience inevitably brought limitations on appropriate material and language. Competition between magazines and between interest groups increased each publisher's concern for retaining his audience.

The broad picture of American magazine editors and contributors shows, however, not a dramatic conflict of adversaries but a gradual process of compromise and change. The most powerful editors were not of the eastern establishment or genteel society; they were practical entrepreneur publishers or upwardly mobile men of letters who made their own professional accommodations with the realities of American publishing. The financial rewards available through magazines drew men and women from throughout the United States. Personal ambition and artistic integrity warred within individuals. Both achievement and compromise were possible and frequent, but neither was inevitable; neither necessarily followed a consistent pattern.

This dissertation attempts to look at the realities and the personalities of those who developed and used major American magazines to establish authorship as a profession in the United States. After a historical survey of nineteenth century magazine publishing, Part I considers the backgrounds and policies of the editors who shaped the Atlantic Monthly, the Harper's magazines, Scribner's Monthly, and the Century Illustrated Monthly Magazine-- journals which dominated American literature in the second half of the nineteenth century. In the slow progress of yearly variations in the public taste and in the contrasts between individual editors and magazines, we can see both the possibilities for innovation and the limitations of the medium. In Part II, four American writers, representing a range of geography and material, provide a perspective on typical magazine contributors. All drawn to literature by opportunities in the magazines, their careers show the range of positive and negative effects in the contributor's role. Figures as diverse as Harriet Beecher Stowe, Edward Eggleston, Bret Harte, and Charles Chesnutt seem to have a great deal in common in terms of their professional roles. This dissertation does not offer a dramatic alternative to the "genteel tradition" concept of warring principles. It does show us men and women perhaps not so unlike ourselves, looking for profession and accomplishment and knowing that compromise is often necessary for survival and for friendship.

CHAPTER I

AMERICAN MAGAZINES IN THE NINETEENTH CENTURY

Despite the tone of discovery in twentieth century writing on the genteel tradition, American authors have long been conscious of separate audiences and levels of sophistication within the American readership. From the beginnings of the nineteenth century, men of letters tried to address and enlarge their audiences through the medium of magazines. Whether in support of a philosophical position or in search of additional income, periodicals were practical means for identifying, guiding, and insuring a consistent readership. The movements toward national identity, a native literature, and indigenous philosophy are inextricably bound in the history of our magazines. As national family magazines found unprecedented audiences in mid-century, the market for literature and the financial rewards of writing became identified with these successful magazines. The development was not unprecedented.

While few joined in the first forays of Noah Webster's 1789 clarion call for Americans to leave colonial subservience and use "the fairest opportunity of establishing a national language . . . that ever presented itself to mankind,"[1] there were soon many who,

---

[1] Noah Webster, Dissertations on the English Language (Boston, 1789), p. 36. Also quoted in Richard Bridgman, The Colloquial Style in America (London: Oxford University Press, 1966), p. 7.

in a variety of causes, were interested in a national literature. From these earliest days, the objection to British and Continental dominance came often combined with the promotion of American writers and writing, distinctive native ideas and subjects, and a sense of "the fairest opportunity of establishing" vehicles to make literature a marketable commodity and authorship a viable profession in America. At the beginning of the nineteenth century, motives toward a national literature and a literary profession began to be manifested in an increasing number and variety of American magazines, with the differences between the journals often a function of regional preferences and rivalries, religious conflict, and direction toward distinct segments of the American audience.

When Charles Brockden Brown, who is generally assigned the title of America's first professional writer, offered his first novel, Wieland, to the public of 1798, he conditioned its reception with an introductory "Advertisement." Brown informed his readers that a "favourable reception" would "induce the writer to publish" more such performances in a projected series. He began what would become something of an American authorial tradition in expressly distinguishing the tale he offered from the class of "ordinary or frivolous sources of amusement." He encouraged the public to accept his work by asserting its factuality and framing it as the work of the anonymous lady whose story it told, claiming for her a purpose only in satisfying the curiosity of interested friends. When Brown found the sale of his volumes would not alone support him, despite the advertisements which cajoled an audience to the acceptability of fiction, he began editing in New York The Monthly Magazine and American Review (1799-1801) which became the quarterly The American Review and Literary Journal (1801-1802). Brown offered nationalism and selections of his own writing and that of his New York literary circle. He edited the magazine toward the values evident in his own fiction: distinctively American subjects, interest in science, and belief that work of quality could appeal simultaneously to the American intellectual and common reader. When the New York magazine failed in 1802, Brown returned to his native Philadelphia, still convinced enough of the viability of magazines to establish and edit The Literary Magazine and American Register (1803-1807), which he turned into a semi-annual almanac, The American Register.

In Boston, the Anthology Club--later to become the Boston Athenaeum--registered its sense that America required higher literary standards and educated authors, and registered its upper class objection to the democratic vulgarity and provincialism of Noah Webster-style nationalism by beginning The Monthly Anthology and Boston Review (1803-1811), which would grow into The North American Review. Addressed to a select American audience and with a consistent Harvard orientation, The Monthly Anthology was associated with William Cullen Bryant, Daniel Webster, liberal religious thought and scathing literary criticism toward all that did not meet its standards. It had a steady, if small, patronage, and never made any money.

Conflict on the proper standards for American literature and the sense of discrete audiences and interests are evident early not only in the New England/New York/Philadelphia nexus, but also throughout the development of regional magazines and increased publishing opportunities for American authors. When in the 1820s and 1830s magazines were begun to serve and suit audiences neglected by the journals of the urban Northeast, their appeals were often argued directly to the potential audience as a requirement for support of vehicles which would offer alternative voices, positions, and interests to serve particular needs. The South developed journals expressly oriented to righting the balance of American writing, presumably otherwise dominated by northern and eastern establishment values. The Southern Review, based in Charleston from 1828 to 1832, promoted distinctively southern subjects and sensibility. The Southern Literary Messenger followed in Richmond, lasting from 1834 through 1864, representing the south and marketing to a southern chauvinism, but also allowing, in 1836, the expression of acrimony toward northern establishment ideals and literature in the writing and critical opinions of its flamboyant editor, Edgar Allan Poe. Poe increased the Messenger's subscriptions from five hundred, a usual number for minor magazines, to thirty-five hundred, a substantial serial audience for the first half of the nineteenth century. The national literary community's interest in Poe's Messenger centered in the critical feuds raging between Poe and the writers of New York's new The Knickerbocker Magazine, named in honor of Washington Irving, and also serving to promote Bryant, John Greenleaf Whittier, Henry Wadsworth Longfellow, Oliver Wendell Holmes, and Nathaniel Hawthorne.

While east coast literary men and intellectuals railed over artistic, philosophic, religious, and sectional differences, James T. Hall took his modest <u>Illinois Monthly Magazine</u>, which he had begun in 1830 and promoted as the first literary magazine west of the Ohio, to Cincinnati and developed it into the <u>Western Monthly Magazine</u>. Looking to a generally provincial audience, Hall opened his venture by decrying British influence on American literature and demanding patriotic patronage from subscribers to whom he promised an emphasis on regional and female writers, information, fiction, elegance, and moral instruction. To his potential contributors--among the first of whom was the young housewife, Harriet Beecher Stowe--Hall offered large dollar prizes in writing contests and the promise of American writers' receiving income from literature like that of their British counterparts. The western magazine rose and then failed in 1836--though not from its regional emphasis or nationalist view of literature, but from an attack by Lyman Beecher, whose feelings and beliefs were represented through the weekly Presbyterian papers. Beecher's personal acrimony and doctrinal dispute helped to replace the <u>Western Monthly</u> with <u>The Western Messenger</u> which, edited by W. H. Channing, lasted from 1835 through 1841 as a religious and literary periodical, with occasional transcendental leanings.

Conflicts over religious issues and transcendentalism added to the proliferation of magazines and the development of writers and literary coteries in the East. Ralph Waldo Emerson had begun to form his own transcendental philosophy and attitudes toward the New England religious establishment in concert with other young clergymen frustrated by their clerical superiors, making some of his early reputation from sermons preached at the invitation of dissenting New England congregations. When Emerson was called on as a substitute orator for the 1837 Harvard Phi Beta Kappa exercises, his address on "The American Scholar" galvanized the younger generation of the Boston/Harvard circle and the New York Knickerbocker to new directions and renewed vitality for the establishment of American literature. Oliver Wendell Holmes called Emerson's address "our intellectual Declaration of Independence"; James Russell Lowell felt it "an event without any former parallel in our literary annals."[1] Its impact and direction were a surge of interest in American literature as literature, and Emerson's urging writers to a "fit audience, though few" reopened, intensified, and specified the controversy between proponents of populist diversity and promulgators of educated standards--and produced a new surge of magazines.

Orestes Brownson attacked both transcendentalism's philosophic base and the anti-democratic isolation of Emerson's "fit audience" through beginning his own dissenting journal, the Boston Quarterly, in 1838. A continual liberal, Brownson used the Quarterly until

---

[1] Quoted in Newton Arvin, ed., "Ralph Waldo Emerson," in Major Writers of America, 2 vols. (New York: Harcourt, Brace & World, 1962), I;5, 501.

1842 and then the Democratic Review to promote the religions which
he successively adopted, a socialist's wide sense of audience, and
his theory that those who suggested America had insufficient culture
to develop a true literature were conspiring to create a self-
fulfilling prophecy. His magazines offered publishing opportunity
to writers unacceptable to other periodicals. When subscriber
complaints, primarily on religious grounds, closed the Democratic
Review to Brownson's writing, he formed Brownson's Quarterly Review,
which continued from 1844 to 1875 and reflected the editor's
variant identification with the Roman Catholic church.

However swiftly and surely the Harvard-connected American
writers could close ranks against those like Brownson or Poe, the
controversies and conflicts within their broader circle were
increasingly evident in the pulls of transcendentalism, literary
nationalism, the proper role of the litterateur to the popular
audience, and sufficient publishing opportunities, and many of the
battles produced new magazines, new audience appeals, and new
controversies.

When Margaret Fuller urged on her compatriots contributions
to and support for The Dial, founded in 1840, her plan of allowing
a hearing for all sides in the transcendental conflicts was
violently attacked by both contributors and readers for failing to
represent a single position and audience. Though the most general
support in the Concord circle for a strictly literary issue was
behind the "ban the nightingale" campaigns which expressed their

dissent from popular versifiers who retained European symbols and values, not even such a seemingly clear issue could effectively align the group's literary position, much less lead them to acknowledge such as Poe whose "Longfellow and Other Plagiarists" was the strongest expression of the indignation at popular support for literary flaks. When Fuller found that editing The Dial brought her only personal obloquy from insiders and outsiders, and no possibility of payment for her efforts, she turned over the job to Emerson. He restricted the magazine's pages to those who agreed in philosophy, taste, and linguistic standards, a policy which did not add to the sparse circulation or quell the calumny of the Fuller period, but which Emerson held to for his minority until he abandoned publication of The Dial in 1844.

Editors and contributors were having better luck in finding both audience and payment with other magazines. Successful journals which printed literature and could afford attractive payments to contributors seemed not to come from doctrinaire editing, feuding over American literary directions, or an audience proved "fit, though few." One of the most successful magazines in the first half of the nineteenth century was Philadelphia's Graham's Magazine from 1841 to 1858. Formed by a businessman from two earlier and lesser journals--Atkinson's Casket, a regional compilation of tidbits from 1826-1839, and The Gentleman's Magazine, later Burton's Gentleman's Magazine, a mixture of news, sports, the arts, British reprints, and short pieces from American writers--Graham's with Poe as its first literary editor parlayed an eclectic mix of contributors with various appeals to achieve a subscribership of thirty-seven hundred, more than a sevenfold increase from the combined total sales of the two earlier magazines. Graham paid his contributors well, and the magazine printed not only such established luminaries as William Cullen Bryant and Henry Wadsworth Longfellow, but also James Fenimore Cooper, James Russell Lowell, William G. Simms, and James K. Paulding. The prestigious contributors were not involved in the direction, philosophy, or critical positions of Graham's, and neither Poe nor his successors (who included Rufus Griswold, a compiler of anthologies of American writers) stayed long enough to personalize the magazine or to identify it with any restrictive interest or philosophy. Graham's maintained its profitability and its ability to get writers by paying good prices, by a combination of appeals to a variety of interests, use of recognized name writers in a mix with others, by lavishly colored fashion plates, and some of the best periodical engraving in illustrations of the 1840s.

As, and then more, successful and long lasting was another Philadelphia monthly, Godey's Lady's Book, which set national standards on fashion and taste as well as offering a mix of well-recompensed American authors who included Simms, Longfellow, Nathaniel Hawthorne, Oliver Wendell Holmes, Harriet Beecher Stowe, Ralph Waldo Emerson--and Edgar Allan Poe. Along with various sectarian journals, newspapers which printed and occasionally paid for literary contributions, and the usually short-lived adversary periodicals of New York and Boston, such magazines represented a substantial share of the publishing opportunities for Americans who wished to sell their writing in the first half of the nineteenth century.

Income and audience from magazine publication were essential to writers who had not caught fire with the popular fancy and whose talents were not oriented toward promotion through subscription book agents. Especially before the Civil War, few writers could rely on trade book volume sales of their work. William Cullen Bryant, for example, sold only 270 copies of his volume of Poems in five years.[1] Emerson and Irving, who did not maintain steady relationships with the most popular magazines, did not begin to see significant financial returns from their writing until, in their sixties and seventies, they established publishing relationships and audiences through the national magazines which developed in the last half of the century.

Complimentary critical opinion or collegial esteem for the quality of one's work was not a condition for entree to the more commercial magazines, nor did it strongly affect popular acceptance and sales of a given author. Editors often followed the popular reception and taste, or at least leavened their own positions and preferences with what had proven its appeal to a broad audience.

---

[1] James Hart, The Popular Book, a History of America's Literary Taste (1950; reprint ed., Berkeley and Los Angeles: University of California Press, 1963), p. 151.

Longfellow, one of the most popular and financially successful poets of the pre-War era, and the poet who would set watersheds of compensation in the 1870s, was continually under attack from critical opinion. As Thomas Wentworth Higginson recalled, Longfellow's early poetry, which "still retained the European symbols . . . just as if this continent had never been discovered," "exasperated" the transcendentalists who in the Dial and elsewhere promoted the native in literature.[1] The resistance of some of the American literary community and negative valuations of his artistry and originality failed to hurt Longfellow's popular appeal or to influence the directions of his art. Howells reported that later in Longfellow's career when "coarse-handed British criticism began to blame his delicate art for the universal acceptance of his verse," Longfellow reacted to "the ill-will that seemed nearly always to go with adverse criticism"[2] and the sneering estimates of his literary quality by ignoring criticism generally. As Longfellow was one of the few who before the Civil War could count on relatively substantial sales of his volumes--with the first dozen accounting for sales over 150,000-- American writers tended to associate his success with the appeal of native subjects, accessibility and underdeveloped audience taste. As Longfellow came to increasingly dominate popular American poetry from major publishers, the criticism became sotto voce in the United

---

[1] Thomas Wentworth Higginson, Margaret Fuller Ossoli (1890; reprint ed., New York: Greenwood Press, 1968), p. 138.

[2] William Dean Howells, "The White Mr. Longfellow" in Literary Friends and Acquaintance, 2nd Ed. (1910; reprint ed., Bloomington: Indiana University Press, 1968), p. 168.

States.

      The importance of American litterateurs' supporting their own and having a range of magazine publishing opportunities came in large part from the peculiarities and monopolies in American book publishing. In 1817, the Harper brothers, New York printers and entrepreneurs, had stepped into the void of reliable native purveyors of literary materials. Beginning with reprints of classic works by centuries-dead authors, the Harpers offered America volumes and then series at prices not much higher than the cost of an almanac or newspaper. By the 1830s, the Harpers were the biggest publisher in the United States, making innovations in production techniques, illustration, and merchandising which firmly established the profitability of their book publishing enterprise and dominance of the national market. On the Harper's list of 234 titles in 1833, less than 10 percent were from American writers. With nc International Copyright, the work of even popular contemporary British authors came relatively cheap to the American publisher, and protection of profit margins and technological innovations worked together to pit mercantile advantage against any demands of literary nationalism. A new printing method, for example, allowed for clearer reproduction of type, but its cost was offset by the increased ease of storing plates--encouraging publication of works likely to have a sustained audience through successive editions. The American books which met the needs of such a volume publisher were relatively few. James Harper felt that "Travels sell about the best of anything we get ahold of," but distinctly American biographies, like J. K. Paulding's Life of Washington, and adventures, like R. H. Dana's Two Years Before the Mast, were also leaders in the Harper's small selection of American work--though Dana, for one, never got a significant share of the profits his book brought to the publisher.[1]

Much as the Harper's mercantile spirit and failure to support American authorship rankled the American literary community, their merchandizing methods and control over the American audience were considered, by applauders and detractors, of even more lasting significance. The Harper methods encouraged consumer loyalty, especially within the expanding market of the upwardly mobile actual or potential middle class family. Not only the classical reprints but all Harper books were marketed in series to Americans in search of family libraries. In elegant editions, with choice of a variety of bindings, the Harpers produced sets of from six to one hundred eighty-seven volumes, priced in single volume and series under the market for books from other publishers. Harper's promoted itself with guarantees that the books were selected by an editorial board of "gentlemen of high literary acquirements and correct taste" and the buyer could "rest assured that no works will be published by J&J H but such as are interesting, instructive, and moral."[2] Some commentators saw the Harper's phenomenon as a boon to the education

---

[1] Eugene Exman, The House of Harper (New York: Harper, 1967), pp. 10-11, 14, 21.

[2] Exman, House, p. 11.

and literacy of the nation; those with less vigorous democratic
sentiments and more direct interest in the enterprise of writing
tended to see Harper's as an unwarranted restrictive force. After
Thoreau's publisher returned to the author most of the print run of
the 1849 Week on the Concord and Merrimack, Thoreau in Walden
directly attacked the Harper's firm for its audacity and efficiency
in determining what Americans would read.

Harper's did not have the early mainstream American book
market entirely to itself. In 1832, William D. Ticknor had established his own Boston book publishing firm in conjunction with
acquiring Boston's Old Corner Bookstore. One of the firm's first
associations with a major New England writer was publication of a
medical book by Oliver Wendell Holmes, but it was Longfellow who soon
became the firm's mainstay and biggest seller. Lowell, Whittier,
Hawthorne, Emerson, and Thoreau were soon added to the publisher's
list, but only Longfellow found enough favor with the book-buying
audience to reap substantial rewards. The infamous controversy
which later developed between Hawthorne's widow and the publisher
resulted from a long-standing practice of cutting royalty percentages
when an author's books were not volume sellers, and the majority of
Ticknor's prestige authors still relied most on income from other
sources and magazine publishing.

While Ticknor marketed to a more educated and urban, and
theoretically more urbane, audience than the Harper's, it was
Boston's Old Corner Bookstore that returned Wuthering Heights to

Harper's, its publisher, because of customer protests over the book's immorality. When James Fields, who came to the American book industry through a clerkship in the bookstore, became a junior partner in the firm in 1849 and half owner in 1854, the firm became even more responsive to the necessity of promoting public acceptance of the publisher and its authors. Competing with Longfellow for sales were Rufus Griswold's anthologies of American writers, produced with the editorial assistance of Fields and dominated by the publisher's authors. Fields encouraged the public to see his Bostonians as major and inevitable American men of letters, developing book reviewing as essentially an adjunct to direct advertising, supplying house-written reviews on his books and authors, and using his personal influence, friendship, and favors to expand sales outside New England.

James Fields's mercantile practicality coincided in many ways with the attitudes of Holmes, *et. al.* to the broad American audience and the future of American authorship. The large audiences necessary to popularity and publishing success were seen as representing an undeveloped taste, easily influenced by the power of the churches, social mores, and publicity. The literary world balanced selecting for them what they would and should read, educating the public through authoritative statement and criticism from prestigious voices, but not outrunning public sentiment. Within this climate, reaction to failures to find favor with a popular audience often came in terms of castigation of the public or of the effects of competition which denigrated the literary enterprise by a lowering of standards to meet the available audience. Hawthorne complained to his publisher Ticknor in 1855,

> America is now wholly given over to a damned mob of scribbling women, and I should have no chance of success while the public taste is occupied with their trash--and should be ashamed of myself if I did succeed. What is the mystery of these innumerable editions of The Lamplighter, and other books neither better nor worse?--worse they could not be, and better they need not be, when they sell by the hundred thousand.[1]

Hawthorne clearly saw his work, as many of his colleagues would throughout the century, competing for the same audience that bought popular, and often pietistic or risque, novels. Hawthorne shortly later wrote to Ticknor again, recanting some of the venom and wholesale nature of his indictment of the women. He had read Fanny Fern's Ruth Hall, and rather admired the deviltry of the woman, Sarah Payson Willis, sister to N. P. Willis, who established a character recognizably her brother, as a man who "recognizes only the drawing room side of human nature."[2] The question of editors like N. P. Willis and story newspapers like the New York Ledger, in which Fanny Fern appeared, recognizing "only the drawing room side of human nature" was especially current in mid-century as national magazines developed to dominate the serial publishing market in much the same way the major book publishers covered the volume market.

---

[1] Quoted by Hart, Popular, p. 93.

[2] Hart, Popular, p. 95.

In 1850, Harper's developed its own magazine, Harper's Monthly, patterned after popular British periodicals. Harper's Monthly Magazine was essentially the first full-scale national literary periodical. Begun as a leader to the business of the firm which dominated American mass market publishing, as a means of both developing and advertising writers and books, the Monthly was controlled by Fletcher Harper, the most venturesome of his generation of Harper brothers. Its immediate success surprised even its publishers, who quickly moved from a print order of seventy-five hundred for the first number to fifty thousand by the end of the first year. In 1852, Harper's Monthly absorbed The International Monthly, a journal which Rufus Griswold, after developing the anthologies for Ticknor and editing Graham's, had begun in 1850 as a direct competitor to the Harper's magazine. By 1853, Harper's was printing 125,000 copies of each issue of their Monthly, recycling much of the profits for expanded and improved illustrations, and proving the existence of a large American audience for family magazines.[1]

Harper's Monthly's early popular success depended on the superb illustrations and on serial publication of major British novels, often managed so that the subscriber would have to renew in order to finish the current feature. Harper's and James Fields had competed throughout the 1840s for identification of their firms with Dickens and Thackeray, and with the Monthly Fletcher Harper kept his personal

---

[1] Exman, House, pp. 69, 77.

relationship with the popular British authors and a "directing hand" over the overall management of the magazine. The Monthly was nominally edited by Henry J. Raymond until 1856 when Raymond left for his newly founded New York Times; Alfred Guernsey, a Harper house scholar and translator, took over the post until 1869, but the journal was always clearly identified with the publisher's overall practices and plan rather than with any individual man of letters. While the Monthly published little creative work from American writers and offered no opportunity to the major Bostonians, its editorial and critical departments were open to the next generation of aspiring writers. George William Curtis was among the first of the magazine's editorial essayists, but his ambitions for American literature were larger than Fletcher Harper's use of it.

In 1853, Curtis and two associates started Putnam's Magazine, named for their first publisher, committed to printing American writers--a deficiency for which Curtis publicly criticized Harper's Monthly even as he continued to write for that magazine, and promoted with advance notices of contributions from the Concord/ Boston circles. Curtis solicited promises of work from Emerson, Hawthorne, Lowell, and others of the Ticknor list; the replies were skeptical. Emerson asked if Curtis thought it likely he could "hold the journal to anything like literature and humanity, and away from that moribund respectability to which everything American tends."[1]

---

[1] Emerson to Curtis, November 1, 1852, Houghton Library, Harvard, quoted in Gordon Milne, George William Curtis and the Genteel Tradition (Bloomington: Indiana University Press, 1956), p. 65.

Though Curtis attempted to develop his audience and bowed sufficiently to respectability that he offended his friend Thoreau by deleting anti-clericism from his manuscripts, the magazine went under with substantial losses in 1857. Curtis moved back to a full-time relationship with Harper's, claiming he had been convinced that "The public of intelligence and moral heroism is not large enough, nor enough interested in such a magazine as Put to make it pay."[1]

Fletcher Harper, in contrast, was doing so well with the Monthly that he added a weekly illustrated family newspaper, Harper's Weekly, in 1857. The Weekly set itself off with the quality and currency of its illustrations and publication of critical essays on literature and a great deal of fiction. As the nation approached the Civil War, the editorial and essay departments had wide influence and readership, enough so that when Charles Norton in 1859 attempted to lure Curtis away from the commercial Harper's to form a new magazine, Curtis declined. He questioned whether there were sufficient new readers left in the market to support the kind of magazine Norton wanted, and claimed there was greater power to lead and persuade in addressing the eclectic broad audience the Harper's illustrated magazines attracted for him. During the war years, the Harper's would boast that their editorials were read by 500,000, with more readers reached through quotation from Harper's magazines in the daily newspapers. Print orders for the Weekly at peaks of interest

---

[1] Quoted in Milne, Curtis, p. 66.

ran as high as 300,000.[1]

"The public of intelligence" Curtis had tried to attract with *Putnam's* and the New England writers he had published were being served with the new Boston-based *Atlantic Monthly*. The impetus to form the *Atlantic* came first from Francis H. Underwood, who approached James Russell Lowell in 1853 about starting a magazine in the abolitionist cause, but Lowell and Underwood were unable to put together a package of policy, publisher, and contributors until 1857, when Philips, Sampson and Company, a publisher previously undistinguished except for having printed two of Harriet Beecher Stowe's books, underwrote the venture. The *Atlantic Monthly* began with a meeting of founding contributors, the Atlantic Club of Holmes, Whittier, Longfellow, Lowell, Emerson, in Boston's Parker House. Holmes named the new magazine, and the founders established a policy of commitment to American Literature and representation of the New England voice in American letters and public policy. Their direction was generally abolitionist, though unconnected with party identification, in policy and dignified promotion of quality in literature. The magazine which evolved under Lowell's editorial hand clearly reflected its origins. With a preponderance of contributors from the immediate Boston and Cambridge environs, the *Atlantic* was heavy with Harvard-based writers' disquisitions on history, classical antiquity, and scientific questions. The *Atlantic* acquired a sterling reputation

---

[1] Exman, *House*, pp. 84, 88.

augmented by the recognition value of its founding contributors, who were soon joined by Harriet Beecher Stowe.

Holmes in his *Autocrat* series ventured into new areas which attracted criticism and also interest and readership. William Dean Howells remembered that in Ohio the *Atlantic Monthly* represented the highest culture and literature, taking the place of Curtis's short-lived *Putnam's*. Emerson's and Thoreau's writing of John Brown identified the magazine with a New England support of abolitionism, but the *Atlantic's* image of prestige and fairness led Abraham Lincoln to feel years later that it would be best to publicize Jefferson Davis's statement that he could continue to fight for independence, not for slavery, in the *Atlantic Monthly* since it would have a "less partisan look" there.[1] Lowell's *Atlantic* never approached the circulation of Harper's mass market illustrated magazines, but with a subscribership of around twenty thousand, it operated at a profit and paid both contributors and editor.

When settlement of the original publisher's estate and failure of the parent publishing firm required selling the *Atlantic* in 1859, Lowell refused to take it on himself, and the journal was bought by Ticknor. Fields was soon involved in management of the magazine, beginning in 1860 the first advertisements in an American literary magazine, encouraging Lowell to move from the heavy scholarly

---

[1] Ellery Sedgwick, ed., *Atlantic Harvest* (Boston, 1947), pp. 239-241, quoted in James C. Austin, *Fields of The Atlantic Monthly* (San Marino: The Huntington Library, 1953), p. 32.

essays to more broadly popular story approaches and contemporary subjects, and generally applying his bookseller's ability to "gauge a man's depth in the public-reading estimation"[1] to suggestions for the magazine. Fields became the Atlantic's editor in 1860, and for ten years changed and promoted the magazine from the courage of his own convictions about American writers and the American audience. Fields's policies made the Atlantic a competitor and a significant force in the American literary marketplace. Subscriptions were up to thirty-two thousand by 1863 and to fifty thousand in 1870,[2] though significant losses were sustained in controversies over work from Holmes and Stowe. Most of the contributors to Fields's Atlantic were well-paid in both dollars and association with the most prestigious names in American literature and society, though not everyone was delighted with the Atlantic's Old Guard or New England orientation.

Howells has reported that many of his Midwestern contemporaries felt the Atlantic was closed to submissions which did not carry a Boston, or at least a New York, postmark, and actually there were few contributors in the first years from outside the Boston area. Accusations of New England insularity in the Atlantic became rather common, along with accusation that eastern publishers were dominating

---

[1] Fields to Bayard Taylor, December 26, 1848, Fields Collection, Huntington Library, quoted in Austin, Fields, p. 25.

[2] Frank Luther Mott, A History of American Magazines (Cambridge: Harvard University Press, 1938), II, 505-506.

and controlling American literature and literary recognition and opportunity. Fields's concentration, as both publisher and editor, on most highly rewarding and promoting the original Ticknor & Fields coterie of Brahmin writers and his willingness to allow them freedom not available to youngsters and outsiders encouraged the new generation's close observation of the old line literary figures and resentment of their attitudes and prerogatives.

Much as Hawthorne had complained of the "scribbling women" in the 1850s, the New York aesthetic group, which is often described as the nineteenth century's genteel circle, complained of the Bostonians. The wealthy Philadelphian roué George Boker wrote to his penurious friend Richard Henry Stoddard in 1864 that they "should not expect to be popular in an age when Longfellow is a great poet,"[1] and that their time would come only when the older generation was gone from the market--and the world. Disappointment with the New England pantheon wasn't restricted to those who felt competition for the public favor. Many of the new generation writers who would develop American subjects and realistic approaches came to literature and to Boston with a combination of hero worship for the literary masters, developed political or social ideas, and some identification with their native regions. They were chagrined to find their heroes abstracted from the concerns of everyday American life, and often

---

[1] Quoted in John Tomsich, <u>A Genteel Endeavor</u> (Stanford: Stanford University Press, 1971), p. 144.

offering pontification or curiosity rather than colleagialty to their new young colleagues. William Dean Howells's memories are the most widely circulated, but his experience is echoed again and again. Rebecca Harding remembered that "I went to Concord, a young woman from the backwoods, firm in the belief that Emerson was the first of living men," but that she found among America's famous men of letters only a rarified, desiccated, lifeless courtesy: an interest not in the men and women of America as fellow souls, not in the reality of American experience or the interests of the American audience, but in a soft experimental theoreticality. Of Emerson, Harding concluded,

> He studied souls as a philologist does words, or an entomologist beetles. He approached each man with bent head and eager eyes. "What new thing shall I find here?" . . . He took from each man his drop of stored honey, and after that the man counted for no more to him than any other robbed bee.[1]

Still, for all the ambiguity they might feel about the social and personal attitudes of the Old Guard and the publishers who gave preference to the established New England writers and to popular British novelists, many of the generation coming forward in the 1860s thought their best chances of publication, payment, and prestige lay with the eastern magazines and publishers. Many of the new contributors who came into the magazines after the Civil War were westerners and midwesterners whose parents had been drawn from the east by the promise of western opportunities. Their sons' and daughters' literary

---

[1] Quoted in Tillie Olsen, "A Biographical Interpretation" with Life in the Iron Mills (New York: Feminist Press, 1972), pp. 105, 107.

aspirations and drives for recognition often reversed this migration. Whether they complained of eastern dominance, restrictions, or the American audience, the young of the frontiers tended to follow the eastern star of literary recognition and its established means and confined routes to overcome their frequent lack of formal education and fears of financial necessity in combinations of journalistic or editing jobs and magazine publication of creative work.

Howells remembered that when he "came to Boston early in 1866, the Atlantic Monthly and Harper's then divided our magazine world between them,"[1] and certainly in the 1860s James Fields in Boston and Fletcher Harper in New York proceeded as if the magazine world was theirs to divide. Their magazines were all the more important since post war inflation in the United States dramatically affected book production costs and put American publishers at a disadvantage in competition with British imports. Harper's Weekly, the magazines, and the daily newspapers editorialized on the crisis situation for American books. For a brief period in 1864, Harper's Monthly's profitability and circulation declined enough so that Fletcher Harper considered dropping the magazine so that it and the trade books' problems would not together harm the firm's financial position, but the combined draws of Dickens's Our Mutual Friend and Wilkie Collins's Armadale revived the Monthly. Fletcher Harper and James Fields began a battle of magazines, in part to compensate the losses

---

[1] Howells, "Literary Boston as I Knew It" in Literary Friends and Acquaintance, p. 106.

on book publishing necessitated by undercutting their own costs to
meet the prices of publishers like Chicago's Donnelly which, in the
Lakeside Press, was doing strong business in cheap reprints, often
priced closer to the popular dime novels than even the cheapest of
Harper's volumes. Both firms developed magazines which were more
national and broadly based to keep and increase their share of
multiple American markets.

Ticknor & Fields had bought the North American Review,
reinvigorating its fortunes but leaving control to its joint editors,
Lowell and Charles Norton. The North American Review was never
profitable, but Fields maintained it (as the Harper's would when they
bought the magazine later in the century) as a prestige, low-budget
item in the firm's spectrum of products. The North American Review
took over the concentrations and interests Lowell had promoted while
editor of the Atlantic, and Fields made the Atlantic into his popular,
though high-toned, literary magazine. The firm also developed Every
Saturday, an eclectic weekly of foreign reprints edited by Thomas
Bailey Aldrich, in 1866, and Fields entered the juvenile market
previously served only by religious journals with Our Young Folks.
Fields encouraged contributors to write for his newest magazines and
succeeded in getting even James Russell Lowell to try composing
fantasies for the children's magazine--though Lowell admitted he had
never even seen Our Young Folks.

Fletcher Harper wrangled his brothers into starting Harper's
Bazar in 1867, not only basing it on the popular German Bazar but also

even using offprints of the German magazine's illustrations. The Bazar combined its fashions and advice with seven or eight serial novels a year, and in the first six weeks achieved a circulation of 100,000.[1] The Bazar's editors assured American women, no matter how removed they were from fashionable or social centers, that the magazine could lead them to the proper clothes, roles, and manners-- as well as providing the most current fiction reliably and at easy prices. Harper's attempted to follow Fields's lead of diversified magazines from one firm more directly with Harper's Young People, begun in 1879. Harper's marketing techniques were evident in the firm's "sending the first thirty issues free to all subscribers of the other three journals, along with subscription blanks,"[2] a price of only five cents an issue, and Harper's willingness to expand the journal, but Young People was never a success, perhaps because independent magazines followed Ticknor & Fields's lead and glutted the market before Harper's entered it.

The three major Harper's magazines were successful and either growing or maintaining their positions. The Weekly, by publishing Thomas Nast's cartoon attacks on Boss Tweed, was earning the praise of the daily newspapers and increasing interest and circulation to bring print orders of 300,000. Though the ring counterattacked by canceling New York's contract for Harper school texts, the firm, at the

---

[1] Exman, House, p. 121.

[2] Exman, House, p. 139.

insistence of Fletcher Harper, held firm to its position and parlayed popular sympathy to increased sales and prestige. In 1869, Harper's moved Henry Mills Alden from the increasingly political *Weekly* to become editor of the *Monthly*, and George William Curtis turned down the editorship of the *New York Times* to stay with the Harper's and concentrate on the *Weekly*. Alden had come to Harper's fresh from Andover Theological Seminary, and he stayed throughout his career, holding, with varying levels of responsibility, the title of *Harper's Monthly* editor for fifty years. Unlike editors of magazines for other firms, Alden seldom had exclusive decision making power or final control over what the magazine published. At Fletcher Harper's death, his role in directing the magazine was taken over by first Joseph W. Harper and then J. Henry Harper, though these two allowed Alden more freedom and flexibility.[1]

For all of Fields's and Harper's attempt to corner the magazine market in the boom years of the late 60s, the resurging economy also drew their attention back to their now more successful and profitable book publishing businesses. The attractions and influence of magazines were also not lost on a number of other publishing entrepreneurs, regional promoters, literary nationalists, and dissidents to the mass publishers' restrictions on American writing. Though none of the competitors ever achieved the stature or circulation of the combined Harper's ventures, the alternative literary magazines which

---

[1] Exman, *House*, pp. 75, 77-79, 87-88.

developed after the Civil War provided publishing options for new writers uncomfortable with or unwelcome in the primary magazines.

A group centered in New York began The Galaxy in 1866, expressly as a counter to the New England focus of the Atlantic Monthly. Though Howells, as the Atlantic's assistant editor, and Fields, as editor, were trying to diversify the list of Atlantic contributors, they hardly treated the Galaxy as a competitor like the Harper's magazines. Many of the new writers Howells brought to the Atlantic in the late 1860s also published in the Galaxy, and Howells even advised colleagues to submit work there when he could not or did not wish to use it himself. While Samuel Clemens was in his Buffalo residence in 1870-71, he conducted an editorial department in the Galaxy, and most American writers of the Howells/Clemens generation had some association with both the Boston Atlantic and the New York Galaxy. When the Galaxy went under, its subscription list was sold to the Atlantic.

Other journals, like the Overland Monthly which did so much to publicize Bret Harte and his California contemporaries, fed into the eastern magazines. Writers often republished work which had appeared in the regional journals in the national magazines and relied on such magazines' publicity to promote book sales outside their native regions.

Charles Scribner & Co., not wishing to miss the profit and promotion opportunities that a national literary magazine offered, began in 1868 to plan an expansion of their modest publicity vehicle,

Hours at Home. Scribner attempted to interest the popular Josiah Holland in editing and developing a major national magazine under the Scribner's imprint. The promotion of magazines by naming popular writers as editors was a growing practice, and Holland had proven himself with sales of over fifty thousand for his Timothy Titcomb series and a consistent reliable sale of anything under his name. Holland resisted a relationship with a Harper's Monthly-style wholly-owned publisher's magazine, and not until he talked over Scribner's plans with wealthy entrepreneur Roswell Smith in Europe, did Holland have an alternative plan under which he would consent to edit a magazine. Holland and Smith proposed a separate corporate entity, with shared ownership and discrete management roles for the partners: Holland having editorial responsibility and total freedom--and 30 percent, Smith having fiscal responsibility and marketing independence--and 30 percent, and Charles Scribner providing name and identity--with 40 percent.[1]

The independence and separation of management between Holland, Smith, and Scribner were unique among American magazines. Although Scribner's was an illustrated family magazine like Harper's Monthly, it compensated for its late entry to the magazine competition by generally using popular writers already well known to subscribers. Holland also saw his journal as superior in mission and effect. In

---

[1] Herbert F. Smith, Richard Watson Gilder (New York: Twayne, 1970), p. 16.

defending his own taste for controversy, Holland claimed he would not "cut the magazine off from the resources of popularity and influence" which Christian leadership could bring, and that "Harper's monopolizes the market for harmless and inoffensive literary pap."[1] So Holland promoted the didactic in editorials, literature, and pop theology. From the beginnings of Scribner's Monthly late in 1870, however, Holland's rigid directions were offset in his assistant editor, Richard Watson Gilder, the young former editor of Hours at Home, who balanced Holland's preferences with his own editorial department strictly devoted to literature and the arts, with support of young American artists, and with an express distaste for authorial preaching.

Perhaps as important in terms of the future of American magazines and their support of professional authorship, Roswell Smith applied his considerable personal political and marketing skills to innovative magazine financial management. Smith not only followed the Harper's with illustrations, but jumped into the burgeoning area of magazine advertising by offering space rates at one-fifth the Harper's prices. Subscribers got a magazine as bulky as most trade books, and Smith offset the increased size by beginning the use of pre-paid bulk mailing for magazines,[2] fostering reliance on selling the magazine by subscription to a widely scattered national audience.

---

[1] Robert Underwood Johnson, Remembered Yesterdays (Boston: Little, Brown and Company, 1923), p. 87 and Holland to Charles Scribner, October 15, 1869, Scribner Company Archives, quoted in Smith, Gilder, p. 17.

[2] Smith, Gilder, p. 18.

Scribner's scattered subscribers opened it to more than the usual variety in charges of favoring one region or one sectional political perspective. Sometimes simultaneous charges claimed Scribner's was dominated by eastern, southern, and northern writers and opinions.

Scribner's actual primary biases were Holland's aversions to what he saw as immoral or politically partisan. While such restrictions meant love stories whose protagonists often seemed sexually neuter and articles on public issues which usually reflected Holland's own judgments, much like the Timothy Titcomb advice and entertainment for young people which had made Holland popular, the magazine's policy of offering what Holland described in the first number as material to "interest and instruct every member of the family"[1] was highly marketable. While subscribers to Scribner's Monthly wrote objections to articles and stories much the same as those which came to more artistically progressive magazines, the overall mixture remained attractive enough to a wide variety of consumers to build a circulation of 140,000 by the end of the 1870s. With advertising revenues usually more than offsetting production costs, the magazine was able to offer contributors some of the highest rates available in American publishing, and many found themselves able to offer something which would meet Scribner's Monthly's standards. Readers found not only some of the Old Guard, like William Cullen Bryant, but also the new generation of Gilder's New York circle,

---

[1] Smith, Gilder, p. 20.

who liked so much to complain of the crass and undeveloped American taste, and regional writers like Edward Eggleston, who wrote his first love stories for Scribner's Monthly even as he edited his own magazine.

When the Scribner sons in the late 1870s pushed for a greater connection between the popular magazine's serial novels and the firm's book publishing, both Holland and Roswell Smith resisted a closer relationship. In 1881, Smith bought full control of the magazine, recapitalizing and reorganizing it as The Century Illustrated Monthly Magazine with the younger and more artistic Richard Watson Gilder as editor.

Scribner's Monthly had gained its success in the 1870s and Harper's Monthly had continued to prosper by concentrating on offering a variety of perspectives and materials. Support of a single critical direction, both in reviews and in selection of material, had been the feature of the Atlantic Monthly, which in the 1870s had represented William Dean Howells's support of realism and native subjects. The Atlantic had gained respect, reputation, and a sort of mentorship over new American writing. It and its editor had also suffered from contributors who wished the magazine to go further in moving away from its Brahmin origins or in vigorously promoting the new literature. Its paying subscribers had faded away. Though the Atlantic was still profitable in 1880, its subscription list had declined to about twelve thousand, and as Thomas Bailey Aldrich assumed the editorship in 1881, it showed no sign of revival.

The writers Howells had promoted were solicited and accepted by Gilder in promoting the new Century. As additions to the prestige of his magazine, markers of the independence of the new editor and journal, and acknowledgement of a changing literary climate, Gilder sought to associate the Century with the primary figures of American literature in his generation. Howells's own novels were serialized, often on the basis of only proposals or outlines, for even though the topics were often risky in considering divorce, miscegenation, women's changing roles, Gilder felt he could count on the judgment of a writer who had himself been a magazine editor. Howells's Century serials came in for quite a bit of criticism, some in terms of a resentment that the novelist had previously been protected by his editorship, but Gilder actually encouraged Howells to further raise discussion and interest with a series of critical articles which promoted the new Americans at the expense of their British counterparts. Gilder also took work from Henry James, though the Century's audience took little interest in it, and Gilder became reluctant to commit himself to James for novels. With the support of Roswell Smith, the editor pursued Samuel Clemens, urging him to let the Century run pre-publication chapters from Huckleberry Finn on the premise that they would help volume sales since the Century's audience was essentially distinct from Twain's usual subscription book buyers.

Gilder's interest in promoting American authorship also opened the Century to new figures from the south, west, and midwest, and the magazine was a loyal defender of what it printed. Contributors soon found, however, that their welcome was conditioned on not continuing any controversy, whether it had begun intentionally or inadvertently. Gilder also insisted on "artistic treatment" and refused both what was obviously preaching and what was pointed in a direction he could not himself follow or understand. More particularly for the criticism which was soon leveled by writers at both the editor and the magazine, Gilder took his concern for public school education and the "family" audience directly into his suggestions for and rejection of manuscripts. Many of the accusations of prudery and examples of indefensible restriction come from writers hoping to publish in the Century but finding Gilder overcareful about physical descriptions, nonstandard language, questionable behavior, etc. Gilder acknowledged the criticism of provincials and Philistines, but himself reminded writers that the magazine audience included children who might not be presumed to know better.

In the post-Civil War golden age of American magazines and in the 1880s when both Harper's Monthly and the Century achieved circulation of 200,000 in the United States and thousands more in Britain, there were publishing opportunities outside these dominant family-oriented magazines. Despite the proliferation of hundreds of independent, regional, religious, and special interest monthlies and quarterlies and the continual expansion of newspapers like the New York Ledger as publishers of original literature willing to pay sometimes triple what was offered by the magazines, both established

and new writers looked to the two large audience monthlies and to
the Atlantic Monthly as publishers of preference. Contemporary
letters and reminiscence are full of references to these three as
significant, publication as a "badge," "diploma," "certification,"
the editor's judgment as significant. As writers complained of the
conservatism of "family" publishing, the commercialism which would
explain reluctance to offend, editors spoke of concern for the
writer's reputation, future. The parameter which excluded from the
magazines what would not be acceptable as reading matter for any
member of the American family--and the general assumption that the
American family was not among the world's most sophisticated--led to
continuous editorial and critical distinctions between what was
magazineable and what was bookable. The terms of distinction were
those which would recur in the twentieth century's indictments of
the "genteel tradition": that the magazine could not and would not
publish anything a father would not read aloud to his daughter and
that the magazine was marketed to the American home, in which the
majority of adult readers were ladies, and ladies who were at least
publicly concerned with convention. Though editors like Gilder
seemed comfortable with the defense and distinction that a writer
could print what he would in a volume and Gilder wrote in the 1890s
that the editor need no longer live under the charge that his
decisions could alone blight careers, many writers were unhappy with
an alternative which generally provided less, and less sure, profits
to them.

In a period marked in American literary history in that men of no independent means were attempting to support themselves--and families--graciously on the proceeds of literature and when the entree to being taken seriously as a writer was acceptance in magazines which printed the acknowledged greats, the impetus to writing what was marketable to those magazines was strong, as strong perhaps as the alternative bitterness toward their restrictions. One of the most effective appeals to editors and audience was the narrative which justified its distance from literary convention or tradition by claiming to be the author's actual observation of the realities of a distinctive segment of American life. Especially for the newcomers from America's regions, the attraction of presenting a fresh subject was itself the likeliest means to editorial attention. Readers could be interested, entertained, or educated by portraits of unfamiliar life, occupations, etc., while their chauvinism was engaged by the movement of representative phases of American life into literature.

While often the scrambling after new American materials and the identification of writers with regional perspectives makes nineteenth century magazine fiction sort more easily geographically than critically, the focus on subject allowed for a broad array of technique and perspective. Local coloring, especially in the gimmicry of regional customs, could foster duplication of plots and recycling of basic stock characters. Remarkable numbers of young girls of good heart but unformed ideas fell in love with a dashing, but unprincipled, swain--only later to recognize the true worth of a devoted clergyman/ schoolteacher/young lawyer/orphan turned philanthropic businessman. The phenomenon is readily explainable when we consider that these stories tend to focus either on events likely to happen at a quilting bee, sociable, corn husking, barn raising, electioneering, or plantation dance or on subjects or major plot lines quite divorced from the love interest. In the stories with dual plots, we often find serious and varied consideration of a variety of subjects which the twentieth century has generally overlooked in considering only the insipid love plots. Government, business, labor, legal and moral issues are prevalent, if not preponderant, in fiction in the three major magazines. Also frequent is an attitude of self-consciousness in the literature, a tendency of writers to frame both action and discussion with references to the reader's expectations from a story, comparisons to other works, clear distinctions between observation and fictional creation and between the author or narrator and the persons being depicted, a kind of fictional attitude which provided its own exegesis and education of the audience.

This sense of the possibility of changing or directing the reader's expectations which is evident within the stories and criticism of the major magazines is also evident in each journal's movement to include newly established writers and approaches. From the early general castigation of the Harper's magazines as strictly commercial enterprises, the Monthly and Weekly came to promote the writers who a decade or two before had seemed so distant from its directions and policies. Other journals took up the slack of printing what the litterateurs would call pap and of garnering the disdain of critics and writers. Even Howells would characterize "Godey's Lady's Book and Peterson's Magazine, /as/ publications really incredible in their insipidity,"[1] but such realizations and condemnations took little pressure off the premiere magazines. Contributors, although attracted by the prices which lesser journals offered, always seemed to prefer to publish if they could in the <u>Atlantic Monthly</u>, <u>Harper's</u> or the <u>Century</u>. Often the competition for space in these magazines was expressed as resentment toward the policies which favored "family" literature and to the literary figures of the first half of the nineteenth century, those we call the Fireside Poets and whom James Fields called the "Old Saints."

---

[1] Howells, "My First Visit," p. 16.

PART ONE

MAGAZINE EDITORS

CHAPTER II

JAMES RUSSELL LOWELL AND JAMES T. FIELDS:

BEGINNINGS OF THE ATLANTIC MONTHLY

The Atlantic Monthly which began publication in 1857 with James Russell Lowell as editor was focused toward representing different interests in literature and politics than any of the commercial magazines which had preceded it in the United States. At the same time, Lowell was conscious of the considerable investment and risk which the publishers had undertaken in fostering a magazine promoting high standards of scholarship, literature, and political liberalism in an economy and culture which had not supported previous similar ventures. As editor, Lowell tried to balance the interests of offering opportunity to American authors against concerns for assuring that this magazine would not go to an early grave or have a subscription list not much longer than its list of contributors.

The publishers paid Lowell a generous editorial salary, twenty-five hundred dollars annually when many editors were getting six hundred dollars, and Lowell rewarded the majority of his contributors on a similarly generous scale--thinking from the first that one purpose of the magazine should be to compensate in some degree for the financial conditions caused by a lack of International

Copyright. Lowell was not one to chauvinistically prefer American writing or always to think the best of it was what seemed distinctively native. He encouraged his countrymen to write what might find favor in England as well as at home, and he solicited some British writers for contributions to the magazine. For at least its first decade, the <u>Atlantic</u> was seen by many of its contributors as a means of addressing readers across the Atlantic as well as on its eastern seaboard in the United States.

For the largest proportion of manuscripts, however, Lowell tended to find the contributors for his mission, his audience, and his rewards almost entirely within the circle of his Harvard/Boston/Cambridge acquaintance and friends. He looked for literary innovation in new developments from established names in Boston letters, and the <u>Atlantic</u>'s literary criticism and social and political thought came as regularly from the denizens of Harvard Yard. In his initial stockpiling of manuscripts to begin the magazine, Lowell accepted or encouraged so many contributions from this base of American writers that by as early as the magazine's second year, he was lamenting the possibility of printing them all in due order while still having space for timely commentary and unexpected offerings of real quality.

Lowell's policies soon brought criticism that the <u>Atlantic</u> was provincially or aggressively a magazine restricted to New England interests and writing. As Lowell also chose and reviewed to reflect his personal preferences, many who met the geographic criterion found the editor idiosyncratic and inconsistent. The editor's personality and habits added to the difficulties of contributors. Better suited, perhaps, for the role of mentor than of editor, Lowell lacked both the organization and patience to carry through consistently on the broad range of editorial responsibilities from reading manuscripts to editing copy and corresponding with contributors. He was liable to misplace and forget manuscripts, to offend those who looked for pattern and justice in the Atlantic's selections, to make major deletions or additions without informing the contributor, and to invoke a concern for audience reaction when sentiments expressed in a piece did not match his own.

For the magazine's general appeal, Lowell relied on the New England authors who had already captured some share of attention from the broad American public. Longfellow was a frequent, if initially reluctant, contributor. Whittier gave the magazine some generally popular poems. But from the first, Lowell felt it was Oliver Wendell Holmes who would make the interest and the fortunes of the magazine. Holmes was the only Atlantic writer whose work went into the magazine without Lowell's prior approval or editing. The regular appearances of the personal opinion and poetry of The Autocrat at the Breakfast-Table and then The Professor at the Breakfast-Table were the feature which gave the Atlantic its initial, distinctive identity in literature and which attracted the attention, and often the criticism, of opinion makers in the press and the pulpit. Holmes's autocratic persona and poetry are generally credited as major factors in Lowell's ability to take the _Atlantic_ to a circulation ranging from twenty to thirty thousand by the end of the magazine's second year, enough to establish the magazine's viability and profitability. Holmes's vigorous statements of opinion also brought him and the magazine what the Dr. later indignantly described as continual "belaboring . . . from the so-called 'evangelical press'."[1]

If Holmes could not assume that all the American press would gracefully grant him as much freedom as the _Atlantic_'s editor, he seldom acknowledged this awareness in any measuring of his scorn toward those who set themselves against their betters in breeding and taste. Rather than bowing to the limitations of the _Atlantic_'s most general public, he instructed the striving classes against applying limited views of "morality" to a world larger than their own. The "Professor" clarified at the "Breakfast Table" issues of all sorts; for example,

> But fashion and wealth are two very solemn realities, which the frivolous class of moralists have talked a great deal of silly stuff about. Fashion is only the attempt to realize Art in living forms and social intercourse. What business has a man who knows nothing about the beautiful, and cannot pronounce the word _view_, to talk about fashion to a set of people who, if one of the quality left a card at their doors, would contrive to keep it on the very top of their heap of the

---

[1] Letter, Holmes to John Lathrop Motley in John T. Morse, Jr., _Life and Letters of Oliver Wendell Holmes_, 2 vols. (Boston and New York: Houghton, Mifflin and Company, 1897), 2:156. Also quoted in Austin, _Fields_, p. 71.

This chapter is heavily indebted throughout to James C. Austin's work on Fields's editorial correspondence.

names of their two-story acquaintances, till it was as yellow as the Codex Vaticanus?[1]

Rather than worrying himself over the reactions of "the frivolous class of moralists," Holmes was continually outspoken about his desire to confront them and to offer alternatives. The "Professor" told the Atlantic readers, "I do not think there is much courage or originality in giving utterance to truths that everybody knows but which get overlaid by conventional trumpery." Besides, there were already more than sufficient "providers of literary diluents, who will weaken any truth so that there is not an old woman in the land who cannot take it with perfect impunity."[2]

Other Atlantic contributors, however, were chagrined to find that it was only Holmes to whom Lowell would grant total freedom from uttering conventional truths. T. W. Higginson, who wrote almost as large a proportion of the early Atlantic as Lowell or Holmes, felt that the editor "strained at gnats and swallowed camels."[3] Typical was Lowell's answer to Higginson's submitting a manuscript in 1858 which asserted "the natural equality of the sexes" in arguing "Ought Women to Learn the Alphabet?" Lowell suggested "the insertion of a qualifying 'perhaps' . . . as much on your own account as mine--because I think it not yet demonstrated." Though Lowell would have

---

[1] Oliver Wendell Holmes, The Professor at the Breakfast-Table with The Story of Iris (Boston: Houghton, Mifflin and Company, 1890), p. 190.

[2] Holmes, Professor, p. 191.

[3] Thomas Wentworth Higginson, Cheerful Yesterdays (Boston: Houghton, Mifflin and Company, 1898), pp. 185-86.

let the sentence stand, if Higginson had insisted on it, the editor made it clear that he felt such an assertion would jeopardize the magazine:

> I only look upon my duty as a vicarious one for Phillips & Sampson, that nothing may go in (before we are firm on our feet) that helps the "religious" press in their warfare on us. Presently we shall be even with them, and have a _free_ magazine in its true sense. I never allow any personal notion of mine to interfere, except in cases of obvious obscurity, bad taste, or bad grammar.[1]

That Lowell did not associate the "warfare" of the "religious press" with the very specific reactions to Holmes's work in the _Atlantic_ was surely as evident to Higginson as was the realization that Lowell's claim to restrain any "personal notion" was more self-serving than accurate.

When Lowell disliked a writer or his opinions, as was the case with Henry David Thoreau,[2] the editor defined "bad taste" and deflected potential objections from "the 'religious' press" by simply deleting from a manuscript whatever he found objectionable. The editor's personal lack of organization and business discipline often meant that such changes were made without informing or consulting the contributor. Thoreau and others reacted by stridently discontinuing their relationship with the _Atlantic_.

---

[1] _Letters of James Russell Lowell_, ed. Charles Eliot Norton, 2 vols. (New York: Harper and Brothers, 1893), I, 287-88.

[2] A succinct analysis of the differences between Lowell and Thoreau appears in Martin Duberman, _James Russell Lowell_ (1966; Boston: Beacon Press Paperback, 1968), pp. 169-172.

Even Howells would later acknowledge that Lowell "was not a good business man in a literary way,"[1] and his conduct of the magazine came under increased scrutiny when the Atlantic was purchased by Ticknor & Fields in 1859. Fields at first limited himself to suggestions for making the Atlantic somewhat less scholarly and more appealing to a general audience. He especially felt the magazine should seek out and print a higher proportion of quality fiction. Lowell opposed any movement away from the "American Scholar" directions Emerson had defined twenty years before, with the advice that "the single man plant himself indomitably on his instincts" and address himself first to the fit few. Lowell wrote to Fields,

> If we make our Magazine merely entertaining how are we better than those Scribes & Pharisees the Harpers? We want to make it interesting to as many classes of people as we can, especially to such as give tone to public opinion in literacy, if there be any such in America.[2]

By 1861, Fields decided to take over the editorship of the Atlantic Monthly. Lowell had anticipated the change, and the parting was amicable, with Fields continually looking for ways to supply Lowell an income from contributions to the firm's magazines. While Fields moved quickly to "popularize" the Atlantic, he combined his publisher's and bookseller's sense of a broad-based audience's literary tastes with continuing the legacy of the Atlantic's Brahmin

---

[1] William Dean Howells, "Studies of Lowell," in Literary Friends and Acquaintance, p. 196.

[2] James Russell Lowell, New Letters of James Russell Lowell, ed. M. A. De Wolfe Howe (New York: Harper, 1932), p. 100.

founders. He shared Lowell's estimate of Holmes's worth and importance. He had agreed to raise Holmes's rate of payment to insure the writer's loyalty to the magazine, perhaps because the obloquy Holmes's *Atlantic* articles raised was matched by increases in subscriptions and by volume sales of the 1858 *Autocrat of the Breakfast-Table* sufficient to make the book a regional best-seller. Fields, however, tried to convince Holmes to turn to writing stories and novels, a suggestion Holmes resisted for years, claiming that he had neither the time nor the need for money which would inspire such a project.

Fields was more successful in convincing Harriet Beecher Stowe to write stories for the *Atlantic*, though he quickly found that she would write whatever inspired her at the moment--regardless of commitments to publishers or advances collected for a specific project. Pushing the "story approach" and encouraging American subjects, Fields was able to get a surprising amount of work from the Old Guard New Englanders whom he affectionately called the "Old Saints." While Lowell had edited their copy and worried over reactions to supposed immorality or impropriety, Fields was not afraid to follow his own taste and to let such premiere writers follow their own. Through much of Fields's editorship, the *Atlantic* was among the most liberal American periodicals--an image which backfired against Fields when Stowe took her *Oldtown Folks*, which Fields had long awaited and subsidized, to another journal, since she said she felt the *Atlantic*'s association with liberal values would exclude the religious audience she wanted to address.

Fields's most powerful and distinctive impact on the _Atlantic_ was his deliberate and successful push toward wider circulation, bringing _Atlantic_ subscriptions during his decade as editor to over fifty thousand, the magazine's highest figure in the nineteenth century. Looking for ways to lighten and popularize the magazine, Fields created an amalgam of original contributors and fresh, young writers. Fields associated general popularity with what was new and amusing. Fresh, distinctly American subjects and a variety of short pieces were his primary formula for the magazine. Fields's demand for amusing stories and new subjects encouraged the flow of local color fiction to the _Atlantic_. Undiscovered authors, regions, occupations presented through short fiction were his favorite means of "leavening" the "heavy" scholarly essays, and he encouraged contributions from writers throughout the country. Many of those who would be Fields's new authors were _Atlantic_ readers and subscribers, for whom the journal supplied a large part of their cultural life in regions without the literary and intellectual advantages of Boston, Cambridge, and Concord. Often directly inspired by the _Atlantic_ writing of Harriet Beecher Stowe, these writers supplied regional diversity to the _Atlantic_'s subject matter and list of contributors. Their fictional collages of local color were often supported by melodramatic, spiritualist, or coincidental plotting, however, and the morality tended to be conventional, the appreciation of nature effusive, and the purpose more didactic than aesthetic.

Howells, who became Fields's assistant editor in 1866, found

the new editor often rejecting Howells's own correct, derivative
poetry, while lamenting to his assistant the lack of enough young
fellows who could write short, amusing fiction. Howells felt the
humor of his situation and shared it with Mrs. Fields, but many of
the young, often realist, writers Howells promoted in Atlantic
criticism and pushed on the editor saw little humor in Fields's
suggestions of more "popular" approaches.

Fields had no consistent literary philosophy of his own and
only a small personal reputation as a writer. As a profit-oriented
publisher and a man who liked the Anglo-American social whirl
(Lowell felt Fields's greatest talent as an editor was his love for
entertaining authors), Fields tended to prefer literary lions who had
caught the popular imagination and made their own publicity. In the
1840s, he had competed with the Harper's firm for exclusive rights
to publish Dickens and Thackeray in America, and in the 1860s, as
editor of the Atlantic, he favored established names who confined
their periodical publishing to his magazine. For the "Old Saints"
who had given the Atlantic its distinctive identity among American
magazines, this meant generous compensation and freedom to publish
what they would in the Atlantic.

In the case of Oliver Wendell Holmes, the combination of
Fields's pushing the "story approach" and favoring established writers
meant the editor pursued Holmes for a novel through years in which
Holmes's resentment of the hypocrisy of clerical moralists built
into a novel for serialization in the Atlantic. Holmes's The

Guardian Angel was directed to a warning to young people of the
duplicity and moral corruption of those evangelical ministers who
had plagued the Autocrat and the Professor like a swarm of gnats.
Rather than being, as Howells's nostalgic memories claimed, unaware
of criticism and his critics, Holmes gloried in finding evidence of
clerical rascality in the midst of those who righteously attacked
him, and in The Guardian Angel, he evened the score against all his
detractors. While Fields was delighted with the initial chapters of
the novel, which pitted a beautiful, potentially rich, female orphan
against all those who would exploit her, the serial developed into
a direct confrontation with the conventionally prohibited subjects
of religiosity and sexuality and a reversal of readers' traditional
expectations of which characters and roles represented the social
frame of morality and decency. The Guardian Angel had a reception
much like Holmes's earlier Atlantic series; it was attacked--always
vigorously, sometimes viciously--attracting attention and notoriety.
The Atlantic's expanded subscription audience, however, now contained
many who had not the broad-minded sympathies which had applauded the
"Autocrat," and the novel which Fields suggested and solicited
effectively reversed many of the gains in circulation and popularity
of Fields's editorial tenure.

    Holmes's attraction to explore what some would forbid, to
pursue underlying and self-protective motives, was a factor in a
second major imbroglio which had an extreme effect on the Atlantic's
fortunes. Harriet Beecher Stowe had a virtual carte blanche to

publish in the Atlantic, having given it not only a number of generally popular works but also significant social statements like her "Reply to the Women of England." Stowe chose to use the Atlantic to print "The True Story of Lady Byron's Life," which reacted to attacks on Lady Byron by revealing Lord Byron's incest and ill treatment of his wife. Stowe depended on her own image and rectitude and Holmes's advice and editing for the article's reception with the public. Holmes knew enough what they were about to write to Fields, who was in Europe, that Mrs. Stowe had wanted advice only on how the material was to be presented, having already determined that she would print her statement. Fields had engaged both Holmes and Lowell as titular advisors to his assistant, Howells, and Lowell advised against the publication of Stowe's defense of her friend. Holmes and Stowe, the two popular favorites, won out over the more conservative former editor, with the young Howells having little to say about the whole matter. None of them anticipated, however, the universality and personal aggression in the calumny which fell on Stowe--or the precipitous loss of about fifteen thousand subscriptions with no compensatory increase in sales. Between them, Holmes and Stowe brought the Atlantic's circulation in late 1868 back to the levels of Lowell's editorship. Fields seems not to have blamed Stowe, Holmes, or Howells, and their relationships continued unabated.

  Such generosity and freedom were not available to the great mass of Atlantic contributors who had neither Fields's personal affection nor his long term belief in their work. While Fields had a reputation for magnanimity and support of the author-oriented International Copyright legislation, the fuller fortunes of his <u>Atlantic</u> administration did not increase opportunities for all. He was willing to call in critical opinions from the Old Saints to support a point against a writer who gave him trouble or whom he would prefer to ease from the <u>Atlantic</u>'s list, especially when the question involved sensuality or the publisher's money. When Bayard Taylor moved from his popular travel sketches to poetry which featured "wine & women," Fields used Whittier to make the final judgment on printing a poem and to write a note of explanation to Taylor.[1]

Julia Ward Howe had published a book with Ticknor & Fields in the 1850s and had consistently supplied the <u>Atlantic</u> with popular pieces, including "The Battle Hymn of the Republic," at extremely cheap prices. She was rewarded in 1862 by Fields's countering a contract offered to Howe by the <u>Continental Monthly</u> with his own proposal that the <u>Atlantic</u> become exclusive publisher of her work. Once assured of Howe's loyalty, Fields lost interest in the arrangement. Howe's letters were unanswered; her manuscripts for a series of poems were printed sporadically; most were left unpublished and unreturned. Finding Fields deaf to all her appeals, Howe finally settled for the return of her unpublished manuscripts, with no compensation for the delays or for her forfeited alternative opportunity.[2]

---

[1] Austin, <u>Fields</u>, pp. 192-93.

[2] Austin, <u>Fields</u>, pp. 101-14.

Though his colleagues claim Fields accepted far more manuscripts than he could print because he was softhearted, he also seems to have used intentional delays in publication and correspondence to discourage intrepid contributors or to lower prices. Fields often cited declines in an author's popularity or in the quality of work submitted as reasons behind ungenerous treatment. Extra-literary factors also seem to have influenced the editor's receptivity to specific writers. Like Lowell, Fields resented any contention from women and granted only the most popular any semblance of equality. Female contributors were increasingly attracted to the *Atlantic*, perhaps encouraged by the feminism of Higginson's essays and the example of Mrs. Stowe. Fields tended to use these writers not only to balance the appeal of his magazine, but also to balance his budget.

While the *Atlantic*'s receptivity to new talent and regional diversity increased dramatically during Fields's tenure, few of these new writers became established first line contributors before William Dean Howells became Fields's assistant editor in 1866. Howells served as both an advocate of and a liason to the new generation of American authors. The *Atlantic*'s eventual importance in developing American realism and in nurturing non-traditional writers comes from Lowell's and Fields's fostering Howells's career as a magazine editor and critic.

In 1860, at Howells's first dinner with Lowell, Fields, and Holmes, Holmes had remarked, "Well, James, this is something like the apostolic succession; this is the laying on of hands." The comment proved not to be the "sweet and caressing irony"[1] Howells felt at the time, but accurate prophecy. When Fields retired in 1870, Howells became the Atlantic's editor-in-chief. For the rest of the century, Howells would be a powerful factor in the directions of major American magazines. Howells has been both blamed and applauded over the years, but no critic has denied his significance, especially as editor of the Atlantic Monthly in the 1870s.

---

[1] Howells, "My First Visit," p. 36.

CHAPTER III

WILLIAM DEAN HOWELLS AND THE ATLANTIC MONTHLY

An unlikely candidate for the "apostolic succession" in the world of New England Brahmins, William Dean Howells had first encountered the Atlantic Monthly as a subscriber in Ohio. In almost every way an outlander, without culture or formal education, Howells's early record combines worship of his eastern idols, a naive and patriotic assumption of their populism and idealism, and his own literary ambition. His "literary ambition, already so strong that my veins might well have run ink rather than blood,"[1] Howells looked to the east and to the opportunities of its literary journals from his first employment as an Ohio newspaperman. With one poem published in the Atlantic, Howells wrote to his sister: "I have my eye on the temple that 'shines afar,' and I will fall up the hill, if I must succumb."[2] Howells's "famine for the old, the quaint, the picturesque" of New England and his veneration for its "great authors . . . the sum of greatness" led him east in 1860, "bursting with the most romantic expectations of life."[3]

---

[1] Howells, "My First Visit," p. 8.

[2] W. D. Howells to Victoria Howells, October 5, 1859, Harvard, quoted in Lynn, Howells, p. 86.

[3] Howells, "My First Visit," pp. 41, 39, 18.

The literary establishment which Howells found deflated most of those high, romantic expectations. Howells was repeatedly reminded of his curiosity value as an uncultivated westerner. In all his talk with Holmes and Lowell, Howells could "recall nothing said of political affairs, though Lincoln had then been nominated . . . and the Civil War had practically begun." His meetings with Emerson and Thoreau were a "rout." Thoreau's "vague, orphic phrases" on a "John Brown type . . . ideal . . . principle" hardly fit Howells's conception of a man who would go to jail for a cause. Despite his disappointments, Howells had come east "as if in return from life-long exile," and he was determined to find a basis for entry into the national literary world. When the publisher Fields listened to his dismay and "got an amusement from it that I could only get through sympathy with him," the young westerner "thought it a favorable moment to propose myself as the assistant editor of the Atlantic Monthly."[1]

The job was filled, and Howells found his basis neither in Boston nor in New York's writers' bohemia. Lowell and Fields were willing advisors to the young writer, but only after a consular appointment in Venice and a stint as a reviewer and essayist for the New York Papers did Howells receive an offer to become the *Atlantic*'s assistant editor. The terms on which Howells came to the *Atlantic* were clear:

---

[1] Howells, "My First Visit," pp. 44, 55, 40, 60.

> . . . the qualification I had as practical printer . . . was most valued, if not the most valued, and that as proof-reader I was expected to make it avail on the side of economy. Somewhere in life's feast the course of humble-pie must always come in; and if I did not wholly relish this bit of it, I dare say it was good for me, and I digested it perfectly.

Howells's writing for the magazine was to be "the four or five pages of book-notices, which were then printed at the end of the periodical in finer type."[1]

Howells's previous book-noticing for New York papers had been distinctive. An early defense of Whitman had refused to join the "Misses Nancy" of criticism who condemned the poet. Howells had also mounted a series of critical attacks against sensationalism, moralistic didacticism, and the Josiah Holland school of pietistic advice to the young. His positive criticism applauded literature which was realistic, democratic, native, and faithful to the everyday details of life.

No matter what Fields chose for the body of the Atlantic and despite the senior editor's personal preference for the popular British novelists leavened by short, light work by young Americans, Howells's Atlantic book-notices were consistent with the young man's independent critical opinions. He encouraged attention to the models of continental realist writers. In sifting manuscripts, he promoted American writers who represented regional life in realistic proportions, with verisimilitude in character, language, and setting.

---

[1] Howells, "Roundabout to Boston," in Literary Friends and Acquaintance, p. 97.

Looking for work which would offset the conception of "romance" as courtship amidst idealistic and sentimental notions of self-sacrifice and character, Howells found many of his contributors in the ranks of American women writers. While he was proudest of identifying the work of such as Sarah Orne Jewett, Constance Fenimore Woolson, and Mary Murfree (Charles Egbert Craddock), Howells, on looking back at "the writers who came forward in these pages during my time," claimed that "if any one were to prove that there were more women than men, I should not be surprised"[1]--a possibility Howells attributed to the proportion of deft realism which came from female hands.

Howells also took over from Fields responsibility for dealings with a number of young writers who had begun to publish in the magazines, but who had not yet developed a popular following. He maintained the house relationship and personal friendships with Charles Dudley Warner and Thomas Bailey Aldrich, but his editorial devotion went to those whose fiction was developing in ways parallel to Howells's own literary credo.

In 1866, Howells's first Boston year, he met Henry James, Jr. They quickly became friends and companions, sharing work in progress and discussion of "the true principles of literary art."[2] James, then

---

[1] Howells, "Recollections of an Atlantic Editorship," in *Criticism and Fiction and Other Essays*, ed. and with Introductions and Notes by Clara Marburg Kirk and Rudolf Kirk (New York: New York University Press, 1959), p. 193.

[2] Howells to E. C. Stedman, December 5, 1866, in *Life in Letters of William Dean Howells*, ed. Mildred Howells, 2 vols. (Garden City, New York: Doubleday, Doran, and Company, 1928), I, 116.

twenty-three, had published "A Tragedy of Error" in the Continental Monthly and "The Story of a Year" and some other short pieces in the Atlantic Monthly. The majority of James's professional writing, however, had been critical notices for the North American Review, edited by Charles Eliot Norton. Fields was not enthusiastic over James's Atlantic contributions, which were not the cheerful, short, lively sketches Fields encouraged young American writers to submit. The editor turned James's offering over to Howells, who gladly supported his friend and ran interference for him. Howells advocated focus on American subjects and settings, and James, who depended on the magazines for both recognition and income, soon supplied his first novella, "Poor Richard," which was published in the Atlantic in three installments. After a number of short contributions, James published a second novella, "Gabrielle de Bergerac," in the 1869 Atlantic. Finally, more than half of James's fiction in his first productive decade appeared in the Atlantic through Howells's support and aid.

    As assistant editor, Howells also encouraged the publication of another New Englander who added to the diversity of American literature. This woman, Helen Hunt (Jackson), Emily Dickinson's friend, would continue publishing with the Atlantic for over twenty years, loyally accepting lower rates than she could get elsewhere and bringing to the attention of the editor other exceptional new talent she discovered. Once with the Atlantic, she began to drop the use of her masculine pseudonym, Saxe Holm, and to turn from poetry to expository prose and fiction. Another American with a ringing pseudonym, Mark Twain, was already publishing without the aid of the eastern magazines. Howells's laudatory review of The Innocents Abroad, however, brought Twain to the Atlantic offices in 1869 to meet and thank the assistant editor who had heaped on establishment recognition--the beginning of a relationship which would last their active careers.

In looking for opportunity for American writers, praising what he found both new and good, concentrating on distinctively native subject matter, and encouraging representation of life in America's regions, Howells critically promoted continuation of the nineteenth century vogue of travel literature. His own early Suburban Sketches are not unlike his Venice sketches, focusing on the high coloring and distinctive characters that attract the traveler, the sojourner, the observer. The tendency of local coloring to be associated with the perspective and distancing of a travelogue is evident throughout Howells's own early fiction and the work of many of the contemporaries he encouraged. In attempts to avoid the sentimental and to bring new subjects to literature, many of this generation began with either a sort of photographic framing of scenes or the heavy plotting of the journalistic or supernatural tale.

Howells's training as assistant editor had not all to do with sifting manuscripts and writing notices. The "practical printer" found "The magazine was already established in its traditions when I came to it," and one of those was the "liberal Atlantic tradition of bettering the authors by editorial transposition and paraphrase, either in the form of suggestion or of absolute correction." The freedom which the <u>Atlantic</u> took with accepted contributions and the system and stringency of its copy-editing were givens in "a school of verbal exactness" with procedures which might well make one wonder to what degree the language of <u>Atlantic</u> contributors can be separately evaluated.[1]

Howells described the process he found when he came to Fields's <u>Atlantic</u> as assistant editor.

> In fact, the proof-reading of the Atlantic Monthly was something almost fearfully scrupulous and perfect. The proofs were first read by the under proof-reader in the printing office; then the head reader passed them to me perfectly clean as to typography, with his own abundant and most intelligent comments on the literature; and then I read them, <u>making what changes I chose</u>, and verifying every quotation, every date, every geographical and biographical name, every foreign word to the last accent, every technical and scientific term. <u>Where it was possible or at all desirable the proof was next submitted to the author</u>. When it came back to me, I revised it, <u>accepting or rejecting the author's judgment according as he was entitled by his ability and knowledge or not to have them</u>. The proof now went to the printers for correction; they sent it again to the head reader, who carefully revised it and returned it again to me. I read it a second time, and it was again corrected. After this it was revised in the office and sent to the stereotyper, from whom it came to the head reader for a last revision in the plates. (Italics mine.)[2]

While Howells comments "there were very few who did not owe something" in their work to the "zeal of our proof-reading," and that

---

[1] Howells, "Recollections," p. 186, 191-92.

[2] Howells, "Literary Boston," p. 119.

"the wisest and ablest were the most patient and grateful," the record does not seem to indicate that even all of the <u>Atlantic</u>'s regular contributors fully understood or accepted the stringency of the process or the thoroughness of its application. Julia Ward Howe replied to an editorial "suggestion" which came to her through Fields:

> I can't mend the lame line--think you find such lines in all long measures. It is like the liberty of spondaic or dactylic lines in hexameters. I think you have over punctuated the line--not like me to pause and grieve.

When Howe saw the proofs of her 1861 article on George Sand, she had also returned them with objections to the "Atlantic tradition of bettering the authors."

> Dear Fields,
> Enclosed please find proofs, with many thanks. Your proof reader is too ambitious of correcting style, and to correct him has cost me some trouble. Please see to it that things are printed my way, and not his. I have never had so many liberties taken with any thing of mine, and cannot write, if I am thus to be called to account.[1]

Howells also recalled that "the deeply lettered Sumner" did not respond graciously to "doubts of his latinity."[2]

With Harriet Beecher Stowe, whose "syntax was such a snare to her that it sometimes needed the combined skill of all the proof-readers and the assistant editor to extricate her," the "proof-reading" process seems more than "ambitious of correcting style." Howells remembered

---

[1] Howe to Fields, n.d. and September 16, 1861, Fields Collection, Huntington Library, quoted in Austin, <u>Fields</u>, p. 103.

[2] Howells, "Literary Boston," pp. 120.

> Of course, nothing was ever written into her work, but in changes of diction, in correction of solecisms, in transposition of phrases, the text was largely rewritten on the margin of her proofs. The soul of her art was present, but the form was so often absent, that when it was clothed on anew, it would have been hard to say whose cut the garment was of in many places.[1]

Still, on the tasks of verifying dates, historical data, etc.--which, according to Howells were essentials of the assistant editor's charge--Harriet Beecher Stowe, who was renowned for missing deadlines, revising commitments, and not reading her own proof, specifically asked Fields for the favor of checking her data. Submitting the manuscript for the "Reply to the Women of England," Mrs. Stowe asked not only that "the usual press corrector of the magazine will do what he has done for me," but also that Fields check a date. "I say *four* years--you must make the figure right four or five as the case may be." and asks "as a favor that you or Mrs. Fields will read the proof sheets and correct any mistakes."[2]

If all the contributors were not always aware in whose and how many hands their work was placed, Howells as assistant and then editor remembered himself as a young contributor almost suffering from the possibility of changes from a variety of hands at different levels of responsibility and different stages in the process. In the *Atlantic* publication of one of Howells's early poems, a copy editor had so far entered into the realistic spirit of Howells's poetic

---

[1] Howells, "Literary Boston," pp. 118-20.

[2] Stowe to Fields, November 27, 1862, Fields Collection, quoted in Austin, *Fields*, pp. 273-74.

dialogue that he changed a "me" to "'Ma'"--a version which horrified young Howells and which the Atlantic then agreed to setting right in the final proof.[1]

William Dean Howells came to be full-charge editor of the Atlantic Monthly in 1871 when Fields retired. Howells would find that his editorial freedom was limited by a number of external factors, including the Atlantic's traditions and the changing economic and cultural climate in the United States. While 1871 was generally a boom year for periodical publishing with the successful introduction of Scribner's Monthly, it was the beginning of a decade of falling circulation for the Atlantic, which never recovered the subscriber losses from the Holmes and Stowe controversies. The series of national economic crises in the 1870s added to the precarious financial position of the magazine and of its new publisher. James Fields had sold his interest in the publishing firm and its various magazines to his younger partner, James R. Osgood. Osgood was an optimist and visionary who "early perceived that if a leading American house were to continue at Boston, it must be hospitable to the talents of the whole country."[2] He began his management of the firm's magazines by greatly increasing the size and scope of its previously modest compilation of foreign reprints, Every Saturday; by encouraging Howells's innovations; and by willingly paying extravagant prices to broadly popular American and British writers who he hoped would

---

[1] Howells, "My First Visit," p. 34.

[2] Howells, "Literary Boston," p. 105.

skyrocket the Atlantic's and the firm's sales.

    Bret Harte was one of the new, national figures that the publisher, rather than the editor, brought to the magazine. Though Harte's work had first been introduced to Fields through the agency of Harte's wealthy California patroness, Mrs. Fremont, the Californian had not yet been east when Howells offered to host him for the Boston portion of his triumphal trip of 1871. Harte's incredible public acclaim had fostered an offer of the editorship and partial ownership of a proposed Chicago journal, The Lakeside Monthly, but before the Hartes arrived in Boston, Howells learned through the newspapers that this opportunity had been bypassed. Howells recalled realizing in the carriage trip between the Boston train station and the Howellses' cottage that the Hartes' was no mere visit to the East, that they, like he, had felt themselves exiles in the West.

    Despite the fable of Harte's success and kingly journey east to accept the munificient offer of ten thousand dollars a year from the Atlantic Monthly, the actual details of the firm's commitment to Harte are more chancy and prosaic. Howells remembered that the publishers "had not profited much" from the sales of "the volume which contained 'The Luck of Roaring Camp,' and the other early tales which made him a continental, and then an all but a world-wide fame," but sold only thirty-five hundred copies in its first six months. And though Harte had asked ten thousand dollars a year plus a generous expense allowance to continue editing The Overland Monthly and had inexplicably eschewed The Lakeside Monthly which seemed to offer so much more, the offers made to Harte in New York were, as Howells remembered, "mortifyingly mean, and others insultingly vague." And yet, though Harte's most popular book had not greatly profited the firm and he clearly had no competitive offer elsewhere, Howells's publishers "were willing, they were eager, to pay him ten thousand dollars for whatever, however much or little, he chose to write in a year." Though Harte's actual contributions have long been argued, both in terms of their quality and whether they met his contractual obligation, Howells's position is that the "net result in a literary return to his publishers was one story and two or three poems."[1]

The story Howells recalls is likely Harte's "The Poet of Sierra Flat" which appeared in the Atlantic in 1871. A second story in Howells's first editorial year, "The Romance of Madrono Hollow," was reprinted from The Luck of Roaring Camp volume and therefore relegated to the back of its issue. Whatever his personal feelings might have been to the over-compensated and under-productive westerner who was amused by Howells, insulted his friend Clemens, and venerated only the most popular Longfellow among the eastern literary circle, Howells editorially followed his publisher's lead in treating Harte as an attractive Atlantic property. He even went so far as to print Harte's second, belated Christmas, story--"How Santa Claus Came to Simpson's Bar"--in the March issue of 1872 rather than have nothing of Bret Harte's in the volume.

---

[1] Howells, "A Belated Guest," in Literary Friends and Acquaintance, p. 252.

Howells's own innovations in the *Atlantic* generated more volume, if no greater commercial or popular success, than the schemes of his publishers. Technical changes in the magazine's format and emphases continued Howells's book-noticing preference by expanding the sections given to review and analysis of important foreign literature. New departments devoted to art and music were added, and for a time Howells even printed sheet music in the *Atlantic*, a feature which was not particularly well-received. The *Atlantic*'s previously occasional policy of signing authors' names to their work became the general practice, a sharp contrast to the custom of the other national magazines. Late in his editorship, after Howells had personally determined to spend more of his time on his own "fictioning," he also added a "Contributor's Club" section to provide less formal and more timely access to writers of both poetry and prose.

Most marked in the changes under Howells's administration was his devoting a major portion of the magazine, its serially published novels, to the new writing and writers he had promoted as a book reviewer and assistant editor. Howells's most prominent beneficiaries were John W. DeForest and Henry James, Jr., neither of whom found consistent favor with any other leading periodical. For James, Howells published a large number of short stories as well as such novels as *Watch and Ward*, *Roderick Hudson*, *The American*, and *The Europeans*. DeForest used the *Atlantic* to publish *Kate Beaumont*, *Honest John Vane*, and *Irene, the Missionary*. The clarity of Howells's preferred editorial directions has been obscured, however, by the coexistence of conventional and traditional writers in the magazine.

Howells's sense of the duties, responsibilities, and opportunities of the <u>Atlantic</u> editorship was based upon sharp distinctions between categories of contributors. While he later nostalgically claimed that it would be difficult to separate his accomplishment from that of his predecessor, Howells's selection and treatment of manuscripts continually reflects a tension between felt obligations to the <u>Atlantic</u> traditions and prior editorial practices and his own commitment to bringing new, national and realist writers before the public. The record of what was published during Howells's editorial tenure and his own reflections on his practices and motives indicate a variant standard for editorial treatment of old vs. new literature.

The Old Guard New England poets--John Greenleaf Whittier, Ralph Waldo Emerson, Oliver Wendell Holmes--soon made clear to the young editor that he would take and put before the public in a way most beneficial to them whatever work they submitted, or stand the ignominy of having no work of theirs at all. Writing of "Literary Boston As I Knew It," Howells related how he was made to learn his appropriate role to such contributors. Discussing Whittier,

> There is great inequality in his work, and I felt this so strongly that when I came to have full charge of the Magazine, I ventured once to distinguish. He sent me a poem, and I had the temerity to return it, and beg him for something else. He magnanimously refrained from all show of offense, and after a while, when he had printed the poem elsewhere, he gave me another. By this time, I perceived that I had been wrong, not as to the poem returned, but as to my function regarding him and such as he. I had made my reflections, and never again did I

venture to pass upon what contributors of his quality
sent me. I took it and printed it, and praised the
gods; and even now I think that with such men it was
not my duty to play the censor in the periodical which
they had made what it was. They had set it in authority
over American literature, and it was not for me to put
myself in authority over them. Their fame was in their
own keeping, and it was not my part to guard it against
them.[1]

Howells soon found that it was not only in accepting "what contributors of his quality sent me," but also in handling the necessities of editing and managing the placement of work in the magazine that these elder contributors required special treatment and a different standard. Rivalries within that generation, and especially between the Concord circle and the Boston/Cambridge group, only added to the ticklish nature of Howells's "duty." Howells reported that after his experience with Whittier,

> I not only practised an eager acquiescence in their wish
> to reach the public through the Atlantic, but I used all
> the delicacy I was master of in bowing the way to them.
> Sometimes my utmost did not avail, or more strictly
> speaking it did not avail in one instance with Emerson.
> He had given me upon much entreaty a poem which was one
> of his greatest and best, but the proof-reader found a
> nominative at odds with its verb. We had some trouble
> in reconciling them, and some other delays, and meanwhile
> Doctor Holmes offered me a poem for the same number. I
> now doubted whether I should get Emerson's poem back in
> time for it, but unluckily the proof did come back in
> time, and then I had to choose between my poets, or
> acquaint them with the state of the case, and let them
> choose what I should do. I really felt that Doctor
> Holmes had the right to precedence, since Emerson had
> withheld his proof so long that I could not count upon
> it; but I wrote to Emerson, and asked . . . whether he
> would consent to let me put his poem over to the next
> number, or would prefer to have it appear in the same

---

[1] Howells, "Literary Boston," p. 117.

> number with Doctor Holmes's; the subjects were cognate, and I had my misgivings. He wrote me back to "return the proofs and break up the forms." . . . I did so, feeling that I had done my possible, and silently grieving that there could be such ire in heavenly minds.[1]

Howells's problems with the Old Guard were exacerbated by their long term history of dealing with Fields and relying on his counsel in the practical affairs of publishing. Though there had been occasional disputes between Fields and the founding contributors, the editor/publisher had retained all responsibility for dealings with them during the period of Howells's assistantship and had countered any reluctance of theirs to contribute with increases in their compensation. Henry Wadsworth Longfellow's loyalty to the <u>Atlantic</u>, even when he was not contributing much to it, was strongly based on his association with Fields. When Fields announced his retirement from editing, Longfellow had written: "I come back to my old wish and intention of leaving the Magazine when you do." The extraordinarily popular poet did continue with the <u>Atlantic</u> after the change of editors, but Fields's private advice and negotiations for Longfellow undercut both Howells's judgment and the benefit to the <u>Atlantic</u>. In advising on Longfellow's placement of a new poem in 1875, Fields wrote

> My dear Longfellow,
> I would not let Howells have the poem at present. And for this reason: he has already printed three pieces in the A.M. lately, &, with little judgment, put <u>two</u> pieces into one number. I would never let him do

---

[1] Howells, "Literary Boston," pp. 117-18.

that again. It weakens the impression of each poem to have two in one number. I would now hold off for a few months. Don't quote me, please, but it seems like squandering your golden thought to appear in any magazine oftener than need be. I would print the "Three Friends of Mine" in the July No. and not before. The last poem you printed in the A.M. has not done its full mission yet. It is constantly reprinted in the papers, and if another comes out so close upon it, the effect is disturbed. I am sure of it.

Longfellow did not follow through on all of the advice contained in Fields's criticism of Howells's editorial management, but the poet soon began to use Fields's offices in placing work elsewhere. Fields arranged for Harper's Monthly to pay one thousand dollars for a poem, but cautioned Longfellow, "Please don't say I had anything to do about the Harper negotiation."[1] Though a single poem hardly returned gains in circulation to offset such prices for its publisher, a new poem from such as Longfellow would be noted and likely reviewed in all the major newspapers and magazines, and the publisher would benefit from the association of his periodical with a prestigious and popular contributor. As New England's "Old Saints" appeared elsewhere as well as in the Atlantic, the Atlantic's commercial benefit from printing whatever they would submit was limited.

Even James Russell Lowell, the Atlantic's first editor and Howells's continuing mentor, though "He was not a good business man in a literary way, . . . (and) I doubt if he ever put a price upon anything he sold," questioned the payment he received for a long poem

---

[1] Longfellow to Fields, July 7, 1871, in Samuel Longfellow, Life of Henry Wadsworth Longfellow, 3 vols. (Boston: Houghton, Mifflin and Company, 1891), III, 177; Fields to Longfellow, February 23, 1875, Fields Collection; Fields to Longfellow, July 1, 1875, Longfellow House, all quoted in Austin, Fields, pp. 95-96.

during Howells's editorship.[1]

Aside from the Brahmins themselves, Howells often had to deal with potential contributors who offered their work to the *Atlantic* under cover of association with the founders. At first, Howells attempted to deal with these seriously, as matters of principle, and he went to great lengths to avoid printing what seemed inferior work without offending the contributor or his supposed sponsor. He recounted, for example, the story of a certain Englishman who had been besieging the *Atlantic* under cover of his acquaintance with Longfellow.

> In the midst of his own suffering, he [Longfellow] was willing to advise with me concerning some poems L. had offered to the Atlantic Monthly, and after we had desperately read them together he said, with inspiration, "I think these things are more adapted to music than the magazine," and this seemed so good a notion that when L. came to know their fate from me, I answered, confidently, "I think they are rather more adapted to music."
>
> He calmly asked, "Why?" and as this was an exigency which Longfellow had not forecast for me, I was caught in it without hope of escape. I really do not know what I said, but I know that I did not take the poems, such was my literary conscience in those days; I am afraid I should be weaker now.[2]

If Howells's "literary conscience" did indeed weaken and weary with time in the editorial chair, it was tried frequently by an ever-growing list of *Atlantic* contributors who took it upon themselves to suggest new writers to the magazine. Howells remembered many cases

---

[1] Howells, "Studies of Lowell," p. 196.

[2] Howells, "White Mr. Longfellow," p. 159.

and categories of supplicants who offered other than literary merit as reasons for being recognized in the <u>Atlantic</u>.

> The poor fellows, and still more the poor dears, were apt in the means by which they tried to find a royal road to the public through the magazine. Claims of acquaintance with friends of the editors, distressful domestic circumstances, adverse fortune, irresistible impulse to literature, mortal sickness in which the last hours of the writer would be brightened by seeing the poem or story in print, were the commonest of appeals.[1]

Howells also charged himself with publishing "that half-barrel of accepted manuscripts which came down to me from the first as well as the second editor of the magazine." Since the magazine's general policy had been to pay for work on publication rather than on acceptance, "such inhibition as fear of the publisher's check had not been laid upon Lowell's literary tenderness or Fields's generous hopefulness when it came to the question of keeping some passable sketch, or article, or story, or poem." Howells remembered, for the ten years of his editorship, making his way through this pile, feeling obligated to publish any piece the author of which was yet alive--and recalling "with what ghoulish glee I exulted in finding a manuscript exanimate."[2]

In the first years of his editorship, Howells was also led by his publisher to follow his predecessor's practice of soliciting work from the most popular British writers in an effort to boost the <u>Atlantic</u>'s fortunes. Just as when Howells was Fields's assistant,

---

[1] Howells, "Recollections," p. 189.

[2] Howells, "Recollections," p. 201.

this often meant the young man was printing work he either considered over-priced and occasionally mediocre or work, like Charles Reade's, of which he frankly disapproved. In all of these contributors, Howells claimed, "we looked for prosperity . . . and . . . we were disappointed of it," and the <u>Atlantic</u> came to leave Charles Dickens and "the monstrous sum" he demanded to other outlets.[1]

The contributors who garnered Howells's most willing editorial attention--and who often required as dexterous handling as the <u>Atlantic</u> founders--were his contemporary male novelists of the "realist" school. Henry James, the continual beneficiary of Howells's editorial and critical influence, acknowledged in 1912 the degree and kind of interest Howells had supplied--

> . . . you held out your open editorial hand to me . . . hospitality that was really the making of me, the making of the confidence that required help and sympathy and that I should otherwise--I think, have strayed and stumbled about a long time without acquiring. You showed me the way and opened the door.[2]

But at the time that both were writing their first long fiction and Howells was editorially showing "the way," James was highly critical of the value of Howells's American directions. Writing to Charles Eliot Norton in 1871, James commented

> Looking about for myself, I conclude that the face of nature and civilization in this our country is to a certain point a very sufficient literary field. But it will yield its secrets only to a really <u>grasping</u>

---

[1] Howells, "Recollections," p. 198.

[2] Henry James, "A Letter to Mr. Howells," <u>North American Review</u>, 195 (April, 1912): 558-59.

imagination. This I think Howells lacks. (Of course I don't!)[1]

There were also any number of particular disagreements between Howells and James, but Howells continued to print the majority of James's work and, frequently, even to encourage his printing what the Atlantic could not use in competing journals. With those whose work he wanted to support, Howells showed none of his predecessor's insistence on loyalty to the Atlantic.

But while writers like Sarah Orne Jewett took Howells's advice and acknowledged his editorial necessities, James, John W. DeForest and others who depended principally upon Howells's Atlantic for publication continually forced the editor to defend his attempts to make them popular.

Neither the general audience nor the critical community shared Howells's interest in Henry James, Jr. until the fame and notoriety which came with the publication of Daisy Miller in 1878. James actively sought the magazine market for his work, and expressed to Howells in the 1870s, as he would later, his despair at not touching the public's sensibilities. Still, when they came to the Atlantic's serial publication of The American in 1876, James reacted rather testily to Howells's suggestion of a more definite conclusion, and his reply has more to do with memories of Fields's objections to James's pessimism and requests for "short, cheerful stories" than the

---

[1] Quoted in F. O. Matthiessen, Introduction to The American Novels and Stories of Henry James, ed. F. O. Matthiessen (New York: Alfred A. Knopf, 1968), p. ix.

actuality of his relationship with his new editor and friend.

> I quite understand that as an editor you should go in for "cheerful endings"; but I am sorry that as a private reader you are not struck with the inevitability of the American denouement . . . . they would have been an impossible couple, with an impossible problem before them. For instance--to speak very materially--where would they have lived? . . . the interest of the subject was, for me (without my being at all a pessimist) its exemplification of one of those insuperable difficulties . . . from which the only issue is by forfeiture--by losing something.[1]

While James many years later found that The American represented experience "uncontrolled by our general sense of 'the way things happen'--which romance alone more or less successfully palms off on us,"[2] his appeal to Howells, including the eminently practical concern for the nuptial domicile, was clearly to work in terms of their shared favoring of "realism." The American was published, in the Atlantic, without the marriage and without revealing the tantalizing "secret of the Bellegardes--something which would damn them if it were known."

James claimed to have won the satisfaction of leaving Claire de Cintre a cloistered Carmelite by promising Howells a "cheerful ending" or at least a marriage at the end of the next novel. Henry Nash Smith cites James's explanation of the exchange in a letter written to Elizabeth Boott:

---

[1] James to Howells, March 30, 1877 in Henry James Letters 2:104-5, quoted in Henry Nash Smith, Democracy and the Novel (New York: Oxford University Press, 1978), p. 134.

[2] Henry James, "Preface to 'The American'," in The Art of the Novel (New York: Charles Scribner's Sons, 1934), p. 34.

> The offhand marrying in the end was commandé . . . it had been a part of the bargain with Howells that this termination should be cheerful and that there should be distinct matrimony. So I did /hit/ it off mechanically in the closing paragraphs.[1]

James's concession was, however, largely a matter of form. In these early years, James often conceived of works in pairs: one with a male and the other with a female center of interest--but with repeated, or parallel, action. As F. O. Matthiesen reported, James "had projected a companion piece to The American, with the situation reversed: instead of Christopher Newman discovering Europe, he would bring back to this country two Europeanized Americans,"[2] The Europeans. In replaying his situation in The Europeans, published in the Atlantic in 1878, James met Howells's request for a final marriage and the editor's suggestion that James use American settings.

But, James hardly made his ending or his novel "cheerful" and he clearly marked for his readers just in what ways The Europeans could be taken as different from The American. While Mrs. Tristram in the penultimate paragraph of The American ascribed Newman's defeat to "their /the Bellegardes/ confidence . . . in your remarkable good nature," The Europeans' first chapter defines its difference in an opening exchange between two of the principals:

> "You are too good-natured, my dear," his companion declared.
>
> . . . "Good-natured--yes. Too good natured--no."

---

[1] James to Elizabeth Boott, October 30, 1878 in Henry James Letters II, 189, quoted in Smith, Democracy, p. 134.

[2] Matthiessen, Introduction, p. x.

And when the novel does come to the concluding nuptials, James handles them not only "mechanically" but also cynically and peremptorily. The action and dialogue hardly meet the criterion of "cheerful endings" demanded by editors to soothe an undeveloped audience. The Europeans' ending has the Baroness Eugenia leaving the scene, answering her brother's question

"Is the play over, Eugenia?"

with

"I have spoken my part."

The disagreement over the ending to The American was not the first such conflict James had had with a magazine editor or with Howells specifically. In the late 1860s, James, with Howells's encouragement, submitted to the Galaxy work which the Atlantic could not or would not print. When Francis Church, the Galaxy editor, suggested that James add a final paragraph to a story which would clarify that the couple had married, James insisted on having his own way:

> As for adding a paragraph I should strongly object to it. It doesn't seem to me necessary. Silence on the subject will prove to the reader, I think, that the marriage did come off. I have little fear that the reader will miss a positive statement to that effect and the story closes in a more dramatic manner, to my apprehension, just as I have left it.[1]

As James became more confident of Howells and of a secure place as

---

[1] James to Francis P. Church, October 23, 1867, New York Public Library, in Henry James Letters, Volume I (1843-1875), ed. Leon Edel (Cambridge: Harvard University Press, Belknap Press, 1974), p. 74.

an <u>Atlantic</u> contributor, he also became more aggressive in responding to what he called editorial "restrictions." Writing to his father on February 1, 1873, James commented on Howells's excising from a story dialogue which "compared the human race to 'cats and monkeys.'" James felt that

> . . . the "immoral" episodes don't artistically affront. With such a standard of propriety, it makes it a bad look out ahead for imaginative writing. For what class of minds is it that such very timorous scruples are thought necessary?

while granting that

> Evidently, too, Howells has a better notion of the allowances of the common public than I have, and I am much obliged to him for performing the excision personally, for of course he will have done it neatly. About his offer to have me write monthly for the <u>Atlantic Monthly</u> I shall directly write to him. I am charmed and ask nothing better.[1]

By March 9, 1874, however, James was at least willing to consider an offer from <u>Scribner's Monthly</u>. Josiah Holland had solicited James through a letter to Henry James, Sr., who handled much of his son's correspondence. James's comments to his parents clearly reflect the degree of his loyalty to the <u>Atlantic</u> and to Howells:

> I am well disposed to accept his /Holland's/ offer, but there is an obstacle. I feel myself under a tacit pledge to offer first to the <u>Atlantic</u> any serial novel I should write--and should consider myself unfriendly to Howells if I made a bargain with <u>Scribner</u> without speaking first to him. I am pretty sure the <u>Atlantic</u> would like equally well with <u>Scribner</u> to have my story and I should prefer to appearing there. It must depend upon the money question, however, entirely and whichever will pay best shall have

---

[1] <u>Henry James Letters</u>, I, 333-36.

the story, and if the Atlantic will pay as much as the other, I ought, properly, to take up with it.[1]

John W. DeForest was another of the new writers who received Howells's public, personal, and editorial attention, and who returned mixed appreciation. Critical praise--from Howells's first lengthy recognition of the Harpers' volume publication of Miss Ravenel's Conversion, "so far he is really the only American novelist," to the late (1895) My Literary Passions in which Howells called Miss Ravenel ". . . one of the best American novels I had known . . . an advanced realism before realism was known by name"--illustrates Howells's own conclusion that "if I have not been able to make the public care for them /DeForest's books/ as much as I did it has not been for want of trying."

Howells's attempts to make the public care for DeForest's work were not restricted to the praise in reviews. From his first discovery of Miss Ravenel, he used the power of his editorial offices to promote DeForest's career. In 1868, as the Atlantic's assistant editor, Howells had invited DeForest to submit stories of the South. When Osgood gained ownership and Howells became full-charge editor in 1871, the new series began with Kate Beaumont, the first DeForest novel to be published in a major national magazine. As DeForest's episodes proceeded to come in and be published, Howells suggested greater brevity. Though DeForest's answer acknowledges the assistance

---

[1] Henry James Letters, I, 435.

Howells had given him, the novelist countered with advice of his own to the young editor.

> My Dear Mr. Howells,
>
> You have believed in me more than most men in authority . . .
>
> I mail today the ninth number of Kate Beaumont. I have tried to make it shorter . . .
>
> I have an idea, by the way, that, if a serial is interesting, the numbers had better be long than short. In the days when I read serials I used to be irritated at getting only a mouthful of sentiment at a time. The veteran English editors, you know, give immense spread of canvass to their stories. It seems to me that the Atlantic has generally lacked in this point; not sufficiently considering the great herd of young people, eager to browse upon romance; editing too much for Mr. Emerson & other select Bostonians; forgetting that our "select few" is a very few.
>
> The great question of course is--is the story interesting? I was almost discouraged the other day by a leader in the Tribune on "American Novels" which said that DeForest is doing good work "almost unnoticed." I see few papers, but I fear the man is right. If you think so, let me know, & I will try to put in more stimulus, or, that failing, to be much briefer. Perhaps, however, the coming volume publication of Overland will help. In this country advertisement & trumpeting are as potent as around Jericho.[1]

The question did come to whether the public found "the story interesting," and the answer was a rather resounding negative. Despite DeForest's having pointed him to the direction of the "veteran English editors" and correcting Howells's sense of audience from "Mr. Emerson & other select Bostonians" to "the great herd of young people," Howells used the Atlantic's own review of Kate Beaumont to chastise

---

[1] DeForest to Howells, May 27, 1871, William Dean Howells Papers, Houghton Library, Harvard University, Cambridge. Hereafter referred to as Howells Papers.

the unresponsive readers, claiming that the United States did not lack a great novelist so much as "a public to recognize him." The volume publication of Overland, an effort of DeForest's to exploit the public interest in western scenery, did not "help." The final chapters of Kate Beaumont seem truncated, and DeForest went on to his next novel, The Wetherell Affair, which he published in The Galaxy, where Overland had appeared serially.

After Osgood had sold the Atlantic to Houghton, Howells tried again with serial publication of DeForest's novel on corruption in the Grant administration, Honest John Vane. During its run, he also commissioned and printed a critical overview of "DeForest's Novels," a lengthy perspective piece of the kind Howells would later recommend to Richard Grant White as a way of reviving an author's sagging public appeal. Neither public recognition nor the monetary compensation DeForest wanted were forthcoming, and DeForest soon began to perceive the early 1870s as having been the peak of his literary reputation. He became increasingly bitter toward just those categories of readers, "the great herd," whom he had suggested, in 1871, the Atlantic editors insufficiently considered. He continued writing toward his own perception of the popular taste, but both his novels and his letters to Howells reflected an increasingly strident indictment of the American public, and especially the lower classes and the female reader. Howells met DeForest's bitterness with the suggestion of an article on army organization, and when The Galaxy went under and sold its subscription list to the Atlantic,

Howells took another DeForest serial novel. DeForest tried his editor by insisting the new novel, Irene, the Missionary, be published anonymously, as he was attempting to curry the public favor in a new way. DeForest's identification with Howells and insistence on making his own conclusions are clear in a letter he wrote from New Haven early in 1879,

> My Dear Howells,
> Your appreciation thaws out a heart frozen by neglect . . . I don't understand why you & I haven't sold monstrously, except on the theory that our novel-reading public is mainly female or a very juvenile public, & wants something nearer its own mark of intellect & taste, as, for instance, "Helen's Babies" & "That Husband of Mine." There is James, to be sure, who belongs to our school, & who yet seems to be forging ahead. But I think that is because he has crossed the ocean & appealed to the maturer public of the old world. At home I suppose that he has only had a "succes d' estime," or rather, perhaps, a "succes de haime," for the women are very mad about his "Daisy Miller."
> I read your "Aroostock" . . . You are gravely right in showing up the American lady who gets on her knees to it. /Venice & Florence society/ It is quite time we should protest against the flunkeyism of the colonie de Paris.

But for all of DeForest's finding the female novel-reading public restricting his success (and for his misreading of the worth of "Daisy Miller" to James's popular recognition), he continued by rejecting Howells's solicitation of an army article.

> As for the article on army organization, I did think of it, & went to reading with a view to it. . . . But . . . it should be written by a thorough specialist. It would cost me months to suit myself on that subject, & I can't afford so much time for the usual fee of an article. . . .

DeForest also objected to the printers' "ramming my narrative and dialogue into solid column" and suggested the Atlantic advertise Irene in "the religious papers." He told Howells, "There is a large public which is interested in missions. I hope that I shall be guessed at as a returned missionary, or a lady."[1]

If the large public was interested in missions, DeForest's missionary, in the words of the New York Times reviewer, made a reader "long for the good old cannibal days." But, of course, Howells and the Atlantic published a most positive review.

Howells's critical reputation and much-vaunted openness to new writers brought him far more manuscripts and potential contributors than he had time and taste or the magazine had space for. To these potential contributors, Howells often addressed himself in essays written both during and after his editorship. He reminded the beginning writer that it was the editor's, not the author's, job to determine what would find favor with the public, and that "The success of American magazines, which is nothing less than prodigious . . . is not only from the courage to decide what ought to please, but from the knowledge of what does please."[2] He asked the eager contributor to admit

> the universe does not revolve around any one of us. . . .
> The thing we strive for is recognition, but when this
> comes it is apt to turn our heads. . . . It is not the
> first business of a periodical to print contributions of

---

[1] DeForest to Howells, March 11, 1879, Howells Papers.

[2] Howells, "Criticism and Fiction," in Criticism and Fiction, p. 63.

this one or of that, but . . . its first business is to amuse and instruct its readers.[1]

Though he claimed himself delighted whenever he found a new light in the stacks of unsolicited manuscripts, Howells soon began postponing his reads through the piles of copy. He later wrote about the guilt an editor felt in accepting a manuscript he could not expect to publish in a reasonable time, but remembered practically that

> . . . at first I could not return a manuscript without a pang . . . in a surprisingly little time that melting mood congealed into an icy indifference, if it did not pass into the sort of inhuman complacency of the judge who sentences a series of proven offenders.

Howells as editor was actually seldom directly accused of ignoring or barring new potential contributors. This may have resulted, in part, from Howells's taking on himself the burden of extensive and often detailed correspondence with any applicant who showed promise. On sifting manuscripts, he recalled,

> The hardest of all to manage were those which had some savor of acceptance in them; which had promise, or which failed so near the point of success that it was a real grief to refuse them. Conscience then laid it upon me to write to the authors and give hopes, or reasons, or tender excuses, and not dismiss any of them with the printed circular that carried insult and despair in the smooth uncandor of its assurance that the contribution in question was not declined necessarily because of a want of merit in it.

Apart from such conscience-bound labor for the contributor of promise, if not final accomplishment, Howells found the practicalities of

---

[1] Howells, "The Editor's Relations with the Young Contributor," in *Literature and Life* (1902; reprint ed., Port Washington, New York: Kennicat Press, 1968), p. 67.

magazine publishing functionally useful in the job of reading manuscripts. He commented that

> It was at first surprising, and when no longer surprising it was gratifying, to find that the vast mass of the contributions fixed their own fate, almost at a glance. They were of subjects treated before, or subjects not to be treated at all, or they were self-condemned by their uncouth or slovenly style, or were written in a hand so crude and ignorant that it was at once apparent that they had not the root of literature in them.[1]

The list of "subjects not to be treated at all" in Howells's Atlantic was, like much of his editorship, a combination of the legacy from Lowell's and Fields's Atlantic and of Howells's personal interest in promoting realistic and native directions in our literature. Both the legacy and Howells's promotion necessarily functioned in the particular position of the Atlantic within the spectrum of American magazine publishing and in the general climate of social, economic, religious, political, and legal forces of American society. The nature and expectations of the Atlantic's perceived audience, both in terms of the direct response of subscribers and of the impact of criticism from other journals and opinion-makers, conditioned the editors' professional choices of material for the magazine.

Howells repeatedly expressed--privately, in his correspondence with contributors, in his criticism, and in his literary essays and fiction--that much of what appealed to him personally, or which he personally read with appreciation of some dimension of the work, was

---

[1] Howells, "Recollections," pp. 188-89.

unsuited to the audience of a "family" magazine. Throughout his career, he directly confronted "the question of how much or how little the American novel ought to deal with certain facts of life which are not usually talked of before young people." In all Howells's discussions--and replies to accusations of American fiction's "prudishness," "truckling to propriety," "limitations," etc.--he generally concurs with the disputants' reasoning that America's literature is conditioned by the fact that "the novel in our civilization now always addresses a mixed company, and that the vast majority of the company are ladies." However, Howells does not allow any excess moralism or need for protection simply to "the sex which is somehow supposed to have purity in its keeping (as if purity were a thing that did not practically concern the other sex, preoccupied with serious affairs)" but expressly to the "young people" among them, remembering that "the vast majority of the company" of readers "are ladies, and that very many, if not most, of these ladies are young girls."[1] What we have, essentially, is the much-discussed "young girl and American parlour table standard of decency," but in the particulars of its influence and motivations, we have dimensions of practical popular publishing which have actually been little discussed.

Henry James claimed, in a story of the 1890s, that it was "the relations between the sexes" that could not be discussed in the pages of America's family magazines, but the actual practice implied

---

[1] Howells, "Criticism and Fiction," pp. 69-70.

much more specific requirements and restrictions, some of which, depending on the writer's perspective, might have been crucial in the battle between realism and romanticism. Howells, both as an editor and a critic, acknowledged the necessity of subjects which in themselves held interest for the general reader. He usually saw such subjects as of two kinds, often expressing the difference as between that which would "inform" and that which would "entertain." The first category contained all those "fresh" subjects available in the treatment of national life: the pictures of distinctive regional customs, characters, scenery and occupations; the histories of incidents and personalities; and the exposition of philosophical or practical positions. In this category, contributors with "subjects treated before" could not be expected to gain the popular interest unless the writer's own reputation, personality, or involvement would itself engage the audience. Work which set itself, in whole or in part, to "entertain" generally required material which, if not "fresh," had "an instant fascination." In the most general sense, Howells explained,

> This is what makes a love intrigue of some sort all but essential to the popularity of any fiction. Without such an intrigue the intellectual equipment of the author must be of the highest, and then he will succeed only with the highest class of readers.[1]

The problem, of course, was in how the writer was to develop "a love intrigue" and yet not "deal with certain facts of life which

---

[1] Howells, "Criticism and Fiction," p. 71.

are not usually talked of before young people." However adamant and various were the opinions of editors and authors as to whether this restriction was necessary or desirable, Howells felt the necessity of its function within the magazine. The way he dealt with its terms in editing manuscripts is distinctive in acknowledging the constraints of the family magazine, reconciling demands between the artist's reality and the audience's possibility, and pushing American literature in specific directions.

Much of what the restriction came down to was writing in a way in which action and motivation could be implied rather than directly expressed. For example, while critics often substantiate Howells's personal prudery by quoting his comment that he could not contemplate DeForest's Mrs. Larue without a shudder, Howells's actual editing of DeForest's work was more in keeping with the perspective Howells expressed in his 1867 Atlantic review of Miss Ravenel's Conversion: "there is too much anxiety that the nature of her intrigue with Carter shall not be misunderstood." For the audience which included "young people," Howells felt it just as well that those not sagacious or experienced enough to understand by inference might miss "the nature" of "intrigue" or "facts of life which are not usually talked of."

Henry James, even in his earliest Atlantic contribution, "The Story of a Year," was adept at ironically exploiting the stricture toward implication. Describing his young people's aspect on returning from a roam in the hills, James had written

> What blinding ardor had kindled these strange phenomena:
> a young lieutenant scornful of his first uniform, a well-
> bred young lady reckless of her stockings?
> Good reader, this narrative is averse to retrospect.

And while Howells admitted that fiction's limitation to depicting "chaste courtship" sometimes resulted in unreal heroines and situations, he clearly felt that the deemphasis of romantic passion more realistically represented life's commonplace proportions, that it was only in the magazines the writer was so restrained, and that the writer's "restriction /was one/ he had put upon himself in this regard; for it is a mistake, as can be readily shown, to suppose that others impose it."[1]

Howells saw many of the "intense effects" of both "guilty love" and sensational action as essentially "cheap effects" for writers who were not serious about fiction's representation of life and readers whose "thumb-fingered apprehension requires something gross and palpable for its assurance of reality." Many of the writers Howells favored used their fiction, as Howells used his own, not only to counter implicitly the reader's expectation for a story to be sensation and adventure, but also to comment expressly in the text on the discrepancies between life's realities, which the serious writer reflects and records, and the highly colored effects and expectations of heroicism and poetic justice, which are the creations of romantic imagination and popular entertainment. Howells looked back with satisfaction on the American books which he read "with

---

[1] Howells, "Criticism and Fiction," p. 71.

perfect comfort and much exhiliration," but which he thought "the average Englishman" (who disliked Howells's critical commentary as much as his preference in novels) would find books in which

> Nothing happens; that is, nobody murders or debauches anybody else; there is no arson or pillage of any sort; there is not a ghost, or a ravening beast, or a hairbreadth escape, or a shipwreck, or a monster of self-sacrifice, or a lady five thousand years old in the whole course of the story.[1]

Howells also felt that no matter whether one "wished to oppose them in their aspiration for greater freedom, or . . . to encourage them," writers exaggerated their case in claiming American fiction, by the agency of the Young Girl, was kept from "the most vital interests of life" and "one of the most serious and sorrowful problems of life." On the one hand, he admitted,

> The manners of the novel have been improving with those of its readers . . . Gentlemen no longer swear or fall drunk under the table, or abduct young ladies and shut them up in lonely country-houses, or so habitually set about the ruin of their neighbors' wives, as they once did. Generally, people now call a spade an agricultural implement; they have not grown decent without having also grown a little squeamish.

He also claimed that the novelist, on "unquestionable proof of his seriousness" and with "scientific decorum" could yet deal with "certain phases of life" as George Eliot did and as Hawthorne did in the Scarlet Letter. He separated the work of such "right-minded" "fine artists" from such as was also available as "entertainment only," "at evil moments when it seems as if all the women had taken

---

[1] Howells, "Criticism and Fiction," p. 61.

to writing hysterical improprieties, and some of the men were trying to be at least as hysterical in despair of being as improper."[1]

Whatever the writer's motive and accomplishment, he was not restricted from publishing--and indeed, Howells frequently remarks such books would be applauded as "virile" and "passionate"--but restricted to publishing it "as a book" rather than in a magazine. "A book," Howells explains, "is something by itself, responsible for its character, which becomes quickly known, and it does not necessarily penetrate to every member of the household." The parent can ask his child not to read the book, lock it up--or as Howells himself did with his French novels, hide it from his children. The magazine contributor's work had, however, to meet a more specialized standard.

> But with the magazine and its serial the affair is different. Between the editor of a reputable English or American magazine and the families which receive it there is a tacit agreement that he will print nothing which a father may not read to his daughter, or safely leave her to read herself. After all, it is a matter of business; and the insurgent novelist should consider the matter with coolness and common-sense. The editor did not create the situation; but it exists, and he could not even attempt to change it without many sorts of disaster.[2]

Such a distinction between the freedom of volume publication and the different affair of magazine serials was unlikely, however, to be met with "coolness and common-sense" by those like DeForest who found volume publication "almost without profit."[3]

---

[1] Howells, "Criticism and Fiction," p. 73.

[2] Howells, "Criticism and Fiction," p. 75.

[3] DeForest to Howells, June 24, 1886, Howells Papers.

Howells made clear that the editorial "revenge in rejecting the contributor who has bothered him to read a manuscript quite through before it yields itself unfit for publication"[1] was not exercised wholesale against work which could generally address "every member of the household" but which lapsed into occasional stronger incident, language, or opinion than the Atlantic generally printed. The roles of editor and contributor in such regard called for mutually responsible acceptable behavior in the literary business. Howells defined the terms for the potential contributor:

> If he is a wise editor, he will wish to hold his hand as much as possible; he will think twice before he asks the contributor to change this or correct that; he will leave him as much to himself as he can. The young contributor, on his part, will do well to realize this, and to receive all the editorial suggestions, which are veiled commands in most cases, as meekly and as imaginatively as possible.
>
> The editor cannot always give his reasons, however strongly he may feel them, but the contributor, if sufficiently docile, can always divine them. It behooves him to be docile at all times, for this is merely the willingness to learn; and whether he learns that he is wrong, or that the editor is wrong, still he gains knowledge.[2]

Aside from guilty passion, the largest category of material that Howells knew to be chancy but did not find always easy to "give his reasons" for restricting was anything to do with religion. The incidents from which the Atlantic had suffered calumny from the religious press, various pulpits, and the newspapers or had suffered

---

[1] Howells, "Recollections," p. 188.

[2] Howells, "The Editor's Relations," p. 70.

the indignation and cancellations of its subscribers were of so many kinds and from such different sources that anyone would be hard put to find a thread of consistency in what was deemed unacceptable. Not even the reputation of the writer or the "seriousness" of the treatment necessarily availed against possible negative public reaction. Howells remembered of Oliver Wendell Holmes's The Guardian Angel, published serially in the Atlantic in 1867-68, "that a supposed infidelity in the tone . . . cost the Atlantic Monthly many subscribers" though on their first meeting, it was Holmes who "had to explain Orthodoxy to me" and "I never heard an irreligious word from him, far less a scoff or sneer at religion."[1]

More from his own sure judgment and wish to set the Atlantic apart from the lurid sensational newspapers, Howells also preferred any violence incident to Atlantic stories to be offstage. He considered the taste for detailed gore to be vulgar and essentially non-literary, felt the popular taste for it well supplied through other publishing vehicles, and preferred to think that the Atlantic's traditions and audience represented a voice for something higher than such sensation.

In making distinctions and editorial suggestions on questionable material generally and on the language of a manuscript specifically, Howells realized the significance of the Atlantic's long-

---

[1] Howells, "Oliver Wendell Holmes," in Literary Friends, pp. 130-31 and "My First Visit," p. 43.

standing copy-editing processes. Throughout his decade as editor, he claimed "I revised all the proofs,"[1] actually preferring the task to those of writing literary notices and sifting through new manuscripts. Howells may well have wanted to keep his hand on the copy-reading to insure as much freedom as possible to his contributors. From his first service as Fields's assistant, Howells had been far more likely to restrain the editorial blue pencil, suggesting that authors should have their way when disputed points were "not likely to meet severe criticism." Writing to Fields late in 1869, Howells had made a joke on his own preceding sentence--"Concerning this last sentence, Mr. Kirk would have written on the margin: 'A scene cannot take place'"--and went on to state his difference of attitude and what would be the difference in his policy as editor: "I believe on general principles that we're proof-read too much."[2] Writing publicly of his editing policy, Howells claimed to reject that "vanity of technique, which is so apt to vaunt itself in the teacher," knowing "that the best he can do, after all, is to let the pupil teach himself."[3]

Combined with Howells's promotion of native, democratic literature which focused on the realism of everyday, this relative editorial allowance of freedom encouraged writers to use realistic

---

[1] Howells, "Recollections," p. 191.

[2] Howells to Fields, 1866, Fields Collection; Howells to Fields, August 24, 1869, Fields Collection and Life in Letters, 1:146-49, quoted in Austin, Fields, pp. 148, 160.

[3] Howells, "The Editor's Relations," p. 70.

American language. Howells felt that the "literary decentralization" of local color, especially in its use of local "dialects," "freshened and revived" our language. While Howells distinguished between the colloquial dialects and slang, he would allow even the latter when its use was forceful and apt. He knew that "perhaps slang has been dropping its 's' and becoming language ever since the world began" but disliked its use merely as an effect or in the "typographical humor" of some American humorists.

> I would not have any one go about for new words, but if one of them came aptly, not to reject its help. For our novelists to write Americanly, from any motive, would be a dismal error, but being born Americans, I would have them use "Americanisms" whenever these serve their turn; and when their characters speak, I should like to hear them speak true American, with all the varying . . . accents. If we bother ourselves to write what the critics imagine to be "English," we shall be priggish and artificial, and still more so if we make our Americans talk "English."[1]

In devaluing the use of "Americanisms" merely for the sake of doing so and promoting the integrated use of native speech in realistic fiction, Howells encouraged the movement of colloquial language and "dialect" and its acceptance in mainstream American literature and prestigious national publishing, rather than relegating it to the realms of popular humor, oral tradition, and sub-literary almanacs and newspapers from which it first developed.

When James R. Osgood's first major financial crisis resulted in his selling off his periodicals, the Atlantic Monthly with

---

[1] Howells, "Criticism and Fiction," pp. 64-66.

Howells went to the firm of Houghton & Mifflin. Houghton's approach to the Atlantic focused on combining the promotional potential of the magazine's traditional association with the older, popular New England writers and the mass appeal of the most successful of the new generation. Of plans for the former, Howells recalled

> When Messrs. Houghton & Mifflin became owner of The Atlantic Monthly, Mr. Houghton fancied having some breakfasts and dinners, which should bring the publishers and the editor face to face with the contributors, who were bidden from far and near. Of course the subtle fiend of advertising, who has now grown so unblushing bold, lurked under the covers at these banquets, and the junior partner and the young editor had their joint and separate fine anguishes of misgiving as to the taste and principle of them; but they were really very simple-hearted and honestly meant hospitality, and they prospered as they ought, and gave great pleasure and no pain.[1]

The occasions Howells remembered honored New England's most popular names: Whittier, Longfellow, Stowe. (Houghton's directions became even clearer--and perhaps less "simple-hearted"--when, during the tenure of Howells's successor, subscribers were offered premiums of portraits of the New England poets for one dollar over the normal subscription price.)

H. L. Houghton also wanted Howells to bring his friend, Samuel Clemens, into the lists of Atlantic contributors, despite the fact that the Atlantic's highest page rates were nowhere near what Clemens could expect elsewhere. The idea had been raised before; Annie Fields's diary of 1868 notes that James Parton had suggested

---

[1] Howells, "My Mark Twain," in Literary Friends, p. 293.

"it would be possible to make the 'Atlantic Monthly' far more popular. He suggests a writer named Mark Twain be engaged."[1] Howells would tactfully ascribe Houghton's eagerness to a feeling of "the incongruity of his /Twain's/ absence from the leading periodical of the country," but also admitted that editor and publisher expected the magazine "to prosper without precedent in its circulation"[2] from printing Mark Twain. The Mark Twain Atlantic materials would be pirated from review copies by the newspapers while the magazine "languished on the news stands," and the publisher had no more direct commercial benefit from the association with Clemens than his predecessor had had with Bret Harte. The association of Clemens as contributor and Howells as editor was, however, very significant as the beginning of a long-standing relationship in which Howells would advise on, edit, and read proof for much of Clemens's fiction, an influence which has been variously construed as aiding or debilitating Clemens's genius.

The immediate editorial handling of Clemens's Atlantic contributions illuminates both the freedom and restriction of 1870s magazine publishing and the nature of Howells's restraint on contributors whose quality he admired but whose literary directions might conflict with the magazine's interests. Clemens met Howells's first request for an Atlantic contribution with the offer of a "Fable

---

[1] Mrs. James T. Fields, Memories of a Hostess, ed. M. A. DeWolfe Howe (Boston: The Atlantic Monthly Press, 1922), p. 111.

[2] Howells, "My Mark Twain," pp. 267-68.

for Old Boys & Girls." Howells telegrammed a reply, now lost, but we can gather its import from Clemens's response:[1]

> I made a mistake in writing you. . . . I was charging about 33 per cent more than I meant to.
> This disgusts me. But I send the "Feble for Old Boys and Girls" anyway. Since its price is lowered I don't know but what you might really come to like it. But hurl it back with obloquy if you don't. I can dodge.
> I enclose also a "True Story" which has no humor in it. You can pay as lightly as you choose for that, if you want it, for it is rather out of my line.

Howells chose the "True Story" of an old colored woman, for which Houghton agreed to pay twenty dollars per page. Twain's "Fable for Old Boys & Girls" was returned, with the following explanation.

> Not, let me hasten to say, that I don't think they're both very good. But the Atlantic, as regards matters of religion, is just in that Good Lord, Good Devil condition when a little fable like yours wouldn't leave a single Presbyterian, Baptist, Unitarian, Episcopalian, or Millerite paying subscriber--all the dead-heads would stick to it, and abuse it in the denominational newspapers. Send your fable to some truly pious concern like Scribner or Harper, and they'll extract it into all the hymnbooks. But it would ruin us.

Howells continued with what he found particular in the "True Story": "extremely good and touching with the best and reallest kind of black talk in it" and made a first general editorial suggestion:

> Perhaps it couldn't be better than it is; but if you feel like giving it a little more circumstantiation (you didn't know there was such a word as that, did you?) on getting the proof, why, don't mind making the printers some over-running.

---

[1] All of the correspondence between Twain and Howells which is quoted may be found in Selected Mark Twain-Howells Letters 1872-1910, ed. Frederick Anderson, William M. Gibson, and Henry Nash Smith (Cambridge: Harvard University Press, Belknap Press, 1967), pp. 20-23, 26, 31, 33-34.

Clemens's and Howells's next letters crossed in the mails, but this confusion would not alone explain the difference between Clemens's assumptions of what the editor's objections might be and Howells's actual recommendations and changes. Clemens had replied to the Howells's letter given above

> All right, my boy, send proof sheets <u>here</u>. I amend
> dialect stuff by talking & talking & <u>talking</u> it until
> it sounds right--& I had difficulty with this negro
> talk because a negro sometimes (rarely) says "goin'" &
> sometimes "gwyne", & they make just such discrepancies
> in other words--& when you come to reproduce them on
> paper they look as if the variation resulted from the
> writer's carelessness. But I want to work at the proofs
> & get the dialect as nearly right as possible.

Howells's concern had not been for any superficial discrepancy in the dialogue or the "circumstantiation" of dialogue such as appears in The Author's "Explanatory" of <u>Huckleberry Finn</u>. Rather, he seems to be encouraging Mark Twain to that circumstancing or framing of portraits of subculture life and dialect that puts an explaining authorial narrator between the general audience and the particular depiction of a reality. The beginning of "A True Story," as it appeared in the <u>Atlantic</u>, provides the same kind of authorial "circumstantiation" that would appear in the local color of Joel Chandler Harris and Charles Chesnutt:

> It was summer-time, and twilight. We were sitting on
> the porch of the farmhouse, on the summit of the hill,
> and "Aunt Rachel" was sitting respectfully below our
> level, on the steps--for she was our servant, and colored.

The character this narrator gives to himself is also far more like the insularly white consciousness of Chesnutt's imagined gentleman farmer than the usual boyish iconoclast Twain assigned to himself.

The porch-sitter of "A True Story," observing that he's never seen "Aunt Rachel" sigh, asks

> "Aunt Rachel, how it is that you've lived sixty years and never had any trouble?"
>
> She stopped quaking. She paused, and there was a moment of silence. She turned her face over her shoulder toward me, and said, without even a smile in her voice:
> "Misto C----, is you in 'arnest?"

Only somewhat after that does "Aunt Rachel" proceed with her dialect story.

The proofs also crossed in the mails between Clemens's moves from Hartford to Elmira, and before Clemens ever received them to see what had been done, Howells wrote to say:

> This little story delights me more and more: I wish you had about forty of 'em!
>
> Please send the proof back suddenly. You can reject any of the proposed corrections.

Clemens seems not to have rejected the "proposed corrections," and he continued to see Howells's magazine as a place for trying things out of his usual line and for developing an audience and reputation apart from and in addition to his established popularity.

After "A True Story" finally made it into the <u>Atlantic</u> late in 1874, Howells was beseeching an <u>Atlantic</u> serial. Clemens first felt himself too busy and without an appropriate idea, but as he entertained Joseph Twichell with stories of piloting on the Mississippi, Twichell commented "What a virgin subject to hurl into a magazine!" and Clemens wrote off immediately to Howells to rescind his regrets and offer the piloting reminiscences as "a series of

papers to run through 2 months or 6 or 9?--or about 4 months, say?"
Clemens had the first installment ready quickly, and the contributor
and editor had no trouble readying the proofs for the January issue
in which Howells had wanted to start a Mark Twain serial. Clemens
sent the first installment with instructions to Howells--"Cut it,
scarify it, reject it--handle it with entire freedom"--and suggested
that they publish the remainder every other month.

    Howells, having already announced continuation in the February
number, replied "I want the sketches, if you can make them, <u>every</u>
<u>month</u>" and held back on preliminary general suggestions.

> The piece about the Mississippi is capital . . . and I
> hope to send you a proof directly. I don't think I
> shall meddle much with it even in the way of suggestion.
> The sketch of the low-lived little town was so good,
> that I could have wished ever so much more of it; and
> perhaps the tearful watchman's story might have been
> abridged--tho this may seem different in print.

When Howells saw the tearful watchman in the print of <u>Atlantic</u> proofs,
he liked the length of it no better, and the <u>Atlantic</u>'s version of
it is much abridged. Howells also could not resist pushing his
friend more strongly to depiction of the actuality of the "virgin
subject."

> If I might put in my jaw at this point, I should say,
> stick to actual fact and character in the thing, and
> give things in <u>detail</u>. <u>All</u> that belongs with old
> river life is novel and is now mostly historical. Don't
> write <u>at</u> any supposed Atlantic audience, but yarn it off
> as if <u>into</u> my sympathetic ear. Don't be afraid of rests
> or pieces of dead color. I fancied a sort of hurried
> and anxious air in the first.

    To the truncation of the watchman's story, Clemens replied,
"Your amendment is good," but he explained away the circumstance

which prompted Howells's general advice to give the "actual fact
. . . in detail."

> It isn't the Atlantic audience that distresses me; for
> it is the only audience that I sit down before in perfect
> serenity (for the simple reason that it don't require a
> "humorist" to paint himself striped & stand on his head
> every fifteen minutes.) The trouble was, that I was
> only bent on "working up an atmosphere" and that is to
> me a most fidgety & irksome thing sometimes. I avoid it,
> usually, but in this case it was absolutely necessary,
> else every reader would be applying the atmosphere of his
> own river or sea experiences, & that shirt wouldn't fit,
> you know.

That Clemens in writing felt unrestricted by "the Atlantic audience" or by Howells's editorial suggestions or amendments is clear just in that the famous incident over the profanity in the second installment of "Old Times" did occur. All the particulars of this episode have been retailed so often as to not need restatement here, but the terms in which Howells identified the problem--". . . the profane words. These she [Mrs. Howells] thinks could be better taken for granted; and in fact I think the sagacious reader could infer them"--Clemens's admission "that I had left it out when reading the MSS. . . ." to his own wife, and the changes the editor made in the proofs indicate the whole process went more smoothly and satisfactorily to all than later critics have made it seem. The text retains such mild, though ungenteel, language as "All I desired to ask Mr. B---- was the simple question whether he was ass enough to really imagine . . ." but the pilots become simply the locuters of "perfect profanity."

Hardly a demonstration of Howells's suggestion to "stick to the actual fact and character in the thing" in its linguistic detail, and Howells himself, in "My Mark Twain," told the story and admitted "I made him observe that I had left out the profanity." Howells's explanation is hardly personally defensive; the situation had to do with the magazine.

> At that time I had become editor of the Atlantic Monthly, and I had allegiances belonging to the conduct of what was and still remains the most scrupulously cultivated of our periodicals. When Clemens began to write for it he came willingly under its rules, for with all his wilfulness there never was a more biddable man in things you could show him a reason for. He never made the least of that trouble which so abounds for the hapless editor from narrower-minded contributors. If you wanted a thing changed, very good, he changed it; if you suggested that a word or a sentence or a paragraph had better be struck out, very good, he struck it out. His proof-sheets came back each a veritable "mush of concession," as Emerson says. Now and then he would try a little stronger language than The Atlantic had stomach for, and once when I sent him a proof I made him observe that I had left out the profanity.[1]

Howells also offered Clemens the same general advice on the public's preference for clear endings that Henry James had taken with such umbrage.

No matter how Howells and his publishers sought the large popular audience, the Atlantic Monthly throughout the 1870s combined concession and courage without adding to its list of subscribers. The fifty thousand who remained after the significant losses at the end of Fields's editorship declined to about twelve thousand by 1881. Expectations of interest from Holmes's returning to his "Breakfast-Table" columns, so popular in the 1860s, were disappointed. The

---

[1] Howells, "My Mark Twain," p. 267.

only noticeable success from the selections of Howells's years came from the Atlantic's printing Thomas Bailey Aldrich's "Marjorie Daw."

James R. Osgood was doing little better than the magazine he had bought and then been forced to sell; in 1878, part of his book publishing enterprise also went to Houghton, and by 1881, he was forced to sell his interest entirely. At the same time, Houghton announced that William Dean Howells was leaving the editorship of the Atlantic Monthly. The new editor was to be Thomas Bailey Aldrich, who had previously managed Every Saturday for Fields and then Osgood, but had not served as an editor since he had been "cut adrift" when Osgood sold his magazines and Every Saturday was allowed to die.

Howells's handling of contributions in the last months of his Atlantic editorship and his correspondence with his successor, Thomas Bailey Aldrich, indicate that he anticipated his departure from the Atlantic Monthly. While Kenneth Lynn, Howells's most recent biographer, and others have made much of Howells's neurotic state of mind shortly after leaving his editorial post, they generally assume his decision was an unforced choice to devote more time to writing fiction and to free himself from the business' incessant labor. The public reporting on the changeover unanimously assured that Howells's move was entirely voluntary, but as Donald Rouel Tuttle observed in his 1939 Western Reserve University dissertation, all the journalists seem to be writing from the same source, likely the official house version and press release. While there is always

some danger in reading fiction too closely as autobiography, Howells's
Indian Summer, with a protagonist whose situation in many ways
paralleled Howells's own, may offer insight. The novel begins with
the musings of Colville, a former editor.

> He had, in fact, taken the prodigious risk of breaking
> his life sharp off from the course in which it had been
> set for many years, and of attempting to renew in a
> direction from which it had long been diverted. <u>Such an
> act could be precipitated only by a strong impulse of
> conscience or a profound disgust,</u> and with Colville it
> sprang from disgust. He had experienced a bitter dis-
> appointment in the city . . . in whose favor he imagined
> that he had triumphantly established himself. (Italics mine.)

The underscored line is remarkable in that it is a general assertion
of a kind rare in Howells's fiction, especially in that it is neither
assigned to conversation between characters nor phrased in terms of
the "he had . . . he had" references which mark Colville's reverie.

Howells used other characteristics of his own transition
from power in drawing Colville. His autobiographical remembrances
and his friends say that for years he dreamt that he was either still
with the Atlantic Monthly or was going back to it. Colville found
himself "from the dream of night, /waking/ with a start to the
realization of the fact that he had no longer a newspaper."

Howells left the Atlantic editorship amidst squabbles
between Houghton and Osgood over rights to his future work, conflicts
which for a time seemed to jeopardize the agreement on the transition.
The split partners fast became intense rivals, and Aldrich, as a
member of the Houghton & Mifflin enterprise, reminded the firm a
number of times that Osgood was or might be getting the jump on them
in negotiations for manuscripts from major figures. Howells personally

decided to contract with Osgood for a steady, annual income with Osgood functioning in part as a sort of agent to place Howells's work where he could. Howells's personal allegiances and literary preferences came into higher relief when his career and aid to authors were separated from the Atlantic Monthly. Without Howells in the editorial offices, the Atlantic changed direction. The premiere writers of his generation generally followed Howells to different magazines and new publishing relationships. Samuel Clemens formed an entrepreneurial relationship with Osgood, with Clemens generally covering expenses and reaping the profits of what Osgood arranged for him. For a short time, Henry James also joined Howells in working through Osgood, promising him first three short stories in 1883 and then, through him, proposing The Bostonians to The Century.

James had rougher going dealing with a new editor who, in publishing both Howells's The Rise of Silas Lapham and James's The Bostonians found, "leaving aside any question as to literary merit, I am afraid Mr. Howells has beaten you in the matter of readers,"[1] and suggested that James both cut and speed up the action. James found himself in the unusual, for him, situation of having difficulty in keeping his schedule for producing The Bostonians serial installments. The popular and critical reaction intensified James's

---

[1] Gilder to James, May 18, 1885, Gilder Papers, New York Public Library, quoted in Smith, Gilder, p. 83.

difficulty with his next novel, Princess Casamassima, finding the details remained vague to him "partly--or indeed wholly--owing to the fact that I have been so terribly preoccupied . . . with the unhappy Bostonians."[1] He wrote to Howells about his hopes that the Princess would be "more popular," and when it was serially published in the Atlantic in 1885-86, Howells privately and publicly supported it as being the best of James's work thus far.

The public reaction made little improvement over the previous disaster, and James wrote to Howells more than once about how the books' receptions had put him back.

> I am still staggering a good deal under the mysterious and (to me) inexplicable injury wrought--apparently--upon my situation by my two last novels, the Bostonians and the Princess, from which I expected so much and derived so little. They have reduced the desire, and the demand, for my productions to zero--as I judge from the fact that though I have for a good while past been writing a number of good short things, I remain irremediably unpublished. Editors keep them back, for months and years, as if they were ashamed of them, and I am condemned apparently to eternal silence.[2]

Howells was receiving similar laments from John DeForest, and he soon attempted to aid both his friends by writing long appreciative essays on them for the magazines.

After James Osgood's final and total failure in the mid 1880s, Howells became associated with the Harper's firm. Though reluctant

---

[1] Henry James, August 10, 1885, in The Notebooks of Henry James, ed. F. O. Matthiessen and Kenneth B. Murdock (New York: Oxford University Press, 1947), p. 68.

[2] James Letters, ed. Percy Lubbock, 2 vols. (New York: Scribner, 1920), I, 135, quoted in Smith, Democracy, p. 135 and Matthiessen and Murdock, Notebooks, p. 69.

to take on any other charge than his own fictioning, Howells was first cajoled by Joseph Harper into conducting the "Editor's Study" for the Monthly, given freedom to express his literary opinions, but reminded that Harper trusted Howells to hear the "little bell" which warned a writer away from unnecessary controversy. After some six years of the "Study," Howells left editing and critical work for a few years, except for some months' association with Cosmopolitan. He returned to Harper's Weekly in 1895 to write "Life and Letters" and remained with the firm, through which Clemens was then arranging publication of some of his books, until Harper's went into receivership late in 1899, the news of which Howells learned through the newspapers. Howells returned to the Harpers late in 1901, when Colonel Harvey wanted to assure his firm's publication of Howells's new novel, The Kentons. Howells also then assumed responsibility for the "Easy Chair" column, worked in the office editing, and was the means through which Henry James finally negotiated the firm's printing The Ambassadors, a decision which had been left hanging for almost three years after James submitted a synopsis in 1900.[1]

Throughout these last decades, Howells was a mainstay of critical support for realist authors. He became popularly known as the "Dean of American Letters," a writer and critic who was familiar to a large audience. He encouraged the Harpers to print Mary Wilkins Freeman, Henry Demarest Lloyd and others. Stephen Crane, Frank Norris,

---

[1] Exman, House, pp. 153-56, 179, 192, 195.

and Hamlin Garland remembered how important Howells's support had been to them. Despite the seeming glory of Howells's reputation and his universally acknowledged influence, the negative reaction was also considerable. Howells remembered experiencing much personal attack for expressing his valuation of realistic and native fiction. He felt the sales of his later novels suffered from the reaction, and from all accounts, his assessment is likely accurate.

For all of this, Howells's influence and the lingering tradition of the Atlantic Monthly are often now evaluated in terms of whom and how he helped in these years. Stephen Crane claimed his own commitment to writing was affirmed by Howells's recognition at the point the young bohemian was about to give up in despair. Crane's work had been brought to Howells's attention by Hamlin Garland, who had been appalled by Crane's demeanor, dress, and life style, but who read the pages the seeming-derelict offered him. Howells worked vigorously to elicit publishers' and public support for the realism of Maggie, though he publicly found the later, instantly popular, Red Badge of Courage a falling-off and mistake.

Garland himself received strong support from Howells through the 1895 Rose of Dutcher's Coolly. Even with Garland's declining quality and facile popularizing in Her Mountain Lover and Cavanagh, Forest Ranger, Howells restricted his criticism to private complaints to Garland that the new work was not up to his standard--and patiently endured Garland's explanations that he needed to pursue a subject in print while it was hot, before the "journalists" wore it out. When Garland attempted to use for advertising himself positive comments in a private letter, Howells protested against his publicizing what was meant to be kept between brother writers. Garland's printed memories of Howells, however, recall little of this aid and tolerance, concentrating instead on personal trivia like the older man's peculiarity in not hosting luncheons or dinners in his home.[1]

If Garland complained of not being hosted, others felt that Howells's critically or editorially encouraging them to follow through on an initial--and perhaps accidental or only temporary--choice of subject matter cut off their own artistic nourishment. Just as Howells, after praising *Miss Ravenel*, wrote to John DeForest eliciting contributions on the South and, when DeForest later needed money, suggested a military article (proposals which DeForest rejected at the time), Howells encouraged many writers of promise to pursue their original, characteristic, and often local, subjects. He convinced H. B. Fuller, for example, to follow *The Cliff-Dwellers* with another Chicago novel--even though Fuller had expressly stated his hatred for the subject. Paul Lawrence Dunbar claimed he had suffered from Howells's promoting the directions of his early, local, dialect verse.

Whether Howells's directions were a magazine editor's tendency to type a writer with a particular approach, the nineteenth century's

---

[1] Garland-Howells and Howells-Garland letters in Howells Papers; Hamlin Garland, *Hamlin Garland's Diaries*, ed. Donald Pizer (San Marino, California: Huntington Library, 1968).

concentration on realism as regionalism, the native realist's focus on subject matter, or the advocate's search for a writer's strength and means to popular acknowledgement, the variety of his advisees and the impossibility of dealing with what might have been make such complaints difficult to evaluate. One could argue that H. B. Fuller's second Chicago book, With the Procession, does now seem more valuable to us than the European romances which he preferred to write. We know also that Howells was not inflexible in viewing a writer's changes in directions, that, for example, when Charles Chesnutt went from heavily and conventionally framed plantation tales, which combined dialect and a "white" narrator, to more direct fiction, Howells found the change "new and fresh and strong as life always is and fable never is." Chesnutt's own complaint, however, was that when his fiction became more realistic and racially conscious, Howells found it "bitter" and white editors and audiences left it unbought.

Howells's personal history and evaluations of genteel restriction on writers are often written not only in terms of indictments like the above but also as explanations of why some were excluded from the roster of his beneficiaries. Seemingly, the most interesting of the absentees is Theodore Dreiser, whose case--with regard to the 1900 publication of Sister Carrie--H. L. Mencken put before the public in his Book of Prefaces. Dreiser offered Sister Carrie, his first novel based on the sensational affair of his younger sister with a flamboyant felon, to Harper's in the year of the "Harper collapse" and reorganization. That firm suggested that

Dreiser try the manuscript on Doubleday, Page, where it was accepted by Thomas Nelson Page at the urging of his reader, Frank Norris. Frank Doubleday was out of the country when Page contracted the book, and both he and his wife disapproved of the novel and the arrangement on seeing the manuscript. Dreiser insisted that the publishers perform on their contract, and the book was printed, though not advertised. Frank Norris continued his advocacy by distributing review copies and praising the book to his associates, but there were few reviews and very small sales.[1] As Howells had previously lent significant support to Norris and would praise both Moran of the Lady Letty and McTeague, despite some expressed reservations over their restricted vision of violence and ugliness, the absence of Howells's advocacy for Sister Carrie has been considered significant. Howells reportedly told Dreiser privately that he "did not like" the book, an opinion which is usually assessed in terms comparable to Kenneth Lynn's "The novel's sexual candor was probably responsible for Howells's attitude."[2]

The legend of the suppression of Sister Carrie and Howells's and others' squeamishness in the face of realism and sexuality was vivified when the book was reprinted in a cheap, popular library British edition the following year. The British reviewers praised

---

[1] A brief, but relatively thorough, account of the early publishing history of Sister Carrie is contained in Claude Simpson, "Introduction" to Sister Carrie (Boston: Houghton, Mifflin, 1959), pp. ix-xi.

[2] Lynn, Howells, p. 317.

Dreiser's revelation of America's real crassness and materialism and assumed the book was rejected by Americans because they were unwilling to be shown--and to admit--the depths of their lack of culture and values. Even among the many who later learned to despise Dreiser personally, Sister Carrie is continually seen as a significant book, and its failure to gain critical attention or popular support as reprisals for violating sexual and moral fictional conventions.

The publishing situation which surrounded the 1900 Sister Carrie and Howells's refusal of involvement may, however, have been more complex and prosaic than the reprisal scenario. Thomas Nelson Page was a former Atlantic Monthly editor who had been lured away by S. S. McClure to join in a takeover of the Harper publishing empire; before McClure found he couldn't raise the capital for his venture, Frank Doubleday left their alliance to form a new firm and took Page with him. The Harpers had gone into receivership under the control of Colonel George Harvey late in 1899, and until late in 1900, Howells had no contract with the reorganized Harper firm and was not writing the critical articles defending realism which in the late 1880s and early 1890s had brought down on him unprecedented personal attacks and declines in the sales of his own books.[1]

Dreiser wrote to Howells in 1902 to state his "spiritual affection for you" and offer "my little tribute and acknowledge the

---

[1] Exman, House, pp. 180-83.

benefit I have received from your work,"[1] comparing Howells to Hardy and Tolstoy. Indeed, both the degree of Dreiser's radical departure from fictional conventions and the difference between his work and Howells's own may have been generally overstated. The handling of incident in Sister Carrie is hardly sexually explicit; Carrie's seduction by Drouet is rendered in indications neither more powerful nor unreserved than the expression of Norris or Crane. The characterization of Drouet--"He was drawn by his innate desire to act the old pursuing part. He would need to delight himself with Carrie as surely as he would need to eat his heavy breakfast."--is certainly no stronger than Howells's own of Jeff Durgin in the earlier The Landlord of Lion's Head, and Howells had attempted, in A Woman's Reason and A Modern Instance, portraits of middle class women with some of the problems and personality of Dreiser's Carrie.

Howells's experience with The Landlord of Lion's Head was a popular and fiscal disaster. Howells had shared with Stephen Crane in the 1890s his despair that it seemed the realists must yet wait their time. Trilby had been the popular novel of the preceding decade. DuMaurier's romantic nostalgia was among the best of what met readers' taste for the popular literature of historical romance, detective mystery, and adventure--a phenomenon which is repeatedly evidenced in the changing directions of even the most accepted and popularly acclaimed literary voices of the era. Howells had even

---

[1] Dreiser to Howells, May 14, 1902, Harvard, quoted in Lynn, Howells, p. 317.

himself followed his Landlord with yet another recycling of the popular March couple in Their Silver Wedding Journey.

Howells's not liking Sister Carrie, aside from the writer's ponderous style which even his advocates acknowledge as a liability, may as likely have had to do with the many assertions of authorial philosophy which underlie and, sometimes, interrupt the novel's action. The lack of human responsibility and the alternative insistence on innate qualities, materialistic greed and lack of reasoning in the character's motivations are certainly not Howellsian. The equation of the beautiful with the ideal and the defense of any means to satisfy "longing for that which is better" were unlikely to satisfy the realist who specialized, in Dreiser's characterization, in "tender kindliness." Howells did not record why exactly he didn't like Dreiser's first novel, but he had before refrained from public comment on books, like Charles Dudley Warner's and Mark Twain's The Gilded Age, which he didn't like or books which were issued when he had no magazine responsibilities to write criticism.

We might also remember that Dreiser's bravery in refusing the "convention" that vice must be punished is actually, in Sister Carrie, only a rejection of the melodrama of punishing the fall with death, and in the case of Hurstwood, does not even reject that. Howells had actually in this sense been braver in his Lemuel Baker, about whose "Manda Grier & Stira Dudley" DeForest had written to Howells in 1886,

> . . . masterpieces of born, unfathomable "lowness," incurably commonplace, egotistic, envious, unappreciative of worth . . . I had expected you would kill her, to get a touching scene & to flatter the soul of the saleslady reader. But you were honester than that, & braver.[1]

The difference <u>Sister Carrie</u> does offer, and which each of Dreiser's succeeding novels would also offer, is the "instant fascination" Howells claimed for "guilty love."

Howells felt that criticism was in many ways of little use, either in influencing an individual writer or in changing the public taste. He reminds us that "every literary movement has been violently opposed at the start, and yet never stayed in the least, or arrested, by criticism" and also that "a book that strikes the popular fancy . . . prospers on in spite of condemnation by the best critics."[2] From those whose reputations or fortunes were actually limited by Howells's criticism, his assessment seems to hold true. Many of the books he thought facile or irresponsible continued to find a large public, and he had difficulty making his audience see the worth of John W. DeForest. But in editorially opening the door and critically sustaining writers of the new "literary movement," Howells helped to establish the role of the magazines in nationalizing and forwarding American literary accomplishment. He helped others to find the opportunity Lowell described and offered to him:

---

[1] DeForest to Howells, December 6, 1886, Howells Papers.

[2] Howells, "Criticism and Fiction," pp. 24-25.

> After all, the barriers are very thin. They are paper.
> If a man has his conscience and one or two friends who
> can help him, it becomes very simple at last.[1]

In the large scheme of our literary history, Howells has been seen as either a pioneering realist or a truckler to middle class conventions who injured his friends Twain and James. In the perspective of his careers with the Atlantic Monthly, the Century, and the Harpers' magazines, we can see instead a professional who combined compromise with quiet courage. While Howells would always consciously acknowledge his own limitations and those of the magazines, he created the confusion which has surrounded his reputation by generously overlooking--and never repeating--the hypocrisy of colleagues who wanted to be equally free to disparage the magazines and to reap their rewards.

---

[1] Stephen Crane, "Howells Fears Realists Must Wait" in The New York City Sketches of Stephen Crane and Related Pieces, ed. R. W. Stallman and E. R. Hagemann (New York: New York University Press, 1966), p. 90.

CHAPTER IV

THOMAS BAILEY ALDRICH AND THE ATLANTIC MONTHLY

In the succession of the Atlantic Monthly editorship from William Dean Howells to Thomas Bailey Aldrich, we can see to what degree personal predilection, taste, and conception of the editorial role could influence the policy of a magazine. The contrast may be drawn all the more clearly here than between any other two editors because Aldrich, like Howells, was neither founder, owner, nor publisher of the magazine he edited. Since, unlike Howells, Aldrich was not directly associated with the Atlantic Monthly's administration before he assumed full-charge editorial responsibility in 1881, the beginnings of his influence are more sharply defined.

The press notices which assured the public that Howells's departure from the Atlantic was voluntary also speculated on what a new editor was likely to mean for the magazine. The general consensus was that Aldrich lacked the critical and literary stature of Lowell or Howells, but that the Atlantic was likely to remain, under his direction, a quality American literary journal. Edmund Clarence Stedman wrote to Aldrich, congratulating him on his appointment and suggesting he had won out over others who had coveted the office. Aldrich's reply suggests that he had given hard thought to what the position would entail.

>When I see you, . . . I'll give you the points of the situation. I have a very clear understanding of the responsibilities I have assumed in taking the editorship of the "Atlantic." I accepted the post only after making a thorough examination of my nerve and backbone. I fancy I shall do very little writing in the magazine, at first. I intend to edit it. I am lost in admiration of Howells, who found time to be a novelist.[1]

Aldrich came to the "responsibilities" of editing the Atlantic with a broader personal experience of American publishing and the vicissitudes of a literary career than had Howells. As a child in Portsmouth, he had the expectations and literary leanings of older generation Brahmin New England. He remembered the most important part of his early education as being his schooling in the science of grammar, and he long held hopes of going to Harvard to study under Longfellow. When the family's finances left him instead apprenticed to an uncle in business, Aldrich focused his ambition for a different life on writing poetry for the newspapers. When he sold his first poem, his uncle greeted the news with the suggestion that Thomas Bailey send one every day to the "damned fool."[2]

---

[1] Ferris Greenslet, The Life of Thomas Bailey Aldrich (Boston and New York: Houghton, Mifflin, 1908), p. 141. Greenslet's authorized biography is the only published collection of Aldrich's letters and contains the statement of Susan Francis, Aldrich's assistant. Hereafter references to this volume will appear in the text in the form of (Greenslet, p.--).

[2] Charles E. Samuels, Thomas Bailey Aldrich (New York: Twayne, 1965), p. 30. The only other volume length study of Aldrich, Samuels concentrates on Aldrich as a poet, relying on Greenslet for biographical material, but adding previously unpublished letters from the New York Public and Widener Libraries. Hereafter references to this volume will appear in the text in the form of (Samuels, p. --).

He moved instead to the practical journalism of the Evening Mirror and N. P. Willis's Home Journal. The latter directed itself toward New York's nouveau riche "society" with columns of instruction on manners, polite conversation, and protocol. Aldrich also remembered that "It was our policy to chronicle the staid comings and goings of our heavy advertisers, and never by any chance to print anything that would give offense to anyone."[1] The first stages of the Civil War saw him as a correspondent for the New York Tribune, which led, in 1862, to the managing editorship of the Illustrated News. He had achieved wide popular recognition with a long poem published in the Journal of Commerce, his "Ballad of Baby Belle," a lachrymose paean to childhood. While his sympathetic biographers make much of Aldrich's early publication of a volume of poetry in the "Blue and Gold Series" which Ticknor and Fields generally reserved for their most prestigious authors, it was the product of Aldrich's determined repeated overtures after initial rejections.

While Aldrich in 1860 characterized his poetry to Stoddard as "innumerable little songs about nothing in particular" that might get a chance "when Longfellow and Bryant get brought down to their proper niches" (Samuels, p. 103), he eagerly solicited for his early volumes the attention of the major old line New England literary figures. Oliver Wendell Holmes responded to receipt of a volume with something less than fulsome praise:

---

[1] Gilbert Donaldson, "Thomas Bailey Aldrich," The Reader 9 (May, 1907), 660, interview quoted in Samuels, p. 33.

> You love the fragrance of certain words so well that
> you are in danger of making nosegays when you should
> write poems. . . . Your tendency to vanilla-flavored
> adjectives and patchouli-scented participles stifle
> your strength in cloying euphemisms.
> (Greenslet, pp. 64-65)

Aldrich took the criticism from Holmes in relatively good temper, though he had earlier withdrawn a poem from the <u>Atlantic</u> when Lowell, as editor, had suggested making changes in it. Along with his attempts to garner the attention of the Boston/Cambridge Old Guard and his natural association with the newspapermen of Pfaff's beer cellar, Aldrich developed in his New York years before 1866 strong personal and philosophical relationships with the city's aesthetic circle. Promoting an "art for art's sake" sensibility, Aldrich, Edmund Clarence Stedman, Richard Henry Stoddard, Bayard Taylor, George Boker, and, for a time, Richard Watson Gilder joined artistic forces in opposing the moral emphasis of earlier American Literature. Aldrich and his friends preferred a poetry of beauty and emotion. In a review of Aldrich's work in 1866, Howells had remarked that the poet seldom addressed "any feature or incident of our national life; for this might have demanded a realistic treatment foreign to his genius."

If Aldrich's genius was not realistic treatment of our national life, he was very much the realist in dealing with the practical opportunities and potential compensations of our national literary life. Aldrich was invited to Boston to edit Fields & Osgood's <u>Every Saturday</u> just a few short months before Fields offered and

Osgood negotiated Howells's contract as the Atlantic's assistant editor. Howells remembered that while "We were of nearly the same age, . . . he had a distinct and distinguished priority of reputation, insomuch that in my Western remoteness I had always ranged him with such elders and betters of mine as Holmes and Lowell . . ." and he was surprised to find Aldrich but a "blond, slight youth." Despite priorities and reputations, their situations were fairly balanced in prestige, for " . . . if the Atlantic Monthly was a somewhat prouder affair than an eclectic weekly like Every Saturday, he was supreme in his place, and I was subordinate in mine."[1] Stedman had recommended Howells to Aldrich, and Aldrich soon found his new acquaintance acceptable. Though Howells characterized the newly-married Aldrich's study as "Aldrich's boudoir,"[2] they shared many friends and literary occasions, and Howells eagerly helped Aldrich to further publication in the Atlantic.

Aldrich gloried in the social benefits of Boston's particular definition of civilization. While Howells remembered the Boston they both found in the late 1860s in terms of a social structure where money was never less important, Thomas Bailey and Lilian Woodman Aldrich quickly picked up on the distinctions within that structure. The Howellses settled in a Cambridge cottage, whose modesty greatly

---

[1] William Dean Howells, "Literary Boston As I Knew It," pp. 103-104.

[2] Mrs. Thomas Bailey Aldrich, Crowding Memories (Boston: Houghton & Mifflin, 1920), p. 102.

amused Bret Harte, but the Aldriches settled on Beacon Street and moved to progressively more elaborate houses and prestigious addresses within Boston's Back Bay. Aldrich continually and elatedly described the Boston difference to his former associates in New York: "to be known as an able writer is to have the choicest society open to you . . . a knight of the quill here is supposed necessarily to be a gentleman. In New York--he is a Bohemian! Outside of his personal friends he has no standing" (Greenslet, p. 81).

The Aldriches were highly social beings. Aldrich's wit-- Clemens claimed "Thomas Bailey Aldrich has said fifteen hundred if not fifteen thousand things as brilliant as the things Talleyrand said." (Greenslet, p. 157)--and devotion to socializing resulted in his having a difficult time making an enemy or not making an invitation. The Brahmins practically god-parented the Aldrich twins, gifting them with inscribed first editions which began Aldrich's connoisseurship of books and pictures, an interest shared with many of the elder Bostonians. Aldrich early and long claimed that he was "Boston-plated," if not Boston born. The assumed veneer was not only a reflection of literature's elder statesmen and Aldrich's long-term ambitions, but also, as he reported to Bayard Taylor, an appreciation of "The people of Boston . . . full blooded readers, appreciative, trained" (Greenslet, p. 81).

Aldrich did not use his propinquity to New England's Old Guard, his appreciative Boston readers, or his freedom from New York newspapers' "heavy advertisers" to promote the literary ideals he and the others had developed in their New York aestheticism. He felt that magazine editing, like journalism, provided a salaried position necessarily and desirably apart from one's own literary production and preferences. Every Saturday was a journal exceptionally well-suited to Aldrich's idea of professional employment. Essentially a compilation of reprinted British and continental literature, Every Saturday required an editor who read widely but who could remain uninvolved with the critical controversies on the work of American contemporaries. Aldrich had always liked to read the current French novels, and his selections for Every Saturday were occasionally venturesome. He published Thomas Hardy before Howells had ever heard of him, and serialized Charles Reade's A Terrible Temptation in 1871. Temptation, which followed Reade's The Cloister and the Hearth and Griffith Gaunt, was condemned from many quarters for its vicarious sensation, but as James Hart reports in The Popular Book, public interest was so high after the Every Saturday serial that the very proper Harpers not only reprinted the novel in the Weekly, but also paid for it.[1] Howells, however, remembered Reade as one of many writers the publisher had expected increased profit and circulation from printing, but who disappointed those expectations.[2]

When James R. Osgood took over the book publishing firm and the magazines and Howells became editor of the Atlantic, Aldrich

---

[1] James D. Hart, The Popular Book, p. 124.

[2] William Dean Howells, "Recollections," p. 198.

continued with *Every Saturday*. Osgood expanded the modest magazine and added illustrations in an attempt to compete with the established and heavily-capitalized New York weeklies. Aldrich complained to his New York friends that he was being worked to death. Among other clever ideas, Osgood had conceived of having Aldrich write weekly a number of different positive reviews of the current issue of his magazine, hoping that newspaper editors would print the pre-written compliments. When Osgood was forced to sell off the magazines in 1874, *Every Saturday*'s purchaser agreed to keep it in print and Aldrich employed for only one more year. Aldrich was bitter over being "set adrift" and would never concur in Howells's nostalgia of Osgood's visionary plans. He claimed to prefer publishers who were more practical, even if their vision was more limited.

Aldrich was, however, finding a growing market for his own writing sufficient to sustain him between periods of editorial employment. In the stories Howells had printed for him in the *Atlantic*, Aldrich had refined his technique for saleable magazine prose, specializing in impersonal fiction with surprise endings. Aldrich also continued to add to his many friends, strong sense of self-protection, willingness to ignore contemporary issues, and respect for Yankee shrewdness and business acumen.

Aldrich's separation of his writing from personal opinion and of his editing from critical advocacy in the twenty years of professional life before he became the *Atlantic Monthly* editor made his administration of that journal quite different from Howells's sense of mission and compromises with tradition. While the New York aesthetics denigrated the Brahmin Old Guard and Aldrich himself felt Howellsian realism was "making a god of the dull commonplace,"[1] he had kept these opinions separate and largely private. He would later claim, in declining to speak at one of those continual dinners of the literary clubs, that "In private I can be as injudicious as anybody!" (Greenslet, p. 172), but his public demeanor was an epitome of the gentleman's separation between private and public life, between the rewards of art and the values of commerce, and between private wit and public reticence or irony.

Aldrich never would form a developed body of criticism nor often express an abstract critical principle. His letters often supply the most general precepts of judgment as well as his assessments of individual accomplishment. He continued, with his New York associates, to find many of the Brahmins overrated in terms of their actual poetic accomplishment. Poetry was always, for him, the highest and purest of arts, rightly concentrating on technically proficient lyrical expression of the eternal and the beautiful. The poet should reach for the highest of which he was capable--"the stanza that makes us _think_ or makes us _feel_," "the verse that impresses a solitary reader here and there." "The verse that pleases merely a set," "the stanza that makes us laugh," "restriction to the contemporary," and "realism" were not part of the artist's "proper

---

[1] Thomas Bailey Aldrich, "At the Funeral of a Minor Poet," The Works of Thomas Bailey Aldrich (Boston: Houghton & Mifflin, 1897), 2:93. Stanza quoted in Samuels, p. 104.

ambition" "to do the largest sort of work within one's own limits" (Greenslet, pp. 154, 165).

From such personal and private preferences, Aldrich repeatedly solicited from among his contemporaries only Edmund Clarence Stedman for contributions to the magazine. So intense was Aldrich's interest in poetic quality that he once thought of printing only four really good poems a year in the body of the magazine. He wrote little himself during his years as *Atlantic* editor and portioned that out to keep himself before the public, but his own poems did not serve his editorial purpose since he insisted, "I shall not print any of my verses in the 'Atlantic.' No man shall say that I crowded him out and put myself in." He encouraged Stedman instead to meet the need, asking him to send on anything he might have "for the maga," claiming that Stedman was the only poet after the Brahmins who was writing anything worth printing (Greenslet, p. 146).

More practically, Aldrich suited his own tastes and personality by adapting the job itself to his own comfort and "fit" in a position rife with the sort of conflicts he preferred to avoid. Feeling himself not bound by the procedures of his predecessors, Aldrich first moved his editorial office up and away from the practical and production workings of the enterprise. His detractors pointed out that he had chosen for himself a view of Boston's oldest cemetaries; even his friends admitted that the *Atlantic* editorial office had never looked so domestic. He also established with Houghton that as editor he would have nothing to do with deciding a contributor's monetary compensation. The separation was so insisted upon and absolute that when Houghton felt James Russell Lowell was not writing for the *Atlantic* because of its usual rates, the publisher engaged Longfellow, not Aldrich, to let Lowell know he was wanted and would be generously used--and this despite the editor's social relationship with Lowell. Even when favorite and frequent contributors reported to Aldrich difficulties in dealing with Houghton, Aldrich refused to involve himself in haggling between writer and publisher.

Miss Susan M. Francis, the *Atlantic*'s office assistant, remembered many other changes which came with the new editor. His work habits tended to be desultory; he refused to plan, and preferred long, tangential story-telling to the work at hand. "As an editor Mr. Aldrich lived from hand to mouth, the box in which accepted manuscripts were kept was never very full, was often half-empty." From Aldrich's "unwillingness to accumulate copy . . . Sometimes destitution seemed to stare him in the face, but with his usual good fortune things altogether desirable arrived at the last moment, and the supply never failed." Even in his most desperate straits, however, "a slovenly or careless style in any sort of article would almost obscure whatever other merit the paper might possess" for the editor. Aldrich's "easy-going" editorial habits meant that the potential contributor never waited so long for a decision as he had with Howells, but the new or unsolicited contributor was also likely to receive less editorial attention and have less possibility of being accepted.

Aldrich read all the incoming poetry himself, making "very quick and very sure" judgments. All the prose manuscripts were first read and sorted by his staff, whose gleanings were accumulated until the editor "on a clearing-up day, of uncertain date . . . went through the mass, and laid aside a few for further consideration." Most often the accepted were "the regular contributors" or "the faithful survivors of the Old Guard," each with an area of expertise which he mined again and again. Of the new writers who were accepted, usually first for the "Contributor's Club" section, Aldrich's preference was for those who had a "distinct literary quality," precision of style and clean copy. Ms. Francis remembered especially the charming essayist whose manuscripts "were never inquired after by the author" but supplied in variety at regular intervals (Greenslet, pp. 143-45).

Unlike Howells, Aldrich also did not involve himself in every detail and stage of the <u>Atlantic</u>'s elaborate sequence of copy-editing. He valued contributors who submitted proof correct to his standards. His biographer, Ferris Greenslet, described Aldrich's attitude:

> To his fastidious sense of phrase and syntax, reading proof was a sacrament. If he habitually delegated the celebration of it to his assistant, his interest in the result was none the less keen, and it fared ill with any split infinitive or suspended nominative--even with such seemingly innocent locutions as "several people"--that fell under his searching eye.
> (Greenslet, p. 147)

Aldrich treated his regular contributors differentially both in soliciting and publishing their work. He was known for somewhat warmer relations than Howells's with the Old Guard poets upon whom the publisher relied in the Atlantic's publicity. While Howells had offended John Greenleaf Whittier at the peak of his--or any American poet's--popularity, Aldrich's relationship with Whittier was strong enough for the Atlantic in the 1880s to publish more of Whittier than of any other poet of his generation. Though Stedman combined a comment that the Atlantic was "steadily improving" with advice that his friend not "permit the old contributors to constantly offer more lyrics of the same kind,"[1] Aldrich instead solicited them, as he did Stedman, for any work of theirs they would offer. Both for their personal publicity and because many of the poems marked public events, the elder poets' contributions were likely to be noted in the papers which reviewed upcoming issues of the major magazines.

While Aldrich would question an unsolicited contributor on whether his thoughts held interest for the "general reader," his "Boston-plated" sensibilities and his veneration for the Harvard circle made the magazine especially receptive not only to the Cambridge poets but also to a constituency of elder Harvard Yard essayists. Aldrich had a long and unbroken friendship with Charles Eliot Norton, and despite the general unpopularity of Norton's humanism, the Atlantic's pages were open to his contributions. Aldrich's Harvard

---

[1] Donald Rouel Tuttle, "Thomas Bailey Aldrich's Editorship of the Atlantic Monthly" (Ph. D. dissertation, Western Reserve University, 1939), p. 443. Tuttle transcribes correspondence and other material in the Thomas Bailey Aldrich Memorial Museum, Portsmouth, New Hampshire, as well as some unpublished letters from the Henry Huntington Library. Hereafter references to this volume will appear in the text in the form of (Tuttle, p.--).

contributors tended to history, biographical-critical retrospectives, memoirs, and recycling of received cultural opinion. Donald Rouel Tuttle in a 1939 Western Reserve dissertation on Aldrich's editorship characterized the essay departments as a combination of something like a museum and a scholarly journal (Tuttle, p. 285).

As Aldrich declined to write literary notices or critical articles, he frequently engaged such safe, elder literary statesmen to write quasi-criticism for the magazine. In choosing what would receive major attention and who would review it, Aldrich seems to have edited according to the conviction he once expressed to Stedman that few writers of significance had developed in the United States since their own early days. Aldrich and his publisher, however, may have been simply feeding their audience's appetite for the older authors who were not producing much new work. Both Aldrich and Houghton attempted to keep exclusive control over rights to previously unpublished material from major figures of the past. The Atlantic's reviews and essay retrospectives held a solid line on appreciative respect for the old Ticknor & Fields writers and for their publishers, a line often held at the expense of both new writers and old.

Donald Tuttle records in his dissertation an extremely strident negotiation between Houghton and Hawthorne's heirs for unpublished Hawthorne material. In his eagerness to get the manuscript and get it at the cheapest possible price, Houghton accused George Parsons Lathrop, Hawthorne's son-in-law, of setting and then misrepresenting his wife's views on the price she demanded. Lathrop's revulsion toward Houghton did not keep the firm from eventually obtaining the rights, but Aldrich's much-publicized refusal to deal with haggles over compensation did not keep Lathrop from reminding the editor that his and the Hawthorne family's dealings with the firm had been a "history of one sided concessions" from Houghton's "beating down prices" (Tuttle, p. 289). It is perhaps no wonder that Lathrop, who had left the *Atlantic* staff in 1877 after a dispute with Howells, but whom Stedman mentioned as a possible alternative to Aldrich as *Atlantic* editor, was not much beloved by the firm, but Aldrich restrained his exercise of editorial "responsibility" and power until Julian Hawthorne published "Nathaniel Hawthorne and his Wife." Looking for a publisher's view of the older generation, Aldrich enlisted Thomas Wentworth Higginson to write the *Atlantic* review (and rebuttal), suggesting none too subtly the direction it might take.

> In your notice of Julian Hawthorne's book I hope that you will find it in your way, or be willing even to go out of your way, to give Julian a rap on the knuckles for his shabby treatment of Fields. It was he who discovered Hawthorne in his obscurity and despondency, and put hope into his heart. . . . The whole is a little piece of small revenge, growing out of a needless quarrel brought about years ago by the pestiferous Gail Hamilton. It seems to me that it is only justice to Field's (sic) memory that Julian Hawthorne's offence should not be overlooked.
> (Tuttle, pp. 291-92)

Higginson's notice easily fit the cut of the editor's order, and it is difficult to tell how far out of his way he went. Higginson's idea of the appropriate public history of literary dealings is amply suggested by the title of his own memoir--*Cheerful*

Yesterdays. Higginson was also, clearly, the editor's choice to be the reviewer, and could presumably be counted on to lean toward the desired reaction. Aldrich's letter, however, reveals an insistence on management and a kind of frenetic overkill somewhat beyond what the single situation might call for. His suggestion that the quarrel's cause was Gail Hamilton, who had helped Mrs. Hawthorne review her accounts with the firm, seems designed to elicit from Higginson his own "little piece of small revenge" since Hamilton, who had edited Fields & Osgood's Our Young Folks, was a frequent opponent of Higginson's on social issues.

Despite Aldrich's willingness to share his publisher's interest in the Old Guard writers and acquisition of their work, he ignored Houghton's dropping "words" of suggestion about other "friends of the house." Ferris Greenslet records a conversation in which a frustrated Houghton informed his editor, "I have written a story and I'm going to send it to you under a fictitious name." Aldrich replied with the suggestion that Houghton "send it to a fictitious editor" (Greenslet, p. 151). Aldrich was more amenable to the lead of his publisher when the question was one of the Atlantic's printing serial installments excerpted from books on Houghton & Mifflin's upcoming list (Tuttle, p. 285)--that is, when the book in question met Aldrich's personal taste.

Aldrich was generally cordial when Howells made suggestions for the Atlantic, but he used his own judgment in discriminating between cases. Aldrich expressed some difficulties over the magazine's using all Howells offered of his own work; in 1884, Aldrich responded to Howells's query regarding a dramatization,

> I find that I cannot do anything about the play--stories in dramatic form haven't been popular downstairs since James's Daisy Miller. But I should greatly like to have that dramatic paper of which you spoke.[1]

Aldrich repeatedly reminded Howells that the Atlantic's top price was fifteen dollars per page, once in combination with addressing the former editor as "haughty spirit."[2] On Howells's urging Atlantic publication for other writers, Aldrich was willing to bend his usual editorial practices when, as in the case of Henry James, Jr., their partialities coincided. But, despite Aldrich's sharing many of John Hay's sentiments on labor and the effects of immigration policies, the editor resisted going so far as agreeing to publish The Breadwinners, despite Howells's importuning.[3]

Even when Aldrich and Howells saw each other infrequently, and their relationship deteriorated from its early warmth to the increasing formality reflected in Aldrich's writing without seeming to expect a response and successively changing the complimentary closes in his letters from "Ever faithfully yours," to "Ever yours," to the final "Yours sincerely" he used on strictly business correspondence, Howells occasionally interceded on behalf of a former

---

[1] Aldrich to Howells, May 10, 1884, Howells Papers.

[2] Aldrich to Howells, January 19, 1885, Howells Papers.

[3] George Monteiro, "William Dean Howells and The Breadwinners," Studies in Bibliography, ed. Fredson Bowers (Charlottesville, Virginia: Bibliographical Society of the University of Virginia) 15 (1962), 267-68.

Atlantic contributor. William Henry Bishop was one who fell from favor during Aldrich's editorship. Though neither Howells nor Aldrich specified the source of difficulty between Aldrich and Bishop, one might suspect that the very private Aldrich had not appreciated Bishop's writing an "Authors at Home" piece on the editor's splendid homes and extravagant style of living for an August 8, 1885, issue of The Critic,[1] especially since The Critic soon joined the more liberal newspapers in criticizing Aldrich's making a "fastidious fetish" of language (Tuttle, p. 428). Still, when Howells solicited help for Bishop, Aldrich responded graciously:

> I wrote to Bishop . . . suggesting a preliminary paper on the Exposition. I would greatly like to serve him, for he is a fine fellow, tho' his proof is a horror! You are good to keep an eye on your stray sheep. I have many a time wished that you hadn't deserted them. I should like to be a favored contributor again. I mean to be some day. I've such a lot of prose and verse piled up in the back of my head.[2]

When it was not a question of Howells's taking care of a "stray sheep," Aldrich was very protective of his editorial prerogatives in dealings with contributors. Even those who had been with the Atlantic from the beginning encountered difficulties if their attitudes, subjects, or style did not meet Aldrich's preferences. When Richard Grant White argued over the treatment of a contribution by suggesting that the publisher would want White to have his way,

---

[1] William Henry Bishop, "Authors at Home. T. B. Aldrich on Beacon Hill, and Round it," The Critic 7 (August 8, 1885), 61-63.

[2] Aldrich to Howells, January 15, 1889, Howells Papers.

that former editors had not subjected him to "leading strings," and that signed work from contributors of his quality stood or fell on its own, Aldrich quickly let White know the editor would not take such criticism. Rather than acknowledging the independence of any contributor, Aldrich clearly stated his own position,

> I am responsible for every word that appears in the Atlantic Monthly. I am supposed to admire what I seem warmly to endorse by printing.

and set it within the magazine tradition,

> I know of no editor who does not reserve the right to strike out a phrase or a passage if it seems to him objectionable, or if the exigencies of the make up require it. Mr. Howells exercised this right to the fullest.
> (Tuttle, p. 162)

Amidst the various pressure to favor this contributor or that contributor, Aldrich developed his own very definite policies and practices to suit the Atlantic to his interests and his ease. He made his selections in terms of a list of "subjects not to be touched,"[1] including religion, politics, economics, social issues, sex, and anything which Aldrich considered vulgar. Himself uninterested in most of the political, social and philosophical concerns of the age, Aldrich preferred not to bother with positions on general questions. He felt it pointless to argue whether God is good or man immortal or to consider the alternative challenges of the various sects. Despite the current popularity of Utopian fiction

---

[1] Aldrich to "Mr. Thayer," quoted in John Tomsich, A Genteel Endeavor, p. 145.

and interest in financial affairs after the upheavals and crises of the 1870s, Aldrich as editor printed instead work which fit his and his early New York associates' definition of art: well-wrought evocations of the beautiful and eternal and avoidance of grounding in the contemporary. In an age which Aldrich, Stedman, Taylor, et. al. felt undervalued poets and poetry, they generally reserved themselves from involvement in the age. When middle-class strictures in magazine publishing and old-line morality restricted the range of emotion they could profitably express, they increasingly chose the alternative of concentration on the classical and impersonal. Aldrich even surprised himself when he once broke from his personal and editorial limitations to write and print in the Atlantic his poem "Unguarded Gates" which indicted the influence of the mongrel, anarchistic immigrant rabble invading American cities and leaving no America for Americans.

Aldrich's distaste for controversy and the contemporary combined with his underlying, but usually unspoken, antidemocratic sentiments and aversion to the commonplace to produce a marked decline in the Atlantic's receptivity to variety in American literature. Much of what Aldrich gainsaid or rejected is what has come to be seen as progressive, native, and of lasting quality in our literature. Among the first to be discouraged was local color which focused on the distinct regional character. Aldrich felt that since his own youth, the local character "has ceased to be parochial; he is no longer distinct; he is simply the Average Man."[1] Not only was this "Average Man" uninteresting and unappealing to Aldrich's refined taste, but the only alternative distinct characters of the American 1880s were those who, as Aldrich termed it to George Woodberry, were making America "the cesspool of Europe" (Greenslet, p. 168). Character in fiction generally was, to Aldrich's thinking, the "moral and . . . mental pose"[2] which was revealed through action, and the actions of the average and the rabble were not the means to "distinct literary quality."

With the eschewal of the local character went much of what was labeled "realism" in the 1880s. Much as he had restrained himself from attacking Howells's critical principles publicly, Aldrich rather sneered at the whole realist credo, and especially its emphases on the average and typical in contemporary experience and its attention to the vulgar classes. A letter written to New York on the death of his dog Trip (whom he loved so well that he took him each day to the office) indicates Aldrich's attitude. Of the dog whose headstone he was planning,

> He wasn't constantly getting drunk and falling out of windows of tenement houses, like Mrs. O'Flararty; he wasn't forever stabbing somebody in North Street. Why should he be dead, and these other creatures exhausting the ozone? If he had written realistic novels and "poems" I could understand "the deep damnation of his taking off."
> (Greenslet, p. 169)

---

[1] Thomas Bailey Aldrich, *An Old Town by the Sea* (Boston: Houghton & Mifflin, 1893), p. 123.

[2] Thomas Bailey Aldrich, "Plot and Character," in *Ponkapog Papers* (Boston: Houghton & Mifflin, 1904), p. 62.

Aldrich's dislike of local coloring, realism, and the vulgar meant that he absolutely refused to print Joaquin Miller or anyone of a like school and that the new realist prose writers could no longer expect any consideration from the <u>Atlantic</u>.

Aldrich was also far more reluctant than Howells or any of his predecessors to contract for serial publication of novels of any kind. He would not commit the <u>Atlantic</u> to publishing as yet unwritten serials--no matter who was doing the writing. Osgood was marketing new books from Howells, Twain, and James to other magazines, but Aldrich encouraged his publisher to compete not for these but for the occasional romance available from the Old Guard or for items like the letters of Emerson. For those whose long work was accepted for the magazine, Aldrich would only very rarely consent to exceed a set maximum number of pages per installment--and this when Gilder was willingly discarding editorial matter from the <u>Century</u> to accommodate the length of Howells's novel episodes. At the <u>Atlantic</u>, Aldrich found he was more likely to get the regular units that suited his needs and to be able to cut where he would "if the exigencies of the make up require it" by discouraging new novels in favor of printing portions of new Houghton & Mifflin books like Francis Parkman's history of Montcalm and Wolfe. Such preferences also relieved Aldrich of the necessity of dealing with contemporary reality or anything on his list of untouchable subjects.

While Aldrich claimed the "widest freedom and the narrowest license" (Greenslet, p. 173) for literature, his own alienation from

general American life encouraged him to see magazine publishing as
a situation in which the writer withheld himself from the unknown
readers. He wrote himself and encouraged in others an impersonal
literature, marked by a reticence not only mandated from without but
necessitated by the writer's own interest not to be revealed and by
his own dignity and sense of decorum. While he would remind fellow
professionals that magazine publication was only a "temporary
matter" (Tuttle, p. 161) and not a final statement, his instruction
to the untried, potential contributor clearly established that one
wrote for a market--"The sonnet is essentially a poet's poem; I don't
believe that the general reader cares for it"--and suggested the
disengagement of an editor who "wondered if we writers of verse did
not give the public credit for more interest in our purely personal
emotions than really exists." He questioned his correspondent,
seemingly confident of only a singular answer:

> Why should we print in a magazine those intimate revela-
> tions which we would n't dream of confiding to the
> bosom of an utter stranger at an evening party? In what
> respect does the stranger differ from the public which we
> are so ready to take into our inmost confidence?
> (Greenslet, pp. 148-49)

If Aldrich's preferences and perceptions restricted from the
Atlantic a variety of subjects and approaches, his tastes for a
"literary quality" in writing and for correct proof meant his copy-
editing policies also kept from the magazine's pages the diversity
of expression in contemporary American language. Aldrich's Atlantic
was one of the most rigorously edited and linguistically uniform
American--or even British--magazines. Aldrich had said he was glad

to have escaped New York while his English was still intact, and he hung vigorously to the only part of his formal education which seemed entree and justification for being received as a gentleman in the society of letters. Annie Fields remembered him as "a worshipper of the English language and a good student of Murray's grammar,"[1] and as an editor he became a prescriptive purist in matters of language and usage. His earliest and sympathetic biographer, Ferris Greenslet, described Aldrich's use of the *Atlantic* tradition of "improving" manuscripts as producing "an excellent magazine for the lettered reader. Under his conduct the 'Atlantic' attained a notable unity of tone and distinction of style," (Greenslet, p. 146) though Donald Tuttle in 1939 found Aldrich's practice reflective of "the impulses of a teacher of composition" (Tuttle, p. 399). Whatever one's judgment, the "Boston-plated" editor who disliked contemporaneity and democratic diversity never hesitated to wield the editorial pencil and would stridently insist on and demand compliance with his corrections, discriminations, fastidiousness, precision, and taste in matters of language.

Aldrich made or had his assistants make corrections in manuscripts or lists of required revisions. Redundancy, failures of taste, imprecise diction, and grammatical and technical errors were frequent editorial objections. He took literally his statement to Richard Grant White--"I am responsible for every word that appears

---

[1] M. A. DeWolfe Howe, *Memories of a Hostess* (Boston: Atlantic Monthly Press, 1922), p. 292.

in the Atlantic Monthly"--and would argue at length even over a disputed spelling of an individual word. No defense a contributor offered held sway over the editorial judgment; even after Aldrich had recognized White as a contributor who had to be handled dexterously, White's argument of precedent in literary history and observation that Aldrich's letter was a "prim condemnatory comment" would not make Aldrich restore the phrase "perforated pimple" in a White description (Tuttle, pp. 143, 150).

Unlike his predecessors at the Atlantic or his contemporaneous editors like Richard Watson Gilder at the Century, Aldrich felt no chagrin at imposing his strictures and brooked no criticism of his taste or judgment. He insisted on his right and his authority in objecting to a writer's logic, indiscretions, or technique. He was so sure of his conclusions that he did not hesitate to use the Atlantic's critical departments, as he did in the case of Julian Hawthorne's offense, to reinforce his own opinions. Tuttle records a case in which Aldrich asked a contributor to "substitute some less disagreeable suggestive phrase for 'graveyard smell'" and the author's attempts to please the editor, which seem now almost a parody of a search for euphemisms. When the contributor restored his phrase in a later, non-Atlantic printing, the Atlantic's review pointed to and specifically reprimanded the bad taste of the description (Tuttle, pp. 400-401).

Contributors who opposed Aldrich's judgment and taste were also likely to find future submissions rejected, even when the work was offered gratis or below the normal rates to "make it available." Often the editor who "lived from hand to mouth" in not maintaining a backlog of accepted manuscripts assured such unwanted contributors that he already had too much material on hand to use what they had submitted.

Aldrich was most stringent in promoting his own taste when the contribution in question was poetry, for him the highest of literary arts. Though he encouraged T. W. Higginson's essay contributions to the *Atlantic*, one of which, the "Letter to a Young Contributor," had brought him some of Emily Dickinson's first public poems, the editor wrote to Higginson: "I don't agree with you on the value of contemporary criticism--excepting when it is mine!" (Greenslet, p. 156). While Higginson admitted to finding Dickinson unclassifiable, one of Aldrich's few critical essays reads as a rebuttal to those who found any value at all in her work and technique. Aldrich did agree to print some of Dickinson's poetry, but rewrote it in metrically regular and regularly rhymed "corrections" which, according to one's view of Dickinson, seem like travesty or burlesque. Dickinson shortly decided publication was not worth the trouble.

Aldrich likewise adamantly objected to Whitman's attitude toward and use of language. Despite the urgings of his friend Stedman that the editor reconsider whether at least some of Whitman's work was worthy, Aldrich felt Whitman was trying to pass off a slovenly mash of words as poetry. Whitman was somewhat more appreciative of

Aldrich's writing; he had told him years before: "I like your tinkles. I like them very well."[1]

If Aldrich would not join his colleagues in the literary establishment in seeing value in Dickinson and Whitman, he also would not follow the "popular taste" in defining poetic accomplishment. Both dialect and humorous poetry he felt to be beneath the levels of art and lasting significance. A poet who promoted himself as a personality was even more abhorrent. While Aldrich claimed that "The only critic whose verdict is worth a fig is the great Public" (Tomsich, p. 143), he had in mind not the large popular audience but the Bostonian true reader. Aldrich's "general public" was defined as those who were not themselves poets--when the editor was dealing in what he saw as the inviolable realm of poetry.

Becoming editor of the Atlantic Monthly seems to have stiffened Aldrich's mind rather than his backbone. His own poetry became rigid and conventional. He had earlier written comic verse with boisterous rhymes and had had some fun writing ametrical poetry on the horrors of ametrical poetry. Often described as a classicist or a society poet, the Aldrich who wrote verse in the 1850-70s and who published much of it in the Atlantic specialized in courtly descriptions of lovely young things, lyrically acknowledging the power of sexual attraction. In the 1880s Aldrich was more likely to compare women to water lilies, and he enjoined similar restraint on

---

[1] William Winter, Old Friends: Being Literary Recollections of Other Days (New York: Moffat, Tard, 1909), p. 40.

most of his contributors.

Aldrich also constrained his contributors to conform to his own taste in metrics and diction. He hated, for example, the Shakespearean sonnet form, feeling that the final couplet reduced the lyric to the epigrammatic. Even regular contributors found their sonnets returned until they acknowledged the justice and perfect taste of this opinion--and revised to the preferred sestet. Aldrich generally required regular metrical arrangements and precise rhyme, usually insisting that even unaccented final syllables match in spelling as well as sound. He also seems to have edited with at least a mental list of undesirable poetic diction, words which he considered unnecessarily or artificially archaic, vulgar, or merely not fitting his taste; for example, neither "e'er" nor "ween" could appear in the *Atlantic* while Aldrich edited it. A contributor who used disapproved diction was unlikely to be welcome back until he-- or more often she--had both removed the offending syllables and expressly acknowledged and thanked Aldrich for "the benefit of your taste" (Tuttle, pp. 407, 415-16, 405).

Aldrich's policies and preferences did not entirely close off the *Atlantic* to new poetic voices, but those most likely to meet the criteria of appropriate subject and style and to be tractable enough to suit the editor tended to be those like the Ohioan Edith Thomas who shared Aldrich's own refusal of a personal and engaged presence in their poetry and wrote brief, technically proficient, and generally lyric tributes to or observations on scenery, sunsets, and flowers. Most appreciated were writers who offered not only poetry but also desirable "fresh and breezy" (Tuttle, p. 324) Contributor's Club pieces. Both new contributors and those with established national reputations had to expect, however, repeated schooling and correction from the editor, who saw himself as the "Enamoured architect of airy rhyme."

It is perhaps little wonder that Aldrich found relatively few poets who consistently met all his requirements. Donald Tuttle tabulated the poetic contributors published in Aldrich's ten years as *Atlantic* editor and found that in a total of 120 poets, 65 appeared once, 22 others only twice (Tuttle, p. 299). In the remaining 33 regulars, we must count the frequent representation of the old line New England poets and Aldrich's early New York associates, like Edmund Clarence Stedman, but these major figures of the 1850s and 1860s often found they could financially do better than publishing in the *Atlantic* with its declining rates and circulation. The great body of regular *Atlantic* poets were women of relatively minor reputations. Tuttle suggested that this "feminine character of the magazine" might be explicable just in that women writers were generally paid less (Tuttle, p. 99), and certainly as Houghton devoted his resources to raising compensation for the living Old Guard poets who leaned toward the enticements of competing publishers, his tendency for "beating down prices" was most often exercised against female contributors. Even established women writers with significant reputations and eager alternative publishers, like Helen Hunt Jackson, found Houghton considered himself ill-used when they asked prices anywhere near what their work was drawing elsewhere. Often they responded to Houghton's implications that they over-valued their work by offering further contributions at reduced prices (Tuttle, p. 101). Aldrich's editorial mode was also, clearly, less likely to offend those who devalued their own taste and accomplishment and so fit neatly with Houghton's market double standard. As Aldrich also did not allow his reviewers to treat a woman rudely (Tuttle, p. 139), his *Atlantic*'s public image may have been more likely to attract women.

Aldrich's tastes in poetry and reliance on a stable of standard essayists helped to establish the justice of applying to his *Atlantic* Finley Peter Dunne's later observation that American magazines displayed "Prom'nent lady authoresses makin' poems at the moon. Now an' thin a scrap over whether Shakespeare was entered in his own name or was a ringer, with the long shot players always agin' Shakespeare . . ."

Aldrich generally denied to fiction the degree of genius or art necessary to poetry. He often saw it as a merchantable alternative in a country where consumerism and materialism were wrecking and neglecting poetry--which is not to say that Aldrich did not give close attention to the short stories he published or that he lacked a theory about what was effective fictional technique. Aldrich felt the audience demanded novelty, but, like Howells, he disliked the sensationalism of American newspapers. Still, he found no entertainment in stories which, as Howells sardonically characterized his own, "nothing happens." For the editor who valued technique above all, "carefully built" was one of the highest of his compliments. In fiction, the building meant concentration on a single effect and a plot which moved swiftly from beginning to middle to end, leaving a vivid final impression in the reader's mind. His own stories all use some sort of gimmick, often a final turn, or final trick, on the reader's expectations--the popular surprise ending which had been pioneered by Aldrich's original New York employer, N. P. Willis--and Aldrich claimed that his own procedure was to write backwards from the ending.

Aldrich's emphasis on plot--the story that could be summarized in what happened--and his fondness for the final surprise are the most general considerations from which he selected what fiction interested him and what he would publish. He also shared with Howells an objection to the interfering author, though while Howells felt it interrupted a story's sense of reality, Aldrich seems to have been more concerned for interruption of the plot, since he seldom objected to or excised introductory authorial remarks (which often identified the writer and clarified his or her distance from the action) or comments following the final plot effect. Aldrich personally disliked excessive long speeches in dialogue, and few of his preferred authors use extensive conversation to forward their plots.

Aldrich's sense of the interest of novelty, action, and surprise endings and disinclination for representations of ordinary life ruled out of his Atlantic major or sustained contributions from the majority of realist writers. Hamlin Garland, who came relatively late to the nineteenth century's magazine opportunities, claimed "Eastern readers were not interested in the monotonous mid-West. They were eager for the plains of Araby and the Vale of Cashmire,"[1] and certainly not only eastern readers, but American readers generally, were showing their interest in romance of the long ago and faraway. While some of this is reflected in Aldrich's Atlantic, his personal assertion of interest and form as primary criteria allowed some old and new contributors to publish in the magazine work which reflected new ideas in American fiction.

Sarah Orne Jewett, who had at 19 first published fluently written New England local color stories inspired by Harriet Beecher Stowe, used Aldrich's preferences for interesting situations and "literary quality" to suggest in the Atlantic her own developing feminism. In 1882, Aldrich published "Tom's Husband," in which Jewett presents a most untraditional couple. Of the woman, Jewett claims,

> Some one once said it was a great pity that she had not been obliged to work for her living, for she had inherited a most uncommon business talent . . . Such executive ability as hers is often wasted in the more contracted sphere of women. . . . Most men like best the women whose natures cling and appeal to theirs for protection. But Tom Wilson, while he did not wish to be protected himself, liked these very qualities . . . to tell the truth, he was very much in love with his wife just as she was.

The story finds the couple not as happy as they expected to be--though

---

[1] Hamlin Garland, Roadside Meetings (New York: Macmillan, 1930), pp. 119-20.

we are assured they are far happier than most--as Tom, who has become an efficient homemaker in his bachelor years, finds he likes the house kept better than his wife seems capable or interested in doing, and she finds herself both incompetent and frustrated in the domestic role. When Tom's siblings and the townspeople urge reopening the family mills at clear benefit to all, Tom prefers his housekeeping-- and his wife very successfully applies her "executive ability" to the business. The conclusion: Tom peremptorily insists that his wife close her affairs--and they leave for Europe.

While hardly doctrinaire, especially in its surprise ending, "Tom's Husband" seems to have encouraged Jewett to continue with more far-reaching suggestions on the possible alternatives of women. In A Country Doctor in 1884, Jewett's heroine, most attractive and presented with a most suitable match, refuses marriage to become a doctor. A White Heron in 1886 puts a young girl in conflict between her wish to save the heron and her love for the ornithologist who threatens it.

Harriet Bates (Eleanor Putnam) also parlayed literary English and structured surprise to extend and ironically clarify her reader's romantic conceptions of old New England. Rather than the sanctity and color of New England customs, she showed prudent, moral spinsters concentrating on the absurdities of miserly housewifery. An observer who participates in the life she describes only to the degree of justifying her knowledge and right to judgment--recalling, for example, that in her childhood "The House of the Seven Gables was no open and

joyous dwelling, where children loved to flock and run about at will"
--Putnam pocked her stories with witty literary allusions: cupboards
"lurked behind the wainscoting, like Polonius back of the arras."
Like many of the stories with local American settings which Aldrich
accepted, Putnam's combine ironic distance with surprise effects.
The story of the cupboards turns within its last paragraph to "How
little did we think . . . that the fate of this haughty collection
was to be sold for mere old silver." Offering readers a glimpse of
a different or romantic world, a touch of drama, and quasi-ironic
distance from their own everyday realities was, of course, the kind
of approach Aldrich himself popularized in "Marjorie Daw."

Aldrich stretched the <u>Atlantic</u> much further in 1887 when he
published "The Goophered Grapevine," Charles Chesnutt's first story
in a national magazine. Though the basic folk tale is framed
through a white narrator with conversation between the narrator and
his wife explaining and determining the old black storyteller's
final victory, the change played by the black writer on the nostalgic
sentimentality of white southerners' popular plantation tales was a
significant development. The body of the story is a powerful dialect
monologue--in the magazine of an editor who disliked dialect and
long speeches--which, like Twain's "True Story" focused on realistic
complexity and ironies in race relations and began Chesnutt's fuller
picture of black experience in America. The conclusion turns the
reader around from the tale to the narrator's realization of Uncle
Julius's motive for claiming the grapevine was "goophered." Chesnutt

continued to develop this particular form, which was very well
received by the white public and critics, for the seven stories
which were eventually collected in The Conjure Woman. He would,
however, be no more satisfied with its limitations than Sarah Orne
Jewett was popularly successful with her feminist novels. In the
long term, Jewett would turn from the revolt against domestic
restriction to historical romance in The Tory Lover, and Chesnutt
would find his increasingly direct and realistic novels unacceptable
to the great white public.

Aldrich left the Atlantic in 1890 when his finances allowed
him to do so comfortably; he hardly looked back on his editorial
days, claiming "What a blessed relief it is not to make a hundred
bitter enemies per month by declining MSS" (Greenslet, p. 161). When
questioned as to whether he would follow Howells in taking up a
Harper's department, Aldrich answered that it would "take a great
deal more money than my poor services are worth" (Greenslet, p. 172).

In all of his years of professional practicality, Aldrich
had focused on received reputations and the poetic traditions to which
he bound himself and the writers he edited. Only in 1897, prompted
by an essay of Hamilton Wright Mabie's, did Aldrich consider whether
the sustained prominence of the elder New Englanders had hampered
his own career; he wrote to Mabie, "Until you said it, I was not
aware, or only vaguely aware, of how heavily we younger writers were
overshadowed and handicapped . . ." (Greenslet, pp. 199-200). When
Aldrich faced the leisure of his last, post-editorial, years, he

found himself first with a lack of ambition and ideas. Finally, he decided to "write prose when I write," discovering that

> Experience teaches a man little in poetry, but it gives him endless themes for short stories. So I shall probably build no more Wyndham Towers, but construct blocks of brown-stone English basement houses and let them out to realistic families!
> (Greenslet, p. 166)

For the man who had defended his own practice of dispersed publication by asserting "To leave the reader wanting more is art; to give him as much as he can hold is stupid" (Greenslet, p. 164), preferences for technically polished art and management by friendship left so many <u>Atlantic</u> readers wanting more that the magazine's circulation dwindled while its competitors' soared. If Aldrich suited his own tastes, his model of leavening the literature of reputations with the "fresh and breezy" suited those who saw the <u>Atlantic</u> as a distinctive and prestigious presence among the mass circulation illustrated weeklies and monthlies, but for an editor who claimed that "Whoever disparages money disparages every step in the progress of the human race" (Tomsich, p. 140), his leadership had offered neither money nor progress to most of America's writers.

CHAPTER V

GEORGE WILLIAM CURTIS AND

PUTNAM'S, HARPER'S MONTHLY AND HARPER'S WEEKLY

George William Curtis was New England's likeliest candidate for continuity in the ideals, literary principles, and patrician backgrounds of American littérateurs of the 1840s. The son of an established and wealthy Eastern family, George and his brother, Burrill Curtis, came early under the influence of Ralph Waldo Emerson and New England transcendentalism. Edward Cary, George William Curtis's biographer, records the memories of Burrill and other Brook Farm associates from the time the brothers were boarders in the experimental community and devotees of Emersonian principles. The Curtises were remembered as the best looking, best dressed, and most courtly mannered of the young Brook Farmers, and as fully engaged in both the social and aesthetic concerns of the group. Curtis developed personal and intellectual relationships with the major Concord figures of the 1840s, and after Burrill and he left Brook Farm, they established themselves in a Walden-like personal experiment near enough to Emerson and Walden Pond to share in a Monday evening "club" in Emerson's library. There the Curtis brothers, Emerson, Thoreau, Hawthorne, Alcott, Ellery Channing and George

Bradford cultivated the "conversations" so dear to the taste of New England intellectuals.[1]

Curtis's first break from the path of a devotee to Concord literary life came with the young man's escapade on a father-sponsored European tour. Initially proposed as two years in European capitals, the travels grew from two years to four, and the itinerary came to include Egypt and the Far East, as the father continued indulgent of his son's changing plans and tastes. Curtis's first public presence as a man of letters dates from the touring of 1846-50 when he joined in the popular vogue of travel literature and Bayard Taylor's style of reporting on exotic climes with letters home to Henry J. Raymond's Courier and Enquirer and the New York Tribune. Armed with a young man's eagerness for observation and experience, money, and sensibility, Curtis was conscious of acquiring material through which he could establish for himself a distinct presence in American letters.

Though the decision to make his mark as a writer seems to have come early in the travels which he recorded in daily journals, Curtis's sense of the possibilities beyond Concord may have been expanded by his meeting Charles Norton in Paris before returning to the United States. Norton introduced Curtis to Lowell and Longfellow, and the four were soon sharing the social delights of Cambridge society[2] as well as their ideas for the future of American politics

---

[1] Edward Cary, George William Curtis, American Men of Letters Series (Boston and New York: Houghton, Mifflin and Company, 1894), pp. 15-17, 22-23, 30-31.

[2] Gordon Milne, George William Curtis, p. 54.

and literature. Curtis's first volume of writing, Nile Notes of a Howadji, was ready within a year after his return. He had little trouble finding a willing publisher in Harper & Bros., convinced as they were of the marketability of travel books by Americans. He claimed that the publication, in 1851 when Curtis was twenty-seven and without any previous claims to literary reputation, "seems all very natural . . . as a sensible tree feels when it sees one of its fruits fallen separate upon the ground--"[1] and he met the generally positive reception and decent sales with the equanimity and confidence of a veteran. Curtis was also beginning what would be a long term and highly successful career as a platform lecturer.

This seemingly easy slide into literary reputation and prerogatives was, however, accompanied by Curtis's first experience of the potential liabilities of expressing oneself before a public larger than one's confirmed friends and cultured acquaintances. A vocal few objected to Nile Notes's sensuousness and sensiblity of preferring artistic over moral values. Though Curtis had attempted to justify his perspective with passages like--

> The harem and polygamy in general are without defense, viewed morally . . . viewed picturesquely under palms, with delicious eyes melting at lattices, they are highly to be favored and encouraged by all poets and disciples of Epicurus.
> Nile Notes, p. 123

--the criticism was sufficient to get back to the father who had subsidized the venture but who had seen neither the manuscript nor

---

[1] Curtis to "a friend in Cambridge," quoted in Cary, Curtis, p. 59.

the advance copies of his son's book. Curtis found it necessary to defend himself to his father, primarily by angrily rejecting the "outcry of immorality or indecency, or whatever it is" from "a conscience void of offense" in only offering a realistic picture of Egyptian culture. He assured his father that the criticism came from New York alone and from a specific class: "Now the moral condemnation of ladies and gentlemen who would sell any daughter to any man, for a sufficient fortune, I do not very highly esteem." Not only was the assault "simply ludicrous" as an "affected and self-conscious exaggeration of the moral sense," but also Curtis could offer proof of the eminent acceptability of his position in that Henry Raymond, now editor of Harper's Monthly, had selected just "the exceptional chapter" for the very proper magazine.[1]

Harper's Monthly and periodical publishing generally soon became useful to Curtis in a number of other ways. He became a regular contributor to the Harper's first magazine, writing essays on literature, society, and the arts which became, by 1854, tenure in the Monthly's "Easy Chair" column which Curtis kept for most of the rest of his life. Curtis also became associated with the Tribune, though he never found the rigors of daily journalism appealing and turned to preparing his second Howadji book for Harper's and to vacationing in the eastern resorts, sending back travel letters to the Tribune which satirized the pretensions of American new society.

---

[1] George William Curtis to George Curtis, March 15, 1851, quoted in Cary, Curtis, pp. 62-65.

Despite an increasing relationship with the Harper Brothers' firm, Curtis became involved in the creation, editing and--eventually--partial ownership of a new magazine, Putnam's, which began publication in 1853 under the guidance of C. F. Briggs, Curtis, and Parke Godwin. Seemingly, neither Harper's nor Curtis saw Putnam's as competition for Harper's Monthly, and Curtis managed to maintain relationships with both magazines despite his publicly criticizing, in Putnam's, the Harper's Monthly promotion of British, rather than American, authors. Putnam's was expressly directed toward publishing American writers and established itself as filling the void of a literary magazine with the highest standards of American culture.

Putnam's offered to potential subscribers the attractions of star writers as major contributors. The editors used their personal and professional contacts to solicit promises of work not only from their own circle but also from a variety of authors who had recognizable names and associations in the public mind. Parke Godwin bragged years after in an address to the Century Club "that among our promised contributors" were not only the expected names of Boston and Concord men of letters but also Miss Sedgwick, Mrs. Kirkland, Herman Melville, E. C. Stedman, Richard Henry Stoddard, William Henry Herbert, and Matthew Arnold. Godwin also remembered, "We had a strong backing from the clergy,"[1] and, in fact, the young Turks of Putnam's got contributions, compliments, and support from most of the major

---

[1] Quoted in Cary, Curtis, pp. 81-82.

figures of American and British literature and culture. One of the few who did not fulfill his promise to contribute was Nathaniel Hawthorne, who had cautioned Curtis in his answer to an initial solicitation, ". . . allow me to hope that your own connection with the magazine will not be very conspicuous--at least, not before it is quite settled that it is to take the top rank among periodicals, a phenomenon which I shall believe when I see it."[1]

In the years of his connection with Putnam's, Curtis was concerned with his own position in the "top rank." He considered not only the traditional route of New England literary prestige of publishing a volume of poetry with Ticknor--despite feeling he had little talent for poetry--and also from "the desire to do something which, by the orthodox and received standard, should be conceded to be a graver work than anything I have done" worked for a time at "a life of Mehemet Ali." Curtis finally gave up on both projects, feeling "the reason is puerile, although the sentiment is good."[2] He followed through instead on the kind of activities which had brought him recognition before: lecturing and writing two separate series of columns for Putnam's, columns which were made into the popular volumes Prue and I and The Potiphar Papers.

Besides the commentary on society, fashion, and literature of the continuing series, Curtis write a great deal of the criticism,

---

[1] Hawthorne to Curtis, October 28, 1852, Houghton Library, quoted in Milne, George William Curtis, p. 65.

[2] Cary, Curtis, pp. 79-81.

miscellaneous articles, and editorial matter for Putnam's. With the
magazine's other principal attractions coming from the contributions
from established figures, the young editorial board could be fairly
cavalier with unsolicited manuscripts from aspiring American writers.
Godwin remembered in his Century Club address that in "our little
conclaves . . . we remorselessly slaughtered the hopes of many a
bright spirit (chiefly female)."[1] Their preference was always for
the company and the writing of their own social and literary compatriots, and Curtis especially moved from his early identification with
the Concord group to friendship and stewardship for the Boston/
Cambridge circle of Lowell and Longfellow.

In copy-editing, Curtis had his difficulties, as Lowell
would after him when editing the Atlantic, when the editor's interest
in his magazine came up against the immovable principles of Henry
David Thoreau. Curtis and Thoreau had known each other long and
intimately enough (Curtis had helped Thoreau build his cabin at
Walden Pond) that the editor might have anticipated his contributor's
attitude toward textual changes, but, nevertheless, as Gordon Milne
reports in his Curtis biography, Putnam's made significant cuts in
the first installment of Thoreau's "A Yankee in Canada." The
deletions of unorthodox religious sentiment and critical observations
like "I am not sure but this Catholic religion would be an admirable
one if the priests were quite omitted" resulted in Thoreau's asking

---

[1] Quoted in Cary, Curtis, p. 84.

for the return of his manuscript and attributing Curtis's actions to a "curt business matter."

Curtis, nevertheless, treated Thoreau's "Cape Cod" even more severely. Milne quotes Curtis as telling his publisher, "Anybody can alter Thoreau's Ms. by his letter," but when the first installment appeared very much cut--and indeed partially rewritten--Thoreau again withdrew his manuscript.[1] Curtis's willingness to alter texts to his liking may have come in part from the general editorial practices of his day and especially of Harper's Monthly, but there is also a possible personal factor in that Curtis's criticism generally does not concentrate exclusively on the work as rendered but is prone to offer suggestions, alternatives, so that his readers might see how a book could have been written. For whatever attempts Curtis made editorially to secure the widest possible audience for Putnam's and to retain the "strong backing from the clergy," the effort to maintain a "top rank" magazine and to make it profitable was faltering.

Putnam's lasted only until 1855 under its original ownership and direction; ownership passed to Dix, Edwards & Co. publishers, and Curtis for a time had little responsibility for soliciting, selecting, or editing manuscripts. When he was more contributor than editor for the magazine, Curtis's attitude and standards changed sufficiently that he recommended a poem and poet far outside the range of his

---

[1] Milne, George William Curtis, p. 67.

usual tastes:

> "The Libres" is Mrs. Sigourney, a very amiable woman and
> a very poor poet. But it's so slight a thing, and so
> without any decided character,--and so sure to please
> many babes of the spirit,--that I am very loath to return
> it to her, because it would be so sad a blow to her really
> kind nature, and because it is so much better than much
> of the verse that has been published in Putnam . . .
> Strain a point. She asks no money. She gives it as a
> free will offering to her personal feeling for me, and
> the supposition that I was the editor.[1]

Lydia Sigourney was hardly herself a charity case, being one of the popular and best-selling female writers that Curtis's circle tended to complain of as competition, but poetry was not her most established genre and she was nearing the end of her active career. The significance of Curtis's asking to "strain a point" is perhaps less in the charity and feelings he expresses than in the shift of his own attitude toward magazines and literature to include a more diverse sense of audience, a larger sympathy for the professional writing community, and a feeling that work which was "slight . . . without any decided character" could probably leaven and enlarge the audience for journals which included other, larger and better purposes.

Despite the reorganization and recapitalization of Putnam's under Dix, Edwards, it was floundering again by 1856. To save the venture, Curtis bought into the magazine. His new money and new position as general partner were not enough, and finally the situation deteriorated, as Curtis reported to Norton, to a point where "To save the creditors (for I would willingly have called quits myself), I

---

[1] Curtis to Dix, August 24, 1855, quoted in Milne, George William Curtis, p. 68.

threw in more money, which was already forfeited, and undertook the business with Mr. Miller, the printer, who wanted to save himself."[1] When the first *Putnam's* finally failed, both Curtis and his new father-in-law found themselves with a substantial debt, which Curtis repaid with years of book royalties and lecture fees. Curtis's experience with *Putnam's* had taken him increasingly away from the legacy of the transcendentalists' view of the American man of letters. He was moving steadily in an alternative direction where social influence and professional practicality encouraged active participation in public affairs and alliance with magazines which appealed to the mass audience rather than the "top rank."

Curtis took the opportunity of an address to the Literary Societies of Wesleyan University in 1856 to define and encourage his alternative to the directions of Emerson's "American Scholar." Speaking on "The Duty of the American Scholar to Politics and the Times," Curtis led his hearers away from concerns with "pure scholarship" and indeed away from literature--pure or otherwise. Instead, "The elevation and correction of public sentiment is the scholar's office in the state." The educated man and woman were to be "the conscience of the state" and not to be led aside by "The very material success for which nations, like individuals, strive . . . full of the gravest danger to the best life of the state as of

---

[1] Curtis to Norton, August, 1857, quoted in Cary, *Curtis*, p. 106.

the individual."[1] Curtis took on the assigned task of "elevation and correction of public sentiment" by increased involvement with the Harper's magazines. His new editorial and literary motive was didactic, and the circulation of the Harper's magazines ensured wide influence on public sentiment. The move marked a sensibility of distinct separation between editor and audience, a new attitude of writing and publishing for the others, not for an audience like oneself or one's peers.

Curtis joined the new Harper's Weekly with a regular column, "The Lounger," continued the "Easy Chair" for Harper's Monthly, provided essays for both magazines, and in 1859 began his first, and only, novel, Trumps, for serial publication in the Weekly. Curtis accepted the variety of writing necessary and reconciled the diversity of quality and intent in the Harper's periodicals in terms of the belief in responsibility he had expressed in the Wesleyan address as "Of what use to a man is a thought that will help the world, if he cannot tell it to the world?" His letters to Norton make it clear that his choice was deliberate and considered. In September, 1859, he explained,

> The "Weekly" now circulates 93,000, and is very thoroughly read. I make my Lounger a sort of lay pulpit, and the readers have a chance of hearing things suggested that otherwise there would be no hint of in the paper. And, after all, an author has something besides his own fame to look after.[2]

---

[1] Quoted in Cary, Curtis, pp. 111-13.

[2] Quoted in Cary, Curtis, p. 120.

Fletcher Harper gave Curtis total freedom and autonomy, though both knew he would only succeed in his purpose by guiding, rather than outrunning, the "popular sympathy." Curtis wrote from his own sense that American society was divided among at least three classes: the best minds, the ostentatious "practical men" whose goal was to "amass wealth and live in palaces," and a vast class in need of enlightenment and susceptible to education. The nature of the Harper's illustrated magazines drew that last audience for him, and he could continue his attacks on the nouveau riche Philistines while endearing himself to, rather than alienating himself from, that largest potential audience. To further his purpose with his new audience, Curtis dropped the sensuous prose style and dogmatic tone of his early travel writings and the abstract discussion of aesthetic principles to develop a conversational, pragmatic, common sense view of literary questions and controversies for the Monthly's "Easy Chair." Suggesting rather than arguing, he led his readers through analogies and comparative perspectives to judge writers and literature in terms of their purposes and varying aesthetics. In 1859-60, Curtis repeatedly confronted the issues of morality, gentility, prudery, and pruriency in literature. While Gordon Milne has seen some "Easy Chair" statements as indicating Curtis shared a genteel offense at earlier and franker literature, I think we can see something more subtle and more consciously didactic in Curtis's asking his readers to see the standards of the day in a larger perspective. The "Easy Chair" in August, 1859, considered

> Does the world grow more decent as it grows older, or is it merely that our standards change, and that we decline upon one side as we rise upon the other? There are parts of the Bible that a man would not like to read aloud in his family. Shakespeare, as we all know, has to be expurgated for families, if not for the stage.

and continued through a perspective of contrasting modern and earlier tastes, including an extended comment on Sir Walter Scott's grandmother's reading Aphra Behn. From his historical backgrounds, Curtis finally leads his reader to positively consider the new literature of his own day.

> The modern novel is reproached for its subjective character--for its constant tendency to explore the secrets of action, rather than to describe action--and a kind of masculine excellence and robust healthiness is claimed for the novels our fathers read and liked. We are told that we have squeamish stomachs--that we want to be coddled with sentiment and dandled with philosophic speculation. But is "Tom Jones," in any sense, a healthier or more manly history than "The Newcomes?"

For those unlikely to read or to feel sympathetically the "Easy Chair" analyses, Curtis developed his balancing act of sentimentality and "respectability" against common sense and human sympathy in the novel, Trumps, which began its serial appearances in the Weekly in 1859. Cary found Trumps a "Sunday-school story" and "depressing reading,"[1] and not in the league of Curtis's earlier Putnam's writing. Milne calls it "sentimental and romantic claptrap"[2] filled with characters existing to make speeches for the author. But read against contemporaneous novels with a purpose, Trumps

---

[1] Cary, Curtis, p. 124.

[2] Milne, George William Curtis, p. 204.

manages to present an upper class model for American cultural values which is, at least, more than occasionally effective in suggesting alternatives to using middle class morality to judge literature.

Curtis frustrated many of his friends and contemporaries by refusing to pursue his own fame in writing and by failing to push stridently the public taste in his efforts to educate it. His early associates and continuing friends regretted Curtis's departure from the ideals of literary quality which had marked Putnam's. They also failed to understand his interest in the brawling of practical county and national politics. Though Curtis through the years reported to Norton on battles over political patronage, party jealousies, etc., such old acquaintances continually tried to draw Curtis away from the Harper's magazines as too commercial a means to pursue either political or literary goals. Fletcher Harper also had a limited understanding of the purposes of his patrician editor. In 1862, Fletcher Harper asked Curtis to consider writing a war history "for popular reading" to gloss a book edition of the war pictures which had appeared in the magazines. Curtis clearly informed Harper that a history of the kind he proposed would be just a "job" to Curtis-- and one in which he had no interest.[1] But in 1863 when the political positions of Harper's Weekly came under attack (The Tribune characterized it as the Weakly), Curtis was willing--even eager--to become political editor of the Weekly to give it a more powerful presence

---

[1] Cary, Curtis, p. 154.

and to use the magazine as a vehicle for his own ideas.[1]

Norton, in 1864, began editing the North American Review with James Russell Lowell, but members of the old Cambridge and Boston circles still had some idea of starting yet another magazine, or perhaps a weekly paper, to promote their own views of politics and culture. In 1865, Norton offered the proposition to Curtis, and Curtis's reply goes far to define both his own position and his concept of the role of commercial mass market magazines in developing the tastes and minds of the American reading public. Curtis had practical concerns about the available capital, the amount of work involved, and the projected market--"Do not the 'Atlantic,' the 'North American,' the 'Evening Post,' and 'Harper's Weekly'--to go no further--address the various parts of the audience that are counted upon for a new paper, and are there not great advantages in having the questions presented in these different forms?" More crucially, however, Curtis attempted to explain the advantages of addressing a mass audience--an audience unlike oneself--and the necessity of retaining those advantages.

> I think upon all public questions in "Harper's Weekly" without the least trouble or responsibility for the details of the paper . . . The audience is immense. The regular circulation is about one hundred thousand, and on remarkable occasions, as now, more than two hundred thousand. This circulation is among that class which needs exactly the enlightenment you propose, and access is secured to it by the character of the paper as an illustrated sheet. I should want some very persuasive

---

[1] Cary, Curtis, p. 168.

inducement to relinquish the hold I already have upon
this audience, for I could not hope to regain it in a
paper of a different kind. Of course, "Harper's Weekly"
is not altogether such a paper as I should prefer for my
own taste; but it does seem to me as if I could do with it
the very work you propose, and upon a much greater scale
than in the form you suggest; nor is the pecuniary advantage
of your offer such as to shake this conviction.[1]

Curtis did not lose his literary tastes or all of his personal ambitions in commitment to public issues and Harper's magazines. In the late 1860s, he wrote repeatedly to William Dean Howells, the new light in the old Boston/Cambridge circle. He sent Howells articles for consideration for the Atlantic when their topics or approach unsuited them for the Harper's columns. Howells returned the graciousness of the critic who had praised Howells's "dreaming" and "romance," and Curtis courteously replied that he was "very glad if you can use one of the articles I sent you."[2] Though the relationship between Curtis and Howells was always rather formal (Howells would write, at the turn of the century, that he felt he had never really known Curtis), the two had a continuous and sympathetic professional relationship through the years when Howells would himself come to the Harper's firm and eventually take over residence in the "Easy Chair."

Their shared interests and associations with magazines often came together in promoting the interests of struggling writers. They traded off helping one another with small causes, however,

---

[1] Quoted in Cary, pp. 190-91.

[2] Curtis to Howells, May 28, 1869, Howells Papers.

rather than promotions of major figures. Though Curtis explained to Howells he felt reluctant to encourage the idea that "magazines, like the Civil Service, are . . . retreats for the unfortunate," he solicited the _Atlantic_ editor for consideration for Lady Blanch Murphy, who had been "shown the door" by her father after she married his organist.[1] Howells, in turn, asked Curtis for aid not only with regard to the Harper's magazines but also in using his influence to secure membership in the Century Club for Howells's protégés. Curtis was continually accommodating, promising, for example, "For your sake and for his sake, whom I have the pleasure of knowing, I shall most gladly do all I can to open the doors of the Century to your friend."[2]

In the literary issues in which Curtis and Howells were both joined, the "Easy Chair" columns show a consistency throughout the century in leading American readers to an understanding of the dynamics of their literary history, of the distinctive role of the artist in social and national life, and of a standard, beyond the restrictions of "morality" and "respectability," necessary to the appreciation of literature. Remarkably, perhaps, in terms of the conception of Curtis as a genteel idealist bound in the standards of the era of Longfellow and Lowell, Curtis is often more forceful in the early "Easy Chair" than Howells is in the later in asserting the limitations of America's early poets and in insisting the audience

---

[1] Milne, _George William Curtis_, pp. 138-39.

[2] Curtis to Howells, March 27, 1879, Howells Papers.

look at the values of literature and literary life in a larger historical and human perspective. Though Howells in "Roundabout to Boston" remembered Curtis for "his fine presence, his benign politeness, his almost deferential tolerance of difference in opinion,"[1] in the personae of the "Lounger" of the Weekly and the "Easy Chair" of the Monthly, Curtis developed the supposed informality, anonymity, and the contrast of opposed opinions in the same publication into an opportunity to engage his readers in reconsidering the prevailing mode of applying Sunday school respectability to judgment of writers and their work.

Answering a Harper's attack on Thackeray, for example, Curtis wrote,

> An article in our April number complained that the tendency of his view of Anne's times was to a social laxity, which might be very exhilarating but was very dangerous; that the lecturer's warm commendation of fermented drinks, . . . was as deleterious to the moral health of enthusiastic young readers disposed to the literary life as the beverage itself to their physical health.
>
> But this is not a charge to be brought against Thackeray. It is a quarrel with history and with the nature of literary life.

Rather than the worst and most dissolute of men, Curtis claimed,

> The literary class is the most innocent of all. The contempt of practical men for the poets is based upon a consciousness that they are not bad enough for a bad world.[2]

---

[1] Howells, "Roundabout to Boston," p. 94.

[2] George William Curtis, Literary and Social Essays (New York and London: Harper and Brothers, 1894), pp. 134-35, 137.

When not defending individuals or the literary life, Curtis tried to explain how American literature had come to be what it was. He saw the generation of Emerson and Holmes and the early magazines as those "who emancipated our literature from its Puritan subjection" and introduced imagination, humor, and grace. The problem came in that "The foundations of our distinctive literature were largely laid in New England, and they rest upon morality." While Curtis combined realistic assessments of the talents of early New England authors with personal respect, he fulsomely laid out the limitations of a society and literature dominated by ecclesiastical interests and the distinctions and necessary effects of a literary "fraternity" which was not bohemian or artistic like the old world's but "distinguished not only for propriety of life and respectability . . . but for . . . the virtues of fidelity, industry, and good sense, which have carried so far both the influence and renown of New England." While Curtis felt the ultimate sorting of American literary reputations was "survival of the fittest," he could hesitate to regret that when "Emerson greeted Walt Whitman at 'the opening of a great career,'" what the elder literary statesman offered was a "personal impression." The elder generation "identified their own preference with the public taste," and did little to insure that "the public taste" met or exceeded their own limitations and standards.[1] Curtis devoted his literary career--and decades of the Harper's Monthly criticism and commentary in the "Easy Chair"--to educating that public

---

[1] Curtis, Essays, pp. 218, 196, 223, 221, 219.

taste and to increasing the audience for literature "among that class which needs exactly the enlightenment."

He had little taste for the details of copy-editing or office work, preferring, in compensation for the time away from home for his heavy lecture schedule, to go into the Harper's offices only on Thursdays. For his Weekly editorials, he often wrote in the composing room, handing his copy directly to the compositor.[1] Curtis's distance from the practical daily workings of the magazine did not keep him from suggesting authors and work to the publishers or lessen his worth to the firm. When Henry Raymond died in 1869 and Curtis was offered the editorship of the New York Times at twice his Harper's salary, Curtis chose to stay with Harper both from loyalty and for the effect he had from the connection; Fletcher Harper, in turn, once Curtis's decision was made, matched the Times salary offer--retroactively.[2]

There was not, however, complete identification between Curtis and his employers. When a Harper's Weekly editorial in September, 1882, appeared in a revised form which essentially reversed Curtis's position, he felt he had been made to look ridiculous and resigned, returning only after Harper's Weekly "disavowed" the error.[3] Though Howells, on coming to the Harper's firm, had, in 1885, refused the publisher's solicitations to take over the "Easy Chair" column, Curtis

---

[1] Exman, House, p. 86.

[2] Exman, House, pp. 133-34.

[3] Cary, Curtis, p. 275.

leagued with Howells on many issues which brought little comfort to their publisher. When Howells in the "Editor's Study" was garnering so much criticism that Howells even felt it necessary to write to his father to assuage his worries, Curtis provided encouragement, writing to Howells on March 5, 1887, "I greatly enjoy watching your fight with the new form of Philisteria, which without the priggish and awful solemnity of Wordsworth reminds me of his."[1] And, while Curtis has been roundly criticized for not joining Howells in his eventual statement on the Haymarket anarchist trial, when Howells first proposed taking a public position in August of 1887, Curtis advised with him on ways and means. Curtis emphasized the need for reason and the influence of Howells's name, commenting from the length of his experience with the firm: "and let us all consider whether it would be well to print it in the Weekly? It would have to be very conclusive, undoubtedly, to strike our friends in Franklin Square favorably."[2] When Howells did finally publish his letter in the New York Tribune on November 6th, it was in response to the urging of the Haymarket defense lawyer, who had thought a public appeal might help his clients,[3] and Curtis did not join in returning to the Tribune as a forum for statements apart from the Weekly.

While Curtis was continually involved in politics and made a major impression in the campaigns for civil service reform, women's

---

[1] Curtis to Howells, Howells Papers.

[2] Curtis to Howells, August 12, 1887, Howells Papers.

[3] Lynn, Howells, p. 290.

rights, and the split within the Republican party over the nomination of James G. Blaine in 1884, his political positions and differences from many of his literary colleagues seem never to have influenced his support of fellow writers or literary issues. After he became, in the century's last decade, Chancellor of New York State University and turned necessarily to other interests, he retained an informed involvement in literary questions. In an address on James Russell Lowell in 1892, he reminded the audience that Lowell, "Like all citizens of high public ideals . . . was inevitably a public critic and censor."[1] Curtis retained for himself, however, the balance he had always urged on his audience, encouraging the value of reasonableness and diversity of motive over promotion of one's own limited interests and ideas. While in politics he felt charity for one's opponents was misplaced; in social and literary life, he urged a largeness of sensibility. In his Harper's essays, he had ventured to distinguish: "The author's success is of a wholly different kind from that of the publisher, and he is thoughtless who demands both."[2] Curtis might well have had a larger effect on the careers of his contemporaries and colleagues if his own directions had not become increasingly impersonal and apart from the usual ambitions of art, fame, and fortune. But for many, the memories of Curtis which are not complimentary or which credit him little with promoting progressive

---

[1] Quoted in Cary, Curtis, p. 312.

[2] Curtis, Essays, p. 139.

ideas come from his insistence that one cannot demand both kinds of success. His reply to Howells in 1892 regarding the proposed Society of American Authors is typical of the directness and the insistence on his own, separate way which kept Curtis functioning as part of the commercial Harper's enterprise years before many of his fellow writers felt comfortable with the corporate world of mass markets. He wrote, ". . . I had declined to take any initiate in it because of what seems to me to be a feeling for publishers which I do not share."[1]

---

[1] Curtis to Howells, May 13, 1892, Howells Papers.

CHAPTER VI

RICHARD WATSON GILDER AND

SCRIBNER'S MONTHLY AND THE CENTURY ILLUSTRATED MONTHLY MAGAZINE

Richard Watson Gilder, the assistant editor of Scribner's Monthly and then editor-in-chief of the Century, has consistently been a popular reference point for critics of the "genteel tradition" and its editorial enforcers. Gilder has been an easy target. He was the son of a Methodist minister, the only male student in his father's Flushing Female Academy, and a very minor poet with an inflated reputation in his own time. In the 1880s, as editor of the Century, the largest circulation and highest-paying literary magazine in the United States, Gilder regularly deleted potentially offensive words from the manuscripts he selected. Since Gilder printed and edited major work from major nineteenth century literary figures, citations to incidents like Gilder's Century "bowdlerizing" of chapters from Huckleberry Finn have engaged and informed the larger audience for American literary history that has little interest in the historical role of the magazines or the long term and essentially symbiotic relationships between the editor and professional authors. With the small production and esteem of Gilder's own creative work, he and the magazines with which he was associated have slipped into literary history as emblems of an age when editorial malfeasance or wrongheaded prudery restricted the expression of American life in literature.

Gilder himself was aware that magazine editors were perceived as arbiters of literary destinies continually open to the charge of suppressing genius. As a journeyman magazine manager and editor, he felt the role was overdrawn, the product of an excess of ambition and imagination. Gilder served a long apprenticeship in periodical publishing. After military service, he had worked on the Newark Advertiser and the Newark Morning Register. While still with the Register, he began editing Charles Scribner and Company's house publicity vehicle, Hours at Home. In 1871 when Charles Scribner developed Scribner's Monthly with Josiah Holland and Roswell Smith, Hours at Home was dropped, and Gilder became Holland's assistant on the larger and more prestigious new journal.[1] Well before he came to have full charge of the new Century in 1881, Gilder had learned to distinguish publishing realities and the variant tastes of magazine audiences from the writer's romantic expectations of recognition and artistic accomplishment.

Scribner, Holland, and Smith made a large success of Scribner's Monthly in the 1870s, succeeding while the fortunes of Howells's Atlantic Monthly were faltering. Gilder saw Holland develop the magazine's policies by combining Holland's personal penchants with

---

[1] Smith, Gilder, p. 15.

sensitive reaction to the complaints--and underlying advice on what was tolerable to his market--which came from the magazine's subscribers. Holland did not avoid controversy, especially what came from his own taste for popular theology. He could not be kept from the expression of his own opinions, no matter how peculiar, but he was willing not to continue an issue which proved unpopular with the paying customers.

The early years of the Holland/Gilder association were marked by dissension between the young, artistic assistant and his more commercial, moralistic and traditional chief. Holland opposed including many articles of substance because, he claimed, the magazine was mainly read by women. Gilder was far less inclined to demean his audience. He noted that the letters from complaining subscribers made their protests on the grounds that questionable material might offend or adversely affect some other category or class of readers, and Gilder's own carefulness was primarily directed to excluding or deleting what might negatively affect the children in the magazine's audience. Gilder concentrated less on defining the rights and wrongs--or even the reasonableness--of this concern than on assuring that writers he thought were talented could present their materials in such a way as to be acceptable to a family audience.

Gilder developed and wrote for Scribner's Monthly "The Old Cabinet," a continuing column which roughly paralleled those which Curtis had made institutions in the Harper's magazines. Gilder and his wife, Helena DeKay Gilder, were very much involved in the artistic life of young New York, and Gilder used the column to report on and evaluate new work in painting, sculpture, illustration and architecture as well as literature. Though Holland at first felt the column insubstantial and unlikely to interest many readers, Gilder insisted on and defended his personal directions without disturbing the two men's working relationship or the identity and fortunes of the magazine.

From the first volume of <u>Scribner's Monthly</u>, Gilder's writing for the magazine provided a lively contrast to Josiah Holland's sanctimonious preachments on public and religious questions, e.g., Holland liked to lament the loss of "the good old fashioned standard of personal honesty among the laboring poor." Gilder's public advice tended to distinctions between flippant or hypocritical protests against received standards and beliefs and genuine, necessary reassessments of life and thought. In "The Old Cabinet," for example, Gilder remarked on what he saw in young poets as "a tendency toward a flippant use of the element and experience of religious doubt." Gilder thought such flippancy ought to be reconsidered not only for the sake of the poetry and the poet, but also for the readers who might be influenced. "The Old Cabinet" argued for a sense of the poet's responsibility and an understanding of the basic sensibility which underlay Gilder's own editorial policies:

> So we think you ought to know enough about it [religious doubt] not to want to hurry any other soul prematurely into the same perlexities which you have nearly, if not quite, emerged from. Is there not darkness enough in the world, that you should go about knocking men's hats over

their eyes? If there is a mountain in the way, don't
forever be harping upon its unscalable heights--
magnifying its dangers by day, its nightly terrors.
If you know the way over, or around, or under, get up
and say so, like a man and a brother. Above all, beware
that you fling no stumbling-block in the way of those
who climb for their lives.[1]

Gilder's philosophy and judgment of literature, from the above quoted "Old Cabinet" in the first volume of Scribner's Monthly through his practice in almost thirty years at the head of the Century, were argued in terms of these distinctions between flippancy and genuine protest. Unwilling to indulge the mannerisms of writers who he felt were hypocritical or self-indulgent, Gilder was both willing and capable of reminding any writer that the large magazine audience was composed of a diversity of souls who could not be presumed to have the sophistication that Gilder himself would desire.

As Scribner's Monthly held a leading and profitable position in American publishing throughout its life in the 1870s, Holland lost interest in dominating the magazine's total policies and gained confidence in his young associate, who took gradually more and more responsibility for soliciting and selecting the magazine's artistic offerings. Though Gilder has traditionally been associated with the school of his poetry--romantic, ideal, mannered, traditional--the young assistant editor early focused on the American short story, a genre which Gilder felt showed our highest achievement and originality.

---

[1] Josiah Holland, "Topics of the Time," and Richard Watson Gilder, "The Old Cabinet," in Scribner's Monthly I (March, 1871) in Scribner's Monthly 1871, with an Introduction by Charles Scribner, Jr., Centennial Reprint Ed. (New York: Charles Scribner's Sons, 1971), pp. 562, 565.

The story writers who came into Scribner's Monthly in Gilder's time, and most often at his suasion, included Edward Eggleston and Henry James, Jr.

Gilder expressed his editorial preferences not on the basis of subject matter but rather in terms of a distinction between artistic and inartistic treatment. Unlike Howells, who looked on submitted manuscripts as finished products and advised rejected potential contributors to try again with something else, Gilder tended to look at manuscripts as work in the making. Much of the critical writing on the genteel tradition works in terms of distinctions between materials and presentation, between "subject" and "treatment." Such separations were an essential base of both Gilder's criticism and his editorial correspondence. He used a very inclusive sense of what constituted treatment or form, including plot, characterization, and language. Since Gilder tended to look at submitted manuscripts as first drafts, first trials of an author's idea and intention which could be modified and improved without disturbing literature's purpose of artistry, he felt he could question and make suggestions for changes without feeling himself to affect the substance of a story. In requesting reforms of stories, he frequently questioned the assignment of non-standard language or values to characters who seemed to be authority figures. He would instigate for a new ending, a less gloomy perspective, a difference of tone overall. Gilder continually claimed that editorial assistance could help even the best of authors see inelegancies or difficulties which had escaped their attention; for the least talented, the instructing and suggesting editor could make tolerable art from a limited talent and idea.

All of Gilder's ideas about editing and literature came from and were oriented toward the illustrated family literary magazines to which he devoted his entire career. Whatever extensions of taste or tolerance he allowed over the years, Gilder was firmly convinced of the essential separation not only between what was magazineable and what was bookable but also between the editor's obligation to construct a composite product which would please his audience and the individual writer's forwarding his own work and directions. Gilder felt the magazine was useful to the writer in that it could supply both a printing and an income at a time when few artists could expect to support themselves by other means. Gilder personally went far further in insisting that the magazines under his direction make a primary commitment to support of American authors, and Gilder prided himself on the number of writers that <u>Scribner's Monthly</u> and the <u>Century</u> introduced to the public. Never, however, did he intend or promise or encourage writers to feel anything that they might offer would be appropriate and welcome to the magazine.

Gilder saw the power of family magazines for the American writer as essentially a result of financial conditions created by the lack of International Copyright. He did not feel, however, that the magazine could make any guarantees.

> I want to see authors have a firmer property and better
> pay, and I am anxious to have all literary values increase.
> But after all that can be done it will always be hard for

a conscientious man to devote his whole time to literature and support his family on the proceeds.[1]

Gilder was personally and professionally a pragmatist in assessing how far the large American public supported such ambition for "literary values." His daughter remembered her mother's describing their surprise at Europeans' esteem for poets since they "came from a land where to be a poet meant to be something one must hide and be ashamed of."[2] And for all the criticism Gilder reaped from being what even Josiah Holland called "very cautious--perhaps overnice," when he was asked in 1891 to address the New York Press Club on "The Future of American Literature," the editor, at the midpoint of his career, spoke of the "magazine sanctum" as a "gilded cage." In forecasting "the effect of the magazine upon the future of our literature," Gilder acknowledged the advantages to professional authorship could be offset by the dangers of restriction.

> In the absence of International Copyright, the magazine and the journalistic syndicate have been in many respects a godsend. A very large proportion of our very best literature has been and will be fostered by the magazines. There is just this danger in the magazine--that its peculiar audience and traditions may unwittingly somewhat cripple the literary criticism of life.

Gilder claimed that in estimating this danger, Americans need also consider the influence of journalism on literature, especially in so far that many writers of the age were journalists in early profession

---

[1] *Letters of Richard Watson Gilder*, ed. Rosamond Gilder (Boston and New York: Houghton Mifflin Co., 1916), p. 396.

[2] Rosamond Gilder, ed., *Letters*, p. 90.

and training. From this connection, he saw "the tendency of modern literature is the same as the tendency of the newspaper--toward realism," but claimed that the realistic novelist and the journalist, when not exaggerating for their own polemic, "know that neither in art nor in journalism can or should there be absolute reality . . . It is not only the voice of conscience, but the voice of social self-preservation!" The conflict that Gilder acknowledged seeing was not between the purposes of variant literary creeds, but the necessity to "stop this side of artistic and moral wreck and ruin," to keep along with "the spirit of the actual" the values of "art and imagination."[1]

For all that Gilder could take very seriously his editorial responsibilities not only to authors and audience but also in terms of the historical literary and social effects of the magazine, he endeared himself to many of his contemporaries by refusing to take himself and his role too seriously and by refusing to allow editorial difficulties or differences in taste to interfere with personal friendships and support. Though Gilder as late as 1909 responded to a reviewer who identified his humor with "I don't know whether I ought to give myself away, but I could publish a book of comic verse if I dared,"[2] the literary fraternity involved with Gilder's magazines hardly found his humor secret. In the earliest days of Scribner's

---

[1] Reported in "Journalism and American Literature," The Critic 15 (February 7, 1891), 71.

[2] Rosamond Gilder, ed., Letters, p. 435.

Monthly, working under Holland, Gilder had seen enough irony in the magazine editor's processes to draft a house memo:

> Send Q. S. The usual editorial answer--that if he will put the twenty-page essay on Esoteric Polarity into the shape of a five-page love-story we may be able to publish it. Or we might use it in the form of a ballad that will illustrate nicely with figures.[1]

Gilder also liked to use dialect for humorous effect in his editorial letters to contributors he knew personally. He joked himself on efforts to conciliate Philistines, Pharisees, and Mrs. Grundy in making and editing selections for the magazine. Whitman remembered how expressly gracious and friendly both Richard and Helena DeKay Gilder had been to him throughout the years, and this despite Whitman's public dismissal of Gilder's poetry as insignificant. When Horace Traubel put together Whitman's reminiscences for the Century, Gilder printed them despite a number of uncomplimentary references to himself. For the editor who has acquired a reputation for imposing his own tastes on writers greater than himself, the strongest continuous imposition of his strictly personal taste was an aversion to writers who were humorless, sanctimonious, or impractical in pushing what Gilder or the magazine should do for their work.

When Gilder began editing the new Century magazine in 1881, he had already suffered graciously through years of his own disappointments in what a magazine might do. In 1908, Gilder remembered for Ferris Greenslet that he and Helena DeKay had one of the first

---

[1] Rosamond Gilder, ed., Letters, p. 388.

copies of the "Rubáiyát" in New York and that, while Gilder had wished to publish it in the magazine, he realized "that Dr. Holland would never let it appear there on account of the wine therein."[1] But with Holland gone and Scribner's Monthly disbanded, Gilder found he had to define himself how far the Century would go on social and literary issues, that he would not be left to expand slowly or subtly in a more liberal direction. Edmund Gosse, the Century's British agent and one of Gilder's earliest British literary friends, pressed on Gilder in 1881 dramatic liberalizations of American magazine policy on controversial religious subjects. Gilder's reply contains a statement which would become typical of his responses to urgent pleas for radical change: ". . . the line must be drawn somewhere, and the editors reserve the right to draw it." He explained to Gosse his view of the magazine's responsibility to its audience:

> We think it no more than honest that a magazine whose principal audience (and an audience that mostly pays in advance, on trust) is of a certain opinion should not too rudely shock that opinion. We constantly go beyond our main audience in the direction of liberality of thought, but generally exercise something of the same reticence of individual opinion that all writers of, say, fiction exercise--Dickens, Thackeray, and, an instance more to the point, George Eliot--in writing for a popular audience.[2]

If Gilder did not please everyone in the degree to which the Century, as he had predicted in its first number, "shall be a better magazine than 'Scribner's' ever was," he made noticeable shifts in

---

[1] Rosamond Gilder, ed., Letters, pp. 434-35.

[2] Gilder to Gosse, December 21, 1881, Gilder Papers, New York Public Library. Quoted in Smith, Gilder, pp. 76-77.

expanding those directions and features of Scribner's Monthly which had been of his making rather than Holland's. The Century maintained the interests of the "Old Cabinet" and "Home and Society" series which Gilder had developed in the earlier magazine, and departments for informal essays and humorous verse were added. Gilder kept his own interest in artistic and literary questions and allowed a variety of "experts" to take on the more economic and social issues. He printed John Hay's The Breadwinners when Aldrich would not have it in the Atlantic, despite Howells's urgings, and promoted the Civil War series and a Lincoln biography, though he left the details of handling this expository work to his associates.

Gilder's most direct effect on the literature of the Century came from his concentration on the "creative" work and "creative" writers within the context of what he saw as the dual priorities of supporting the most talented American writers and of creating an overall combination which would make the magazine successful. As Gilder wrote to Maurice Thompson in 1886, he believed,

> What makes a magazine "go" in a business and moneyed point of view, is not the individual writers; it is the combination which is made by the editors backed by the publishing enterprise. . . . We put a poem or an artistic story in next to a war article and that number of the magazine has a large circulation, but it is the war article that gives it the circulation and us the power to pay authors, rather than the individual story.[1]

Gilder did not use this pragmatic perspective as an excuse to underrate or underpay the Century's writers of poems and stories, and

---

[1] Rosamond Gilder, ed., Letters, p. 395.

though he was not at all fond of conflict, he supported his contributors through the inevitable, and not so inevitable, controversies which arose from work published in the Century.

Gilder experienced the rigors of controversy early in the Century's history when he himself in 1882 became involved in what has been called "The Cesnola Affair," a public artistic brawl over whether officials of the Metropolitan Museum had profited from intentionally adding fraudulent pieces to the collection. Gilder seems to have come out of the experience willing for the Century to support a righteous cause, but determined that the magazine would not become associated exclusively with a particular faction, partisan viewpoint, or permanent political position. For many of the writers who came to the Century looking toward a large, general forum to plead a cause, this meant that an initial, considered statement would be welcome, but that Gilder would not allow an individual or a group to continue discussion through the Century. His critical emphasis on artistic treatment and the importance of form in poetry and fiction meant Gilder would also dissuade writers from using "creative" work to promote partisan discussion or solutions to social questions. This view of the mission of belles lettres and his disinclination to associate the magazine with a continuing crusade brought Gilder much of the criticism in his own time from contributors he respected and thought to have talent.

One of the Scribner's Monthly writers of whose work Gilder was exceptionally fond was George Washington Cable. Gilder had done much to promote Cable's stories in the magazine, and both the author and publisher had won popular attention and success from the Scribner's Monthly serialization of Cable's first novel, The Grandissimes. Gilder considered Cable one of the best and most popular of the new writers he had helped to put before the public. The novel manuscript Cable offered to the new Century--originally titled Bread, later Dr. Sevier--unfortunately, however, ran against Gilder's few absolute principles of literary artistic treatment. Gilder's letter of advice apologized for the attack it made, but clearly outlined the editor's general and particular objections to the treatment. Gilder wrote

> To me it is the least good work you have ever done. And yet it has in it some of your best work, and it is free from your greatest fault, namely confusion.
>
> I will not condemn myself by suspecting that you imagine that I object to the inculcation of morality, religion, or any kind of spiritual truth in a work of art. . . . I am sure that we both agree that it may be done, and that the question only is, is it well done! It seems to me that in the present story (if it is a story) your heart has got the better of your head.

The editor warned that the novel, as written, was not only unacceptable but also disfunctional--and likely to ruin the career Cable had so recently developed. His advice, identifying the proper goals for literature, the best parts of the story, and possible audience reactions was taken by Cable as a blueprint for the first of a series of revisions. The letter's details give an indication to what degree and in what direction Gilder's attitude and directions could change the shape of individual works offered to the magazine.

> . . . The story to me fails of its end--because the motive is too apparent. The reader feels that it is

a "put up job";--that the characters, are dragged from misery to misery in order that the writer can preach his theories through them. The Dr., the clerk, & the nurse are the only real persons in the book. The two principal characters are lay figures--"objects" of sympathy.--You have turned your mind lately so completely into philanthropical work that for the time being you have lost your sense of art. I do not object to philanthropy either in life and act, nor in the book--but its expression must--in a work of art--take an artistic form. You and I do not object to the morality and spiritual teaching of Hawthorne nor to the patriotism and philanthropy of Torugueneff (whose writings it is said, freed the Russian serfs) because the form is always artistic.

Gilder warned Cable that his direction could "injure" the talent and career that had been given to him and urged that his "direction" should be to carry "spiritual food no less than intellectual stimulus and wholesome pleasure." Gilder was willing to sort out what in Bread met the various criteria. He questioned the author from the perspectives of editor and reader, asking why there could not be

> . . . a less obviously heart-wringing & "reformatory" an ↓aspect and ↑ end. Why on earth should that woman keep away from her husband during the /illegible/ of his prosperity. and then--worse than all--why spoil everything by making an infidel of her--an infidel to the true love of her life! Her marrying the Dr. seems to me under all the circumstances a most wanton and cruel infliction upon the sympathies of the reader.
>
> There are several minor points I will write to you . . .
>
> P.S. Narcissi is one of your very best creations. . . . Then the description of the beginning of the war is most valuable--excellent--but utterly thrown away in this tract." . . . you could use the good material that is in this work in a fuller and more careful matured work--or else somehow make a real story of it--instead of a

[damnation ground?] without plot or artistic reason for being.[1]

Despite Cable's being in the seemingly enviable position of riding the success of The Grandissimes and his having previously been able to place in other magazines work Gilder had rejected, the novelist replied with the intention of rewriting the manuscript to meet the editor's concerns. Gilder repeated and added to his praise for the parts of the work he felt were well done and coached Cable through a series of revisions until the novel was finally serialized in the Century as Dr. Sevier some years later. When Cable wished to express his views on the southern question as an expository opinion piece for the Century after the novel was accepted, Gilder took and printed the essay, "The Freedman's Case in Equity," and defended both the writer and his opinions against a host of objections and threats of reprisal. Gilder at the time fought out the controversy equally with the writer who had fomented it, but he became hesitant to encourage, either as editor or friend, the southerner's use of literature or the magazine to pursue solutions to social causes. When Cable offered the novel, John March, Southerner, to the Century, Gilder was wary of another inartistic novel like the first manuscript of Bread, and on reading the manuscript, he found his concerns realized. Though Cable was again willing to go through a series of revisions, he could not bring the novel to the form Gilder would find

---

[1] Gilder to Cable, February 1, 1882, Richard Watson Gilder Letter-Press Book, vol. 1 (Nov. 16, 1880-Jan. 13, 1886), Gilder Collection, New York Public Library. Hereafter referred to as Gilder Collection.

acceptable, and John March was never serialized in the Century. In
Cable's pursuit of the magazine's publication both for himself and
for other southern spokesmen, including Charles Chesnutt, the distance
between the editor's sense of art and the role of the magazine and
the writers' offerings grew increasingly unbridgeable.

By September of 1889, "play material" which Cable had sent
struck Gilder as so far off the mark that the editor replied not only
with his own opinion, but citing consultation with Madame Modjeska,
Bozluta, and Jefferson:

> What these three experts say is exactly what I feel.
> Better be discouraging than misleading. . . . In
> general a detail I never read anything so obviously
> unadapted to the stage. . . . If any one with stage
> experience endorses these acts--it is simply unaccount-
> able.
>
> The "lay-out" strikes all of us as simply unfeasable.
> . . . The prolonged use of the mule, the opening talk--
> where the whole situation must be told--& is told--but
> in a manner which no audience could follow.[1]

The personal relationship could also become somewhat strained. Gilder
wrote to Cable regarding a rumor which had been attributed to Cable
that Gilder's sister-in-law, Mrs. Bronson, was married to Browning.
(They were close.) While Gilder assured Cable that he was sure
Cable had not said it, he asked him to track down the rumor and
squelch it.

Gilder's relationship with many of the other southern writers
whom the Century "discovered" and promoted ran a similar pattern,

---

[1] Gilder to Cable, September 4, 1889, Gilder Collection.

especially in the matter of bringing their unique material to an
"artistic treatment." Thomas Nelson Page--encouraged by Gilder's
associate editor, Robert Underwood Johnson--published some of his
best known stories in the Century, but as Page attempted to continue
and expand the relationship, Gilder felt again the disappointment of
work which had fine elements, but failed formally. He returned the
manuscript of "Soldier of the Empire" in January of 1886, complimenting
it as "capital," but pointing out "a grave defect; there is no climax,
therefore no story. It is too much like a story for a sketch, but
as a story it lacks dramatic completeness such as all your other
stories have had."[1] Page was encouraged to revise the manuscript to
meet the editor's criterion, a necessity which he encountered with
other editors as well.

Joel Chandler Harris was treated somewhat more gently by
Gilder, primarily because the author was unlikely to resubmit manuscripts which had been returned for revisions. Still, when it was a
question of the Century's publishing a work of any significant
length, Gilder saw in Harris's work the usual difficulty of southern
fiction and sent the usual reply combining praise for the story's fine
elements--"full of life, and the heroine is not sentimentalized nor
lifted out of her plane . . ."--with a number of suggestions for
streamlining and strengthening the plot.[2] Joel Chandler Harris did

---

[1] Quoted in Smith, Gilder, p. 57.

[2] Smith, Gilder, pp. 61-62.

not need the Century's recognition to establish himself in the 1880s. Uncle Remus had been a best seller in volume sales in 1881, and other magazines were eager for Harris's work. Still, he trusted Gilder's judgment on artistic questions and was willing, at his most vociferous, to explain patiently to Gilder the writer's alternative reasoning when they disagreed, but when the Century offered Harris an exclusive contract, he declined.

For all of Gilder's and the Century's difficulties and rapprochements with southern writers and the editor's tightrope walking between supporting Cable's case for the freedmen and excising Page's racism, both the man and the magazine were continually accused of favoring southern literature blindly and to the detriment of other American writers. For a time, the Century was as clearly and as frequently indicted for representing only the south as the Atlantic Monthly had been for seeming exclusively New England's. By 1890, Gilder felt it necessary to reply personally to criticism from James Lane Allen.

> Without intending in any way to make a pet of southern literature, it has forced itself upon the attention of the editors of "The Century" to such a degree, that we are supposed to make a specialty of it, and I had a northern⟨er⟩ ↓author↑ ask me, not a great while ago, when I was going to give the North a chance. So far, in the North, as well as in the South, short stories seem to have reached the greatest perfection, although some very notable novels have been written since the War ↓north and south↑. I regard a ↓good↑ short story, not only in itself as a ↓notable work↑ of art, but as having no little importance as a separate scene in the great panorama of contemporary life. No painters of such scenes

have been more successful in America than the new ⟨group⟩ ↓generation↑ of Southern authors.[1]

In Gilder's defense of the short story and his care that the southerners not be seen as a "group" nor as competitors with northerners, we can see a particular application of Gilder's more general editorial values and precepts. He wished to devote the Century to the promotion of American writers and to publish what was to him the best available work. The increased production of and public vogue for southern literature allowed the new Century magazine to find a profitable identity in the market. But at the same time, Gilder, as we have seen, was unwilling for the Century to support the southern writers in whatever direction they chose to go. The initial value of material in adding another "separate scene in the great panorama of contemporary life" was extendable to a continuing publishing relationship only if the writer could work within the terms of artistic treatment and suggested emendations which came from the editorial standards. In many ways, it seems that the continuing southern presence in the Century resulted in part from the malleability of the southerners in contrast to other Americans of like levels of talent and professionalism.

Gilder actually gave more helpful tolerance and publishing aid to two other categories of writers that both contemporaries and historians have given less attention: the personal friends and

---

[1] Gilder to Allen, January 18, 1890, Richard Watson Gilder Letter-Press Book, vol. 4 (Aug. 20, 1888-Sept. 8, 1890), Gilder Collection.

"popular" writers whose work he respected and the major progressive literary figures of his age. The outstanding figure in the first category is Frances Hodgson Burnett, an Englishwoman married to an American who is most famous for her Little Lord Fauntleroy, a popular St. Nicholas magazine serial which was a best-seller in volume publication and a huge success in the play adaptation written by the author. Years before Fauntleroy, Burnett was a principal contributor to the Century and a social friend of the Gilders. They carried on a sizeable, friendly, chatty correspondence on both personal and literary issues. Writing to Gilder from Long Island in 1881, Burnett observed that the Long Island people didn't seem to find her respectable, and considered whether a sign on her back with her name and "authoress" would help the situation or make it worse. Gilder, however, had enough faith in Burnett's respectability and talent that, as one of the Century's first serialized novels, he contracted for and began printing an uncompleted novel without even having a definite plot prospectus. The novel, Through One Administration, headlined the new volume of the new Century magazine, developing a plot in which the sympathetic hero is quite madly in love with a woman married to someone else. Subscribers and the press waged a war of complaint against the novel, the novelist, the magazine, and the magazine editor which can justifiably be seen as emblematic of the risk American magazines ran in affronting middle American sexual morality in the nineteenth century. Gilder felt the criticism was justified, given the image and role of the family magazine, and asked Burnett for changes. She refused, and the novel and calumny continued.

There is no record, however, that Gilder ever blamed Burnett for the controversy or referred it to her after the initial editorial request and her refusal. Their personal and professional relationship continued unabated. The Gilders traveled to share social occasions like boating excursions, musical evenings, etc. with Burnett, and she continued to correspond with him about decisions she was making in her writing. She shared fully in the projects and prerogatives of the most favored American literary groups. When Gilder, Howells, Clemens, et. al. set out to write a committee novel, the basic concept was determined by Burnett. As Gilder wrote to Clemens, her place in the circle was clear:

> I was talking a day or two ago with Mrs. Burnett about the story project. She suggests that a large family be taken, and the various members scattered throughout the country--in some cases, two or three remaining together, as husband and wife and child. She thinks this would avoid repetition, and add to the interest, and show equally the effect of varied surrounds upon the same sort of people. . . .[1]

When Gilder wrote to Clemens again in October of 1884, trying to convince him to give the Century half or three quarters of Huckleberry Finn to serialize in the magazine before the volume publication, he offered Mrs. Burnett as one example of an author for whom Century publication had worked well, even when it violated custom and precedent:

> Its against your rule. Yes, but we find that the best thing we can do now & then is to break a rule--or we

---

[1] Gilder to Clemens, April 24, 1884, Mark Twain Papers, University of California Libraries, Berkeley. Hereafter referred to as Mark Twain Papers.

did when, for instance, we . . . reprinted Mrs. Burnetts
Louisiana from the back numbers of Peterson's Magazine![1]

It was not that favored contributors like Mrs. Burnett had total freedom with the magazine. She did not buckle under to, and from an artistic sense did not need, the kind of wholesale editorial suggestions that Gilder habitually made to the southern writers. Everyone who wrote for the Century, however, had his or her manuscripts edited, and emendations and deletions were frequent, especially in removing strictly personal or partisan statements of opinion, strong language, libel or potential libel of living figures, and details of physical description which could in any way be conceived as sexual. Though Mrs. Burnett fought it out--and won--with Gilder on a question of whether she should and could use details of the private lives of public figures, to the end of their relationship and Gilder's editorship, she acknowledged his right to edit copy and to make cuts for space and form. Gilder often joked publicly about the scourge to authors of the editorial blue pencil, and in submitting the first seventeen chapters of The Shuttle, Burnett returned the jest in kind:

> . . . In your sainted hands alone would I trust it to be run over by the blue pencil in your eye--what a hideously uncomfortable place for a blue pencil. I am afraid it will be hopelessly long for serialization but I do not want it to be. The fact that one can restore everything in the book after the serializing makes it possible to gaze on blue pencils with calmness.[2]

---

[1] Gilder to Clemens, October 10, 1884, Mark Twain Papers.

[2] Burnett to Gilder, April 6, 1906, Gilder Collection.

Though Gilder expressed repeatedly and in a variety of forms his conviction that the best writers were also the most amenable to editorial suggestions and criticism, his preference for her work and that of his most prestigious contemporaries had more to do with their ultimate quality than amiability. Gilder early conceived of the Century as a factor not only in promoting the profession of authorship in the United States, but also in using the opportunity the magazine presented to bring together and establish the historical and artistic importance of major American literary figures. In pursuing his aim, Gilder in the 1880s relied heavily on both the creative production and the critical perspectives of William Dean Howells, who had just moved from the editorship of the Atlantic Monthly. In encouraging Howells to write for almost every issue of the Century in the early years, Gilder urged him to follow his own directions, to try "not something in 'our line'--we would rather improve upon 'our line'."[1] With Howells's involvement with the magazine, as American audiences and editors would inevitably find, followed Henry James.

Howells's relationship with the Century, from its founding until he joined the Harper's establishment in 1885, was productive both for Howells and for the image of the magazine. On the basis of only general proposals, Gilder accepted a series of Howells's novels for the magazine and allowed the former editor almost total freedom

---

[1] Gilder to Howells, March 26, 1881, Howells Papers, quoted in Smith, Gilder, p. 107.

in the treatment. Howells's Century novels took on, in turn, topics which are generally considered taboo in the genteel construct. The first, A Modern Instance, dealt with chicanery in journalism and business dealings, divorce, and uncomplimentary views of the jealousy and passion in the husband-wife and father-daughter relationship. Gilder not only printed the novel, but a Century editorial called attention to it as a serious consideration of the contemporary divorce "problem." The second Howells Century novel, A Woman's Reason, looked toward the situation of a woman dependent on her own activity and her own nature for financial and psychological support in the context of a rather realistic--and somewhat cynical--portrait of Boston society. The third, The Rise of Silas Lapham, combined a study of business ethics with the conflicts of values and culture between Brahmin Boston society and the new manufacturing rich. Aside from some discussion of alternative titles and very minor points of publishing mechanics, all these three went through the Century essentially under the artist's sole control. The only recorded editorial incident was Gilder's request that Howells rewrite a scene in Silas Lapham which mentioned dynamite as a potential resort of working class dissidents, and this because the explosive had become an issue in domestic troubles in the British political economy.

Though Gilder thought Howells's novels for the Century were a major step forward in their serious and realistic confrontation of significant issues and in their artistry, many critics of the day attacked both Howells and the books, with some relish for evaluating

Howells outside the protection of his Atlantic editorship and publishing. Despite a comparably rather grand and general success for Silas Lapham over the other two Century novels, Howells remembered that Francis Parkman, who was "immutably of the Boston social and literary faith," talked to the author about The Rise of Silas Lapham,

> in a somewhat troubled and uncertain strain, and interpreting his rise as the achievement of social recognition, without much or at all liking it or me for it. I did not think it my part to point out that I had supposed the rise to be a moral one . . .[1]

Despite a very mixed and measured reception for Howells's work, Gilder was as continually supportive as Howells had ever been for his favored contributors to the Atlantic. He urged and allowed Howells other contributions in various kinds, and the editor rejected only a long play Howells proposed and one novel when the choice came to be one of two Howells's novels.

Along with Howells's creative work for the Century, he began in 1882 a series of extensive critical articles on major figures in American literature. The first, on Henry James, praised his friend and countryman at the expense of traditional and contemporary British novelists. The uproar which ensued, especially in England, was sufficiently strident and personal that Howells himself tried to avoid the controversy, but Gilder was delighted with the attention it attracted. He encouraged Howells to continue when he would a series which would associate the most talented figures of their

---

[1] Howells, "Literary Boston," p. 121.

generation with the Century, wanting such as James and Twain discussed and even defended. Despite Gilder's lack of personal association with the realist school and the realist cause, partially from a perception of their talent, partially from the relationship with Howells, partially in compensation for the closure of the Atlantic Monthly which came with Aldrich's editorship, the Century became the place to find the writers Howells admired. Gilder was as likely as Howells to cite Tourgeneff and other standards and masters to writers he felt had not made the best use of their materials, but in dealing with Howells himself and with James and Twain, Gilder became almost obsequious in serving as editor to talents he thought far greater than his own.

Henry James came to Gilder's open invitation to the Century in the personal tradition he had established with Howells at the Atlantic: pushing an editor to, and then beyond, his limits. James's earliest work for the magazine, a sketch and story in 1882, pleased the editor, though the story was exceptionally long by Century standards, and James set his prices at the peak of the market, asking more for a magazine contribution than even the ever popular Mark Twain. In no practical sense could Gilder justify either the fees or the attention he paid to Henry James, but he felt the writer and his work were important and that the public--especially with the aid of Howells's critical essays--could be educated to a different, and higher, standard of literary taste. Gilder accepted James's The Bostonians for the Century on the basis of a prospectus and the

first two chapters, even though James had put him through the same
sort of defining what the magazine would and would not do that Gilder
had gone through with Edmund Gosse at the Century's beginnings.
Gilder explained the difference between a separate volume, which made
its own fame and fortune, and a magazine serial, which was sold on
faith to a pre-paid and identifiable audience. He reminded James
of the editor's responsibility not to shock greatly this audience
while advancing before it and leading it to a more liberal and
artistically sophisticated sensibility.

The risk Gilder took in contracting for The Bostonians was
a rather large and predictable one, though not in terms of the
magazine constraints they had discussed or any considerations of
shocking middle American gentility. Though the "situation" of the
novel, especially in the suggestions of lesbianism which have attracted
the attention of later critics, might be presumed to be something
which would shock the Century audience, the editor's problems with
the novel were almost exclusively that both the large public and the
critics seemed inutterably bored with the serial. The whole and the
individual episodes were extremely long and lacking in action by any
magazine standards, and Gilder tried very delicately to induce the
author to speed things up or cut them down before the audience simply
stopped reading the serial. James was unswayed by Gilder's tentative
suggestions, and the novel plodded on to such a disaster of reception
that even Robert Underwood Johnson, one of James's strongest supporters and admirers in the Century office, would recall joking that one

could count The Bostonians' readers on one hand.

If Gilder could not make a good thing, for the author or the magazine, of publishing James's novels, he thought the Century's publishing Mark Twain enough of a good thing that he was willing to pursue the author and take the chance of shocking the audience. Though books from subscription publishers were generally ignored by the major periodicals, Gilder was willing to violate all precedents by publishing excerpts from Twain's current volumes in the Century. Clemens and Gilder had considered the publicity advantages of printing a chapter of Huckleberry Finn in the magazine before the book was ready for sale, but Gilder conceived of a far more ambitious plan and pressed it on Clemens:

> Take a long pull & a strong pull and a pull altogether & listen to what I have to say & dont get wrothy till you get through. You say Huckleberrie won't be ripe for the public for a month or two;--make it a bit longer before the book comes out & let us have a good lot more of it. Here is what I propose . . . delay the book--& let us print half or three quarters of it with a whole lot of pictures in The Century!
>
> . . . We could just skim through that book, make up a jolly thing of it for four or five numbers . . . interesting & in every way 'creditable to you & the magazine--then you could in announcing the book through agents &c. say that the book version contained twice as much matter--or one third--or one fourth as much. It would not kill the sale in book form for two reasons--one is that it would not all be in the magazine--& the second is that a very large part of your audience lies outside of the magazine's regular readers.
>
> Then, please take this into consideration: the advertising and notoriety of the serial publication could not hurt & might help your winter readings. You could moreover, as did Cable, with Levier, run ahead of the serial publication in your reading and thereby secure greater novelty & freshness for these.

Gilder acknowledged he was "thinking largely of the magazine's interest--mainly thereof . . . trying to get an unusual & highly desirable 'card,'" but was also convinced that the "scheme" would not injure Twain's interests. The editor offered even to "let you precede in your publication the issue of the book by subscription, if you so demand."

Though Gilder admitted "I want this badly and if I could button hole you, I would get you to cast a vote for," his proposal did not gloss over any of the realities of magazine publication oriented toward "regular readers" who were generally not part of Twain's usual audience.

> There are some few expressions "not adapted to our audience" (I do not find many) that we would wish the liberty of expunging, and a good deal would have to be omitted on acct. of space--and in omitting we might also have a regard for our audience. But I have a pretty "robustous taste," (for a pharisaical dude) and wouldn't mutilate your book you may be sure. I can only think of one expression that would be of the kind that I would expunge--as far as I have read--the two lines at top of page 44 about navigation.

Gilder knew Clemens well enough, however, to anticipate that the author would be concerned about the effect of a serial on the volume sales figures in which he took so much pride, and so the editor offered both a contingency plan and as much financial incentive as he could.

> If we can only use one installment it may be somewhat awkward to select as the story runs in and out. I am thinking of that part about the feuds--but it would be hard to dove-tail it in--can you suggest a way--without making it a mere extract from the book.

> In naming a price please remember that you have the largest audience of any English writer above ground-- also dont name a price so high that all advantage to the magazine would be discounted in advance.[1]

Clemens did not warm to the idea of a projected serial of Huckleberry Finn in the Century, and Gilder gave way gracefully, though "with profound regret," hoping that Clemens might take up the offer "with another book." The magazine would proceed with the feud episode for the December, 1884 number, and Gilder explained to Clemens his general plan for "an eleven or twelve" page excerpt:

> We use as prelude the description of the river . . . "Here is the way" p. 157 to dern the dern fog p. 159-- the story begins p. 130 . . . omits the next paragraph about the snake-skin -- to resume with the words "the place to buy" & continue without omission to end of page 156 . . . But will not Huckleberry send a brief introduction to tell where he is, & who Jim is--& let me have it by return mail.[2]

Clemens gave Gilder both the December feud episode and two other excerpts from Huckleberry Finn which appeared in the Century early in 1885 for the price Gilder had paid for earlier Twain contributions. The dealings throughout the magazine publication were amicable, the author giving the editor essentially a free hand to choose from the book whatever he thought would stand alone in the magazine and to edit--and "expunge"--with "a regard for our audience." That all went easily is especially remarkable in that this is the time when Clemens, for his new publishing company, took from Gilder and the Century the plum of publishing General Grant's memoirs.

---

[1] Gilder to Clemens, October 10, 1884, Mark Twain Papers.

[2] Gilder to Clemens, October 13, 1884, Mark Twain Papers.

But as the treatment of Twain's work has become a touchstone for evaluating the judgment of editors and the restrictions of a "genteel tradition" on American writers, the publication of the Huckleberry Finn excerpts in the Century has consistently attracted more critical attention than any instance of actual dispute and acrimony between author and editor. The strongest charges against Gilder concern the "bowdlerizing" of the third, and final, Huckleberry Finn episode to appear in the Century, a compilation of the various materials on the Duke and the Dauphin. Gilder's latter day defenders have tried to deflect the indictment by focusing on the editor's bravery in choosing such a problematic section for use in the magazine, but from Gilder's clear concern in the letters to Clemens about finding sections from the book which would stand independently, it seems that the editor's use of the Mississippi "royalty" was more a matter of coming to the end of his options in being allowed three episodes, but not a continuing serial, from the book. Gilder may have also, in looking for his unusual "card," been tempted toward those sections which seemed most distinctively Twain and most unlike other Century contributions.

The variants between the Century and volume publications of Huckleberry Finn have been documented and discussed (at length) elsewhere. I was interested, in view of the obvious unconcern of the author, in getting some sense of what difference in effect came from reading the Century's version, which deleted words that could in any way be considered profane or vulgar, the lines on the Royal

Nonesuch poster about "LADIES AND CHILDREN NOT ADMITTED" and the King's interest in the ladies, and the adjective "naked" from the description of the King's Royal Nonesuch "costume." Though it was rather difficult to find adults who had never read Huckleberry Finn or even heard of the Royal Nonesuch, I finally unearthed a number of men and women who fit the criteria. Universally, they found the Century version of the Royal Nonesuch not funny, because they could not understand what was going on. The general reaction to a second reading of the book version was "Oh. That's funny." None of these latter day readers saw one version as cleaner, more decent, more refined than the other.

Apparently, for all of Gilder's quite deliberate editorial expunging, a number of the Century's readers also did not observe the differences--and they certainly didn't think the episode was funny. The following subscriber complaint was one Gilder took to be typical:

> Doubtless the editor of the Century, in common with other editors, receives a vast amount of gratuitous advice. Every one imagines he would make a better editor than any one else. As a matter of business, if one does not like a piece of goods, he has the privilege of letting it alone. It is a satisfaction, however, to be allowed to protest against the quality. Your correspondent has been a paying and enthusiastic reader of the Century for many years. The magazine is one of his most valued friends. As such it is as mortifying to have it commit a fault as for any personal friend to show lack of discretion and well ordered behavior.
>
> I must emphatically object to any more Mark Twain articles of merit, or demerit, and tone of those that have recently appeared in your otherwise most excellent periodical. They are atrocious, and destitute of a single redeeming quality,

and wholly unworthy of a great magazine like our beloved
Century. They are hardly worthy a place in the columns
of the average country newspaper which never assumes
any literary airs. If written by any one else but Mark
Twain, such ⟨articles would⟩ silly, pointless wit and
puerile literary attempts would be relegated to the most
convenient waste basket. Mark Twain has written some
readable and laughable books and sketches. Either he has
"written out" or is speculating on a name.

This is the first time that I have ever written to an
editor or public teacher or servant relative to his work.
But my allegiance to my duty as a teacher, my interest in
placing high ideals before the youth of our land, and my
desire to see a refined and discriminating literary taste
fostered among the people ⟨has⟩ have induced me to turn
free adviser and venture a protest which I am sure is amply
sustained by many other readers.

Though Gilder would later write that the editor, like a congressman, "thinks that, while he has heard from only two men, as many thousands may hold the same opinions, but haven't taken the trouble to write" and that "there's nothing a publisher is more sensitive to than the criticisms of readers,"[1] he replied to his subscriber defending Twain in the terms in which the Century promoted the reception of its most valued authors and emphasizing the editing done to Twain's work.

. . . We understand the points at which you object in
Mark Twain's writings, but we cannot agree with you that
they are "destitute of a single redeeming quality." We
think that the literary judgment of this country and of
England will not sustain you in such an opinion. I ask
you in all fairness to read Mr. Howells' essay on Mark
Twain in the September number of the Century for 1882.
. . . Mr. Clemens has great faults; at times he is
inartistically and indefensibly coarse, but we do not think
anything of his that has been printed in the Century is
without very decided value, literary and otherwise. At
least as a picture of the life which he describes, his

---

[1] Richard Watson Gilder, "The Newspaper, The Magazine, and the Public," Outlook 61 (February 4, 1899), 319.

Century sketches are of decided force and worth. Mark
Twain is not a giber at religion or morality. He is a
good citizen, and believes in the best things. Nevertheless there is much of his writing that we would not
print for a miscellaneous audience. If you should ever
carefully compare the ⟨difference between the⟩ chapters
of "Huckleberry Finn," as we printed them, ⟨and⟩ with
the same as they appear in his book you will see the
most decided difference. These extracts were carefully
edited for a magazine audience with his full consent. . . .

Gilder packed off both the complaining subscriber's letter and a copy of his own reply to Clemens. His covering letter explained that the reply was "not written for your eye," but that he was sending the "complete correspondence as a sample of what often occurs here with regard to your writing for the Century." Gilder's motive was a hope that Clemens would use his strength, his writing, to create a public image of "a good citizen," edifying and educating his audience more directly to the high, serious motive which Gilder saw in Twain's writing. Seemingly, from Gilder's specific suggestion, the Century audience would be most easily persuaded by pathos. The editor cajoled Clemens,

Perhaps you will be angry. You must be tired of this
sort of thing, knowing the sincerity of your own motives,
but it has occurred to me to make a suggestion:--While
Christmas still lingers in your memory, write now for
the Century (to be used next year) a Christmas story or
sketch which will be so human, so beautiful, as to melt
the hearts even of the Philistines. Think deeply on this
thing and go to work while the spirit moves, if it does
move you to anything but cursing the particular Philistine
whose letter I send you.[1]

Gilder had precedent even within his own circle for referring Mark

---

[1] Gilder to Clemens, January 8, 1886, Mark Twain Papers.

Twain controversies back to the author. Jeannette Gilder had sent a copy of the Critic and a "communique" Clemens might be interested in to the author in December, 1881, with the offer: "Need I say that we would be most happy to publish any reply you may care to make."[1] While Clemens published neither direct answers to the Philistines nor the sort of Christmas story Gilder suggested, the relationship between the author and the genteel editor grew in both warmth and mutual advantage, without any objection--or even real discussion--from Clemens on the magazine's restraints.

Gilder was again willing to break his policy of not printing excerpts from current books when Clemens offered to repeat the Huckleberry Finn scheme by publishing an extract from A Connecticut Yankee in King Arthur's Court in the Century. Gilder had some problem again finding a section which would read independently as a complete text, and again consulted with the author on adding materials to fill in the context for the Century readers. When Clemens finally gave Gilder a full serial for the magazine, it was Pudd'nhead Wilson, hardly the safest or most genteel of Mark Twain's novels. Combining the melodrama and detective effects of popular fiction with Twain's most developed female character, Pudd'nhead Wilson would seem a fertile ground for an expurgating editor, but Gilder made almost no changes in the text serialized in the Century.

The kinds of difficulties Clemens and Gilder encountered in

---

[1] Jeannette Gilder to Clemens, December 6, 1881, Mark Twain Papers.

dealing with each other as professionals were clearly not matters which resulted in Clemens's withdrawing or Gilder's rejecting contributions. Gilder was always direct about his concerns for propriety and his reservations about some aspects of Twain's humor, but the letters which passed back and forth from the editorial offices seem evidence that the editor tried for the least change he thought necessary and expected no objection from the author. An example less weighted with critical freight than the changes in Huckleberry Finn shows Gilder citing both principle and example so that both men might know where they stood. In October, 1889, Gilder wrote,

> . . . I have been closely considering the Meisterschaft experiment; and am convinced that it wouldn't do to go before our two million readers with the German ungroomed. Our German experts are so lost in distress over that they can't raise a laugh--no, not a smile. Surely the bad German is not a part of the fun in this case--but rather a distraction. Note the following--enclosed exhibit marked A . . . I told him to do his worst which he has now done on a separate sheet pinned to the Ms.
>
> Now further I have run my own chaste lead-pencil through a few expressions which would run off very well on the stage, I dare say, but when served up in cold Century typo would surely grieve. There is so much necessarily of ⟨the⟩ colloquial ↓slang↑ in the boys' talk that when it comes out in their speeches as well there soon gets to be a ⟨monopoly⟩ ↓monotone↑ of it. I have therefore in two or three places expunged such phrases as "puppy-love" take "the hair off a dog," "fetch Omnipotence."
>
> . . . The play is now all right: & you will much oblige me by sending it right back. It's all right now & don't you forget it.[1]

---

[1] Gilder to Clemens, October 29, 1889, Mark Twain Papers.

Though Gilder's revisions in his own letter indicate some feeling for not wanting to appear schoolteacherly hyper-corrective, e.g., the change of "the colloquial" to "colloquial slang," he was sure of his prerogatives as an editor of a major magazine. The only real incident of something approaching Gilder's feeling that his best and most treasured contributors overreached in their use of him and the Century concerns not their own writing, but their exploitation of the literary fraternity's practice of recommending other contributors to the magazine. In a letter addressed to "Samuel L. Clemens, Esq., Editor The Century Magazine, Hartford, Conn.," Gilder expressed some of his irritation on this count.

My dear Editor:

Leman's paper shall have strict attention in this office. But I dont know whether it can be made to suit all the editors of "The Century." There is Howells, for instance; he has been editor of "The Century" for several years. He has his own way of looking at things and may not like it. Stedman, also, is a distinguished editor of "The Century;" and how can I tell whether he will like what Leman does? So, after I have got through with it, you see it will have to run the muck of Clemens, Howells, Stedman, and, according to the Newport paper, Mr. Roswell Smith also. All these persons are editors of "The Century," to say nothing about Johnson, and Buel, and Carey, and Tooker, and Mrs. Herrick, and Mr. Ellsworth, and as we occasionally get letters addressed to Dr. Holland I dont see why he should'n have something to say about it also. If I were the editor of "The Century," as you are, I would write more for my own magazine. If you will send on a contribution from your own pen I will try to get the other above-named editors to agree to it, and we will keep Mark Twain's boom booming.[1]

---

[1] Gilder to Clemens, May 24, 1886, Mark Twain Papers.

With Howells and James no longer regular contributors to the Century and Cable, et. al. becoming more polemic, Gilder was turning for diversification and talent to the midwestern and western authors promoted by these many "editors of 'The Century'." Edward Eggleston, whom Gilder had solicited for stories for the first volume of Scribner's Monthly and who had rejected Josiah Holland's and Gilder's advice on emendations in the serial publication of Roxy in that magazine, reappeared in Gilder's Century with the serialization of two major novels: The Graysons and The Faith Doctor. Gilder proposed few improvements or changes in The Graysons, and publication of that semi-historical novel on the life of Lincoln went smoothly. On reading the manuscript of The Faith Doctor, however, Gilder had serious reservations about some aspects of the novel, though he generally felt it well worth his pursuit. His general editorial objections were to the novel's scathing treatment of wealthy Christian Scientists and frequent references to living real persons. Though Eggleston and Gilder had a personal relationship to the degree that Eggleston did not hesitate to name "a certain amount of nervous prostration" as reason for the delay of the novel ms. and shared with Gilder his experiences in trying to get the Washington Post to publish a "Fable" on the copyright issue they both supported,[1] Eggleston was strictly business on the question of whether his literary manuscripts could be edited by other hands and tastes.

---

[1] Eggleston to Gilder, July 3, 1890, January 26, 1889, Gilder Collection.

Though he promised to give serious consideration to Gilder's objections, Eggleston insisted the final decision would be his own. As in the case of the earlier Roxy, the author had his way on all substantive points, and the novel was serialized in the Century essentially as he had written it.

With the younger writers who had no established public persona like Dr. Eggleston's and of whose talent Gilder was less sure, the editor responded to manuscripts generally with either rejections or detailed critiques and lists of suggested revisions. Many of these young writers were realists whom Howells was praising in his "Editor's Study" department for the Harper's, and Gilder often felt Howells was overly hopeful in assessing their potential. It is generally within this group of writers that the volume indictment of the "genteel tradition" in magazine editing gets its thunder. Stephen Crane could not get Gilder to publish Maggie in the Century, though Gilder took other work from Crane. An often-quoted, but so far undocumented, exchange has Gilder answering Crane's charge that the magazine had published similar work with the distinction that such stories were not written by "an American."

Hamlin Garland also came to wide, literary recognition through publication in the Century, and from his memories in A Son of the Middle Border (1917) and Roadside Meetings (1930), many of the early critics of the "genteel tradition" took evidence of the restrictions of editors and magazines. Unfortunately for the cause of accuracy, Garland's memoirs tend to be self-serving. In distinguishing his ethical vs. aesthetic ambitions and editors, Hamlin Garland, in 1917, remembered "A Prairie Heroine" as "a tract . . . and realizing this, knowing that it was entirely too grim to find a place in the pages of the Century or Harpers I decided to send it to Arena,"[1] but Garland did submit "A Prairie Heroine" to the Century. Gilder thought it too obviously a tract and selected instead "A Spring Romance" which came in the same batch of manuscripts from Garland. Despite B. O. Flower's willingness for the Arena to publish all that Garland offered, his ambition for reform was "subordinate to my desire to take honors as a novelist" and the Century paid more in prestige, audience, and dollars than Flower's radical Arena; so Garland's practice was generally to send to the Arena only work written specifically to its editor's political interests or stories which had been rejected by all his other outlets. Garland saw the Century and Gilder's standard of artistic treatment as "another and more distinctive avenue of expression,"[2] and his success in both this "distinctive avenue" and in the grim tracts which Flower preferred came quickly and rather easily. In his first active year as a writer, Garland placed a number of stories in Harper's Weekly, in the Arena, and then in the Century. When Gilder rejected Garland's proposal of a play for the Century, Flower took it for the Arena, and when Flower wanted to publish a volume

---

[1] Hamlin Garland, A Son of the Middle Border (New York: The Macmillan Co., 1917), p. 410.

[2] Garland, Son, p. 412.

of Garland's stories, Garland added to the previous magazine pieces
two novellas which no periodical editor had wanted.

    Garland promoted himself as a regional writer, using many of
the standard techniques of local color and dialect in combination
with his distinctive view of the hopelessness and isolation of life
on the midwestern prairies. In Gilder, he found an editor who had
little understanding of the ambition or despair of the young men
and women who felt trapped by the conditions of their lives. Gilder
felt Garland could make his points more clear and "useful" if he
could somehow incorporate into the stories themselves the explanations
and alternatives by which readers unfamiliar with the life he
described could come to an understanding of his characters' motives
and feelings. Such additions or restructurings struck the editor as
infinitely preferable to Garland's tendency toward repetition and
toward heroically worded final paragraphs which Gilder felt detracted
from the effect of the story's conclusion.

    What Garland remembered in <u>Roadside Meetings</u> as "the heart"
of Gilder's editing was not such general advice, but the particular
instance, in preparing "A Girl in Modern Tyre" for the <u>Century</u>, of
Gilder's reminding Garland of the magazine's role in bringing culture
and refinement not only to the wide national audience but also to
the children within it--and therefore of the necessity to balance
the interests of realism in language against the need to present and
represent standard English. While Garland willingly argued with
Gilder the merits of dialect and common language and the demerits

which ought to be assigned to hyper-correction, he made the changes Gilder required in all the manuscripts printed in the Century--essentially a matter of removing dialect and slang from the story's narrative voice or value center character.

Garland did not contribute the volume of work to the Century of his elders among the magazine's contributors, but the influence of the magazine and of editorial restriction generally was the base for a widely-promoted argument that Garland "declined" from realism and from his early social protest. In the revisions of his early Harper's Weekly stories for subsequent editions of the first story volume, Main-Traveled Roads, and in the magazine fiction Garland wrote after his first dealings with Gilder in 1889-1901, Garland did indeed carry through some of Gilder's recommendations: eliminating the postscript "explanations" and their heroic language and assigning little dialect or nonstandard language to the narrative voice or principal value center character. He also seems to have a fuller awareness of the kinds of distinctions Gilder often argued with Garland's brother in regard to the theater. As Gilder once reported to Hamlin Garland on one of these discussions, "I don't know whether he full understands the differences between realism and realistic. The real in art leads to real dogs, for instance, on the stage."[1]

Garland would come to many such distinctions on his own as

---

[1] Gilder to Garland, January 28, 1890, Gilder Collection.

he wrote and gained yet more confidence. Any assessment of Garland's particular development and changes needs to go beyond the editing of his manuscripts--or before--to Garland's own desire for distinction and a place alongside the masters of a previous generation, his pride in using original materials and his self-acknowledged changes over the years away from "the proselytizing zeal"[1] of the fights for social issues and sexual candor. On Gilder's part, it seems he never considered Garland in the league of Howells, et. al. and knew him as not dependent only on the Century for printing or largess.

Gilder would probably have been amused or irritated by the idea that he would--or could--change a good writer's literary directions. He certainly would argue that polemic was inartistic and despair of Cable's choice of that direction in writing novels, but he saw himself, as a magazine editor, determining only what work and what words would appear in one magazine, a magazine which he felt with relief was becoming only one of many possible outlets for American writers. Gilder wrote in the Outlook for February 4, 1899:

> There is one thing that one does not hear so much about now as formerly--namely, the suppression of genius. There are so many periodicals that it would be difficult for any one of them to suppress any given "new genius." He or she is not only sure of getting a hearing, but of getting a printing. The editor, therefore, is no longer the terrible being who decides fates. This is well, for I suspect he never quite deserved his fame as a distributor of literary destinies.[2]

---

[1] Hamlin Garland, January 3, 1926, Hamlin Garland's Diaries, ed. Donald Pizer (San Marino, California: The Huntington Library, 1968), p. 196.

[2] Gilder, "The Newspaper," p. 321.

Gilder's awareness of and sensitivity to the charges that an editor's rejections could result in the neglect of true talent or a real comer and his pride in the number of new American writers introduced in the Century had frequently made issues of the magazine look like a Reader's Digest of contemporary Americans who wanted the recognition and social and financial rewards of being published in the Century. With the large revenues brought in by the magazine's advertising, the Century's page rates also attracted the largest number of submissions of any of the nineteenth century magazines. Sometimes receiving hundreds of manuscripts for each space in the magazine, Gilder's openness to new authors and continuous support of some of his major contemporaries often meant the editor's vault was overstocked. Gilder frequently made ironic jokes that the best way to kill a book for a generation was to have it accepted for the Century and wait its place in line for publication. Some writers preferred to withdraw their work rather than to wait years for publication, and the longer the work, the longer the likely wait. Especially with the magazine's popularity often dependent on expository series, like the extended illustrated war histories which boosted circulation for both the Century and the Harper's magazines, the possible two to three year backlog was most likely to affect novelists looking for serial publishing contracts--and most likely to affect those novelists who lacked a large popular following. The situation, especially with the lack of International Copyright to which Gilder himself attributed the peculiar development and importance of American magazines, could seem desperate--especially to writers who needed or wanted the income and prestige which came only from the large national magazines.

John W. DeForest, who had "been such an invalid" for the six years after Howells left the editorship of the Atlantic Monthly that he was out of touch with the practical realities of magazine publishing when a writer did not have a magazine editor devoted to developing a school or an individual's reputation, wrote to Howells in 1886 about a new novel which "has been for eight weeks seeking a publisher."

> Prospects, by the way, are discouraging. The Century professes to be full for years to come. The Atlantic has three or four serials. Harpers kept the Ms. six weeks, & then decided that they can't make room for it till /88, which of course won't do. I fear that I shall be driven to volume publication, which at present is almost without profit. What a doleful situation our book market is in! I never saw it so swamped with foreign reprints & cheap pamphlets. Congress apparently means to reduce American literature to mere periodicals & journalism. Do you know if there is the smallest chance for an International Copyright?[1]

While certainly DeForest was facing more competition than he had in Howells's editorial years when the Atlantic would print almost anything DeForest offered, part of the novelist's specific problem with the manuscript, A Daughter of Toil, might have been a "coincidence" he explained to Howells earlier in the letter that his story of "the struggle of a city working-girl for life & respectability" was remarkably similar to Howells's then current Lemuel Barker. Any

---

[1] DeForest to Howells, June 24, 1886, Howells Papers.

editor would be unlikely to use two so parallel books from writers of the same school without a substantial interval between the publications. Policies like Gilder's willingness to introduce, but not continue, controversial questions further limited the acceptability and timeliness of magazine publication for writers who were not first with distinctive material.

Looking back on twenty years of making daily editorial decisions between writers and works, Gilder acknowledged the drawbacks of acting as "a judge, almost an executioner, of my fellow writers," the necessity "again and again to inflict pain upon members of a peculiarly sensitive race," and the "editor's hell . . . paved with rejected manuscripts which he wishes he had accepted." But he felt the editor was likely to become "over-anxious or over-conscientious" in his eagerness to make no mistakes and to discover new talent, the danger becoming more one of "coddling the commonplace than of neglecting genius." The situation had become such, Gilder believed, that

> The new writer, nowadays, instead of too little is apt to get almost too much chance. . . . The consequence is that there is a patter of new names on the public mind, none of which names makes much impression. A good many people can, especially with some editorial assistance, write one or two fairly good things; the continuous procession of miscellaneous names, while it does not make reputations, is in danger of interfering with the impression made by more serious and able writers--men and women who are likely to have literary careers; who stick to their work from year to year, and often improve in their art . . .

Gilder's concern for guiding and developing the audience for "serious and able writers" was balanced, however, with an insistence that the writers show some concern for that audience and the responsibilities of the editors frequently criticized for censoring literature as Philistines and hypocrites. In his age, Gilder found

> "Reality" is a word to conjure with; any one who raises a "blue pencil" against reality is in peril of losing his literary standing. . . . But if there is any greater humbug and hypocrisy than "realism" can be I do not know what it is. Take, for instance, the single detail of profanity in the "conversations" of a story. Did any one who has ever heard the thing in all its luxurious and picturesque reality ever see it "really" reported? . . . Say what you will there is no realist who does not draw the line somewhere; and that line is at least as debatable as the one between Venezuela and British Guiana.

The energy of the editor, the author, and the audience, Gilder felt, should go toward maintaining the "character of the individual citizen," saving him "from the flashy, hysterical, and gross"--the readers showing their "good sense by allowing a certain honest freedom and unconventionality in editing, at the same time that they demand decency and a wholesome and helpful tone."[1]

  Perhaps Gilder's clearest statement of the problems and directions of his long editorial career, the above shows the editor's willingness to draw lines between "genius" and "the commonplace," between artistic freedom and the family magazine's censorship, between the professional writer and the dilettante, between humbug "reality" and good taste--and his willingness to admit that others, both American and British, might well disagree and did definitely feel such editorial policies injured literature. Gilder's editorial

---

[1] Richard Watson Gilder, "An 'Open Letter' about Editing," Independent 48 (December 10, 1896), 1670.

suggestions and required deletions were often severe and specific. He seems to have felt that the writer needed both to prove and take care of himself. He could answer a contributor, "As to the phrase that you want to retain, make it as mild as you can,"[1] but would generally insist that changes be made if he felt the issue enjoined was publication of "the flashy, hysterical and gross." Textual emendations and changes in "treatment" were pushed more aggressively against the contributor who pursued the Century than those the editor himself wooed, but Gilder would likely argue that the majority of the most sought after authors were the most amenable to "friendly editorial suggestion."

To all, Gilder focused his interest in the broad American citizenry and the magazine's educational role into injunctions to think of the youth in the Century's audience and to share the concerns of their parents, America's emerging middle class, in bringing these children up with educated tastes and standards. Less likely than any other editor to refer specifically to the "American girl" as a primary cultural consumer, Gilder seldom distinguished between subject matter which would appeal to the "ladies" and that which would not. His Century volumes contain a great deal of the mediocre and much major work from established figures. With both, he allowed a broad range of subject matter, after disallowing the strictly personal or the partisanly political. In "treatment," he used his "blue pencil."

---

[1] Rosamond Gilder, ed., Letters, p. 401.

PART TWO

MAGAZINE CONTRIBUTORS

CHAPTER VII

HARRIET BEECHER STOWE

The magazines' ability to create and dominate a nineteenth century American literary career is especially evident in the case of Harriet Beecher Stowe. Stowe's first contacts with literature reflect her American generation more than the overbearing Puritanism of her family heritage. She read and was fascinated by Lord Byron, beginning herself to write at 14 a blank verse tragedy in what she perceived as the Byronic mode. She read Mme. de Staël's <u>Corrine</u> and retained from it for her own writing the use of aphorism and the idea that women had also a role to play in society. Stowe's uniqueness among the women of her era is that she went beyond listening to Puritanism and reading romance to see in the developing regional and Church magazines her own opportunity for financial freedom, recognition, and alternative to continuing with her sister the supervision of young "animals" in the Beecher kindergartens and primary schools.

Removed from her native New England to Cincinnati when Lyman Beecher decided to save the West for God and then bound there for almost twenty years by her marriage to Calvin Stowe, Harriet Beecher Stowe responded to James Hall's appeal in his new <u>Western Monthly</u>

Magazine for American writers to take for themselves the opportunities and compensation of their British counterparts. With the majority of American book publishers favoring British reprints because of the profits available from a lack of International Copyright, Hall urged both his subscribers and his potential contributors to see the future of American writing as dependent on magazines like his own. When Hall combined his national and professional attractions with announced sympathy for women writers, preference for elegant and instructive literature, and offers of then rather substantial prizes of fifty dollars in contests for essays and stories, Harriet Beecher set to writing in earnest and to order. Hall's essay winner was another's "Themes for Western Fiction," but Stowe managed both to win the story prize and to have accepted additional stories and essays. She also produced with her sister a popular children's geography and expanded her offerings to the various journals and Presbyterian weekly newspapers with which the family was associated.[1]

The work for Hall's literary magazine was reprinted in the Cincinnati newspapers along and equal with the productions of Miss

---

[1] For basic biographical information on Harriet Beecher Stowe, I have relied on Anne Fields, Life and Letters of Harriet Beecher Stowe (Boston: Houghton, Mifflin & Co., 1898); Charles Edward Stowe, Life of Harriet Beecher Stowe (Boston: Houghton, Mifflin & Co., 1890); Charles Edward Stowe and Lyman Beecher Stowe, Harriet Beecher Stowe: The Story of Her Life (Boston: Houghton, Mifflin Co., 1911). John R. Adams, Harriet Beecher Stowe (New York: Twayne, 1963) and Forrest Wilson, Crusader in Crinoline: The Life of Harriet Beecher Stowe (Philadelphia: J. B. Lippincott Co., 1941) provided a more contemporary synthesis and interpretation. For the Beecher family and religion, I am indebted to Charles H. Foster, The Rungless Ladder: Harriet Beecher Stowe and New England Puritanism (Durham: Duke University Press, 1954).

Catharine Sedgwick and Mrs. Lydia Sigourney. Mrs. Sigourney was also published in national religious papers, and Mrs. Stowe soon followed her to papers like the New York *Evangelist* and to places in the various gift books and annuals. Stowe deliberately followed the market, querying editors on proposed articles, stories, or series and then producing a variety of effects to fit the tone and practice of the particular journals. Work in the religious papers tended toward lay sermons and household advice; for *Godey's Lady's Book*, she wrote local color and romance. Throughout this period of developing reputation and repertory, Stowe maintained an absolute pragmatic correlation between writing and the periodical market. When she was later asked to write the traditional series of advice to aspiring writers, Stowe equated writing with profit, directing her readers to target their material to a specific magazine, audience, and editor and assuring that the ultimate test of merit was the market. There is no record that Stowe as an adult wrote without a previous commitment from an editor or publisher; almost nothing of hers appeared in volume form without previous periodical publication. She preferred and, as she grew more prominent, insisted on separate publishing contracts for periodical and volume publication. Periodical prices were negotiated to a set dollar amount per installment rather than the more typical page rates or single total fees for a novel or series. She refused to sell book rights for a flat fee rather than percentage royalties and was among the first writers to arrange personally simultaneous British and American periodical publication and to use her trips abroad to register copyright in Britain.

Stowe's personal situation and view of the periodical market and popular audience early conditioned both her literary method and her public persona. Finding periodical markets and testing the popularity of subjects and methods, Stowe never set out until after Uncle Tom's Cabin to write a novel or even to plan a sustained sequence for her current writing. Uncle Tom's Cabin was itself begun with a query to the editor of the abolitionist National Era proposing some few sketches to illuminate the emotional realities of slavery. The National Era had taken short contributions from Stowe before, but there was nothing in her relationship with the journal or its policy of printing Lowell, Melville, and Whittier right along with Mrs. E.D.E.N. Southworth that would necessarily direct Harriet Beecher Stowe to her first long and internationally recognized work. It seems, rather, that from the magazine's practice of printing Mrs. Southworth's serial novels, it was willing to let Stowe continue through multiple installments. The committed audience attracted by the journal, enflamed to interest and discussion by the Fugitive Slave Act, responded to her sequential additions to the tale. That Stowe was now back at home in New England and that her brothers' interest in abolition provided reason and justification for continuing a story added to Stowe's comfort in an ambition which may have seemed unwarranted had the literature not had a purpose.

In the years between her first publication in 1833 and the

serialization of Uncle Tom's Cabin in 1851, Stowe had made a living from authorship equal to or better than those of her prestigious male New England contemporaries who also appeared in the National Era. Her public image, however, still was that of the non-professional "young housewife" which her sister Catherine had used in 1843 to introduce The Mayflower, an unsuccessful collection of sketches. Stowe seems to have assimilated some of this public image and to have associated success exclusively with magazine publication. It was the readers of the National Era who first suggested that Uncle Tom's Cabin be offered as a book, and none of that unshocked audience nor any established American publisher anticipated the interest or success which the lady's story would find with the national and international audience. A fledgling entrepreneur offered to publish the volume, but was so uncertain of the venture that he asked the Stowes to assume half the expense and risk of publication in return for fifty percent of any profits. Harriet was finally willing to accept the terms but, never before having ventured any writing not contracted for a specific fee in advance, she allowed her husband to convince her that they could not finance a share in the project. Her publisher eventually conceded to take the risk entirely by himself and to pay the author a 10 percent royalty--a conclusion which would cost the Stowes tens of thousands of dollars.

    The unexpected and astronomical sales of Uncle Tom's Cabin in 1852 paralleled other publishing surprises in the decade, like the soaring fortunes and circulation of Fletcher Harper's Monthly

Magazine and the floundering and then decline of George William
Curtis's Putnam's Magazine. American writers and publishers seemed
to be shown that the financial rewards and wide influence of broad
popular appeal came from a mixture of social issues and standard
literary formulas with tangible and publicly available authorial
personalities. To Harriet Beecher Stowe, the success of her book
meant fame, money, and increased opportunities. She would never
again have to make a proposal to an editor, but could choose among
the proposals offered to her, generally with a carte blanche as to
subject and method. Uncle Tom's Cabin also, however, began a pattern
of public attacks on Stowe following each of her major works and
every departure from the safe domestic moral formulas she had
developed in her magazine sketches. Stowe did not retreat from such
controversy. In the tradition of her family's contentious religion,
she obliged herself to defend her rectitude against the aspersions
of the unrighteous and misdirected. She also circumvented much
calumny by presenting herself to the general audience, in articles
and prefaces, as an essentially passive and unremarkable scribe to
whom had been given the accident of opportunity to observe, describe,
and explain the workings of Christian sufferance in America.

The combination of righteous self-defence and the persona
of the passive observer is evident in A Key to Uncle Tom's Cabin.
Stowe had published some of what she would include in A Key as
separate pieces in the National Era. She and her book publisher,
John P. Jewett, had originally planned to append some pages of such

data to the two-volume 1852 edition of Uncle Tom's Cabin which included an "Author's Preface" that placed the story in a literary tradition which sought out "the common and gentler humanities of life" to fill out the traditional literary portrait of a dominant culture. The attacks on Stowe's accuracy and personal motives in writing Uncle Tom's Cabin spurred her instead to A Key, an additional full volume of data and defense, which Jewett published in 1853. The positive benefits of personal renown and notoriety were not, however, lost to Stowe in the surprise attacks or the necessity she felt for rebuttal. With her earnings, she toured Europe, feeling the Uncle Tom's Cabin controversy settled by her last word, and published in 1854 a two-volume collection of her foreign letters as Sunny Memories of Foreign Lands. She continued to feed the market and force of argument of Uncle Tom's Cabin with Dred in 1855, alternating the story of slavery with yet more magazine articles and travel letters to periodicals like the Independent.

  The volume of Stowe's production was considerable, as was her range from articles like "How to Make Friends with Mammon" to applications of Biblical motifs to housekeeping. She became something more than a popular literary phenomenon like Mrs. Southworth or Mrs. Sigourney and more than a socio/political and religious phenomenon by joining the founding circle of the Atlantic Monthly shortly after Francis Underwood combined his interest in a national abolitionist magazine with James Russell Lowell's and Oliver Wendell Holmes's literary ambitions and Stowe's current book publisher, Phillips &

Sampson. Stowe's presence in the Atlantic is generally seen as tempering the magazine's literary quality and dignity, an aberrance especially in the early years of Lowell's editorship and the Atlantic's association with Harvard scholars and New England philosophers and poets. Stowe's association and appearance together with many of the august New England literary men was, however, of much longer standing than their coming together in the pages of the new Atlantic Monthly. Despite differences of doctrine, audience, and literary ambition, the fact that periodicals provided the only reliable compensation for authors outside subscription publishing continually brought together all the Americans who did sustained writing or who attempted to sustain themselves by writing. Whittier had been an associate editor of the National Era at its founding in 1847; the other New Englanders published there, in Godey's Lady's Book and the Independent right along with the "scribbling women" and the preachers. Mrs. Sigourney, who has retreated in our memory to associations with sentimental women's novels, had begun in 1824 the practice of vernacular New England stories with a distinctive male narrator who resembles in genre, if not in content, Lowell's Bigelow papers of the 1840s.

Mrs. Stowe's first major contribution to the Atlantic was the serial novel, The Minister's Wooing. By the late 1850s, all of the American periodicals recognized the value of serial stories from famous writers both for attracting and retaining subscribers, and the Atlantic had something of the kind in the popular, but often criticized, continuing columns of Holmes's *Autocrat* and *Professor at the Breakfast-Table*. Mrs. Stowe, as the founding group's fictionist, was urged to provide a serial story, and in *The Minister's Wooing* supplied one which confirmed her record of combining popularity with controversy. She also developed the basic cast of characters and plot outline for the rest of her New England fiction. Stowe's early *Western Monthly* romances worked around the situation of a single acceptable male choosing between two girls, one pretty and social, the other educated, moral, and practical. *The Minister's Wooing* offered alternated visions of the American girl's possibilities with two less simply defined girls: a mild version of the town flirt and a Christian and deserving, though romantic, heroine. Their available suitors increased to three, providing a range of attractions which Mrs. Stowe, a cast of advising older female characters, and a male vernacular observer/narrator sequentially favored and evaluated for the situations they offered and the associations they engaged in female minds. The masculine types developed in *The Minister's Wooing* reappear throughout Stowe's fiction. The Byronic sophisticate is valueless but physically attractive--in detailed descriptions for which Mrs. Stowe has seldom been given credit. The older clergyman lacks for romantic or practical engagement, but offers a reliable alternative and the possibility for doing good. The young, independent, unsaved, but redeemable contemporary ultimately wins the favored lady, often after being miraculously returned from a rumored death. For all that Stowe would seem to present a relatively inconsequential preachment on courtship, much of what she offered in her own voice led to a decidedly non-romantic and non-Puritan view of love and marriage. She warns the reader early on that love, once aroused, bears little relation to the reality of its object and that marriage inevitably results in "disenchantment," when "the ideal is gradually sunk in the real"--though the value of love is regardless of the worthiness of its object.

Like all of Stowe's work, however, The Minister's Wooing frustrates both formal analysis and search for consistent philosophy or point of view. She agreed to write extended stories rather reluctantly, preferring the series of sketches organized around some general principle, narrator, or topic, and the novels verge increasingly toward compendia. There was enough in The Minister's Wooing to supply attacks on Stowe for inaccurate history and impious doctrine. Stowe also supplied a variety of incidents and treatment which would reappear in later, more artistic, novels from other hands. (Stowe's attractive Aaron Burr, for example, discusses the character of the heroine's innocence and upbringing with a French-speaking sophisticated lady in much the manner that John W. DeForest developed Colonel Carter and Mrs. LaRue in Miss Ravenel's Conversion.) Much as Stowe might have been personally discomfited by the aspersions and personality of the controversial reactions to her books, she, like her friend Holmes, came to acknowledge it as the concomitant to large success and to seeing literature as both mission and profession. In the outbursts against The Minister's Wooing, she had also the comfort and rebuttal of established relationships with major periodicals. The Independent continued the editorial practice of defending Stowe, which had begun in her printing there letters in the Stowe-Parker libel controversy and parts of the Key, by weighing the charges offered against The Minister's Wooing. The Atlantic Club acknowledged the growing contribution of its female writers and especially Mrs. Stowe by inviting the women to an 1859 meeting, often referred to in reminiscences and biographies since the men amused themselves by circumventing Mrs. Stowe's prohibition of alcohol in her presence by drinking their wine from water glasses--and apparently, from the accounts, having all the more of a good time.

Stowe continued as an Atlantic regular after The Minister's Wooing, though, despite her growing friendship with James and Annie Fields, she resisted the publisher's requests for another long story. Fields pursued all his contributors for novels or story approaches to topics, but his next success was with Holmes, who produced The Professor's Story (later Elsie Venner) as a serial offering to follow Stowe. Fields was not able to impose on Stowe his other general requirement that a major figure write exclusively for the Atlantic. Aware that the magazine was limited in what it would pay for a single contribution, Stowe asked not that her rates so far exceed the others', but insisted that inflation forced her necessarily to make contractual commitments to more than one journal. With options available to her, Stowe became increasingly independent in choosing what of her work would appear in the Atlantic and what she would

assign to her sequence of primary alternatives in the _Independent_
and later the _Christian Union_. When she agreed to write novels again
in 1862, she offered to Fields and the _Atlantic_ her favorite idea,
the proposed Italian story, _Agnes of Sorrento_. Her characteristic
New England two girls/three men romance, _The Pearl of Orr's Island_,
went to the _Independent_. Stowe had trouble maintaining schedule on
both stories and came to apologize to both her readers and editors
at the _Independent_ for temporarily suspending their story. Her public
justification had, again, to do with her image of housewife and
mother rather than working professional or successful author.

    Concentration on the household was also the alternative Stowe
offered in response to Fields's next requests for a serial novel.
Proposing to write sketches of domestic life for a monthly fee, she
urged Fields to see this not only as something which would be popular
with an audience torn by war and the daily news, but which would be
good for the _Atlantic_. When the first year of her series concluded,
she proposed a continuation of the loosely related sketches, arguing
that she had offers to do the same for other journals--offers which
were themselves products of the extending popularity of this sort of
writing from Stowe's promotion of it in the _Atlantic_. Though Fields
continued to press for a story, going so far as to withhold answer to
Stowe's proposals of a continuing domestic column even when she
offered to write exclusively for the _Atlantic_, her determination to
do the writing which came most easily to her and reluctance to work
within the confinement of a plot eventually won out. Though critics

generally deprecate the three years and three volumes of household papers Stowe wrote for the Atlantic in the narrative persona of Christopher Crowfield, they were one of the elements in Fields's diversifying and lightening of the magazine which took circulation to a peak in the 1860s. As he printed Stowe's random essays, however, Fields reluctantly admitted that he needed to turn to other major New England writers for a serial novel. Some of Fields's effort was dissipated in his looking to the same writers for contributions to the firm's children's magazine, Our Young Folks, an alternative publishing opportunity which both Stowe and Lowell used.

While Stowe generally concentrated on her Atlantic pieces, except for continuing a sideline of writing short biographies of patriotic Americans for the Watchman and Register, she fell increasingly into the practice of dictating all her work, using her daughters as copyists for finished sections, sometimes not reading the completed ms. drafts or her own proof. Looking for efficient returns on the value of her popular reputation, family memories, and imagination, Stowe not only repeated her familiar ideas, formulas, and characters but also commonly wrote only a single draft--as she had for the important "Reply to the Address of the Women of England." She seldom kept her schedule, and she relied on magazine editors to do what they would and had time for in correcting and preparing her copy for the printers. Her biographers and critics have often remarked on the differential quality and care in writing evident in Stowe's essays and stories in the prestigious Atlantic Monthly, but the difference seems to be less Stowe's own than a result of the magazine's meticulous editing policies, and, after 1866, the wholesale revisions of the Atlantic's new assistant editor, William Dean Howells.

Stowe had less care for the manner in which her work finally appeared than for the surety of being paid for it and the freedom of addressing what she wanted to say to the particular audience she chose for it. When she did turn, in 1868, to Oldtown Folks, the New England story Fields had sought for years, the Atlantic had already experienced its first dramatic loss of subscribers in the clerical and popular reaction to Holmes's The Guardian Angel, and the magazine had become associated in the religious papers with a liberal and heretical point of view. The New England sketches came from Stowe's working through her husband's reminiscences of his New England childhood. She was again using a male narrator in Horace Holyoke, a device which had proven popular. But instead of printing the episodes as they came to him, Fields--though encouraging Stowe with letters and financial subsidies--accumulated the manuscript until he had the whole book before him. The publisher was as pleased with Oldtown Folks as he initially had been with Holmes's novel, but rather than offering Stowe her usual contract, he suggested a flat fee of six thousand dollars for American and British serial rights and first year book rights.[1] Whether Fields was looking for

---

[1] Austin, Fields, p. 288.

a return on his years of encouragement, felt the Stowes--after the great financial success of Calvin Stowe's Origin and History of the Books of the Bible--were not as needy, or was merely tired of Harriet Beecher Stowe's special arrangements is not clear, since all the documentation comes from interested parties. What is clear is that Stowe was unwilling to accept the arrangement, and for once limited herself to book publication alone, claiming the Atlantic's liberal religious associations would keep her work from the readers for whom she had written.

Stowe's relationship with the magazine continued, though with James Fields's increasing absence from the daily management through his foreign travels and Stowe's own moves, it was less continuous and less of a major commitment in her publishing. In a contrast of purpose and audience which she had begun to clarify in her service to the Independent and a brief period of editorial writing for Hearth and Home in 1868-69, Stowe came to view the Atlantic Monthly as a vehicle for what was too liberal, too literary, too elitist, or too idiosyncratic for her other markets. The Atlantic got Stowe's tribute to the Duchess of Sutherland; it also got the now infamous article, "The True Story of Lady Byron's Life." Why Stowe chose to defend Lady Byron and to reveal Lord Byron's incest has been the subject of so much and such disparate discussion that we need not recycle it here. Stowe knew the Atlantic would publish what she offered, and by the time she consulted Holmes for advice on the manuscript, she had already determined that the piece would be published and wanted assistance only in determining the manner in which it was presented. She kept the manuscript with Holmes and away from Howells, who was acting editor while Fields was in Europe, until close to the printer's deadline. Both Stowe and Holmes anticipated strong public interest in the Lady Byron revelations, but apparently Stowe not only felt the necessity of defending her friend but also counted on her presentation of herself and Lady Byron as Christian charitable proper upright women as a guarantee against aspersions from many quarters. The personal calumny that fell to Stowe and the loss of some fifteen thousand subscribers to the Atlantic might have indicated some jeopardy in her continued welcome by the American audience, but Stowe lost more of her British literary friends than her American market. Fields published for her a volume defense and list of sources, Lady Byron Vindicated, which paralleled her earlier Key to Uncle Tom's Cabin, and while Stowe hid from the uproar in the seclusion of her Florida estate, she continued her writing and magazine contracts much as before.

The major difference lay in her brother's coming to be editor of the Christian Union magazine in 1870. With novels and serial stories always her most desired and marketable product, Harriet Beecher Stowe now devoted much of her energy to supplying Henry Ward Beecher with a popular draw for his magazine. Most of the Beecher family wrote for the Christian Union, and Harriet supplied a new permutation on her usual formula, with My Wife and I and a sequel, We and Our Neighbors. She also continued the Oldtown Folks series with occasional pieces in the <u>Atlantic</u> and the <u>Independent</u>. Her most popular work--New England Christmas sketches and travel letters from Florida--would be reserved for brother Henry. Stowe's final New England local color sketches, continuations of Calvin Stowe's stories with her own largely romanticized memories of New England childhood, are now her most appreciated. Stowe had finished her major writing with these sketches in the late 1870s. Henry Ward Beecher no longer edited the <u>Christian Union</u> after the 1878 Beecher-Tilton divorce scandal and trial in which Henry was accused of exploiting his clerical and literary position to forward an affair with his best friend's wife. So the Beechers and Stowes moved out of the magazines and out of their place as a center of controversy and charismatic popular appeal.

For all of the acclaim now given to Stowe's New England sketches of local color and humor and for the social importance and literary phenomenon of <u>Uncle Tom's Cabin</u>, Stowe's sense of herself as a writer gave little precedence to either of these accomplishments. She wrote so much, and so much which was never reprinted either in the posthumous sixteen-volume collected <u>Writings</u> or anywhere since, that we have tended to look at her major achievements and see the majority of magazine work as filler or supplement. From Harriet Beecher Stowe's own cultivation of alternative subject areas, personas, and magazine markets, it seems instead that she wrote all that she did pretty much of a piece, distinguishing between work that was easier or more difficult for her by what she charged for it--and thereby leavening one with the other. Not only did she dislike making commitments to write novels, she wasn't sure she entirely approved of novels, and therefore excused herself righteously whenever her moral purpose seemed to exceed her art. With no express literary principles other than the market price, she lapsed in and out of what would be called realism and sentimentalism, claiming, when pressed, that the value of fiction was in the imagination's capacity to create refuge from the most hard and terrible of reality.

Though her work appeared alongside the intellectuals of the founding Atlantic Club and the new young writers of 1860s and 1870s realism and American humor, she kept her production separate from their literary discussions. Henry James, Jr. in a Nation review attempted to treat Stowe's Christian Union serial, We and Our Neighbors, in his usual critical terms, but finally admitted "It would be rather awkward to attempt to tell what Mrs. Stowe's novel is about." He also, in finding Mrs. Stowe's "ladies and gentlemen" speaking vulgarisms in a dialect never heard in society while talking in set pieces unrelated to the narrative, clearly missed the difference of Stowe's usual appeal and method.[1] Her audience was not society, but a broader and eclectic public who rewarded her prolific, if various, production with purchase, not praise for art. Her characters, whenever they needed to go beyond recalled folktale or reminiscence of family life, always spoke set pieces--and some of

---

[1] Henry James, New York Nation, 21 (1875), 61, quoted in Adams, Stowe, p. 87.

those pieces recurred in only slightly different form in works as various as the housekeeping essays and the New York society novels. But Harriet Beecher Stowe cared little for any absolutes about what literature or the novel should be. In her maturity, the only care and precision she devoted to a manuscript went to Calvin Stowe's scholarly writing and those few revisions in the Lady Byron article she made at Holmes's suggestion. Her career had been a choice among limited options which brought surprising rewards, though Harriet had predicted both her attitude and achievement when she observed in the 1830s: "If I choose to be a literary lady, I have, I think, as good a chance of making profit by it as any one I know of."[1]

---

[1] Anne Fields, *Stowe*, quoted in Adams, *Stowe*, p. 8.

CHAPTER VIII

EDWARD EGGLESTON

Edward Eggleston, best known as the author of <u>The Hoosier School-Master</u>, has long held the public image of an Indiana clergyman who wrote to redress New England's dominance and midland America's lack of representation in <u>belles lettres</u>. Eggleston's preface to the first book edition of <u>The Hoosier School-Master</u> in 1871 began this image of persona and purpose: the country man, sharing the values of his community, out to break the monopoly and give his region its due.

> It used to be a matter of no little jealousy with us . . . that the manners, customs, thoughts, and feelings of New England country people filled so large a place in books, while our life, not less interesting, not less romantic, and certainly not less filled with humorous and grotesque material had no place in literature. It was as though we were shut out of good society.

As late as 1890, Eggleston characterized his particular accomplishment as "only drawing on the resources which the very peculiar circumstances of my life had put at my disposal." In his introduction to the short story collection, <u>Duffels</u>, in 1893, Eggleston claimed that he had only come to write stories for adults because Richard Watson Gilder, as assistant editor of the new <u>Scribner's Monthly</u>, had urged the task upon him, despite Eggleston's demurral that he had neither the time nor the experience for such writing.

Eggleston seems to have known--without being told as Lowell told Howells in 1865--that in post-bellum American publishing, the audience, if not the editors, would favor a writer who was identified to them as western. Eggleston's awareness was not, however, a product of a search for position and audience any less deliberate than Howells's own. Eggleston had himself solicited Lowell's interest and advice by sending him a listing of Hoosier dialect words for assessment of their usefulness in literature. Lowell had replied, "Remember that it will soon be too late. Railways are mixing and the school-master rooting-out" and reminded Eggleston "that Mr. Biglow was not writing to illustrate a dialect--but using his lingo as a cudgel," an exchange which hardly squares with the image of a reluctant author who resented New England establishment literature and came late to the idea of writing regional fiction.

Eggleston's life before *The Hoosier School-Master*, editorial work, and dealings with other editors does go far, however, to define the opportunities of American Literature for non-establishment writers who had both determination and a clear sense of the value of periodicals. Far from being himself a Hoosier school-master, Eggleston had spent only a few weeks in his first job teaching in a Madison, Indiana, primary school. His next employment as a Methodist circuit rider, the subject of *The Circuit Rider*, lasted only six months before Eggleston left for a pastorate in an established church in Minnesota. Frustrated by pressure within the church for numbers of evangelical conversions and for sparsely-compensated travel as a Bible agent, Eggleston soon came to feel that anyone content to try to raise a family on a clerical salary had only his own incapacities to blame. His diaries and journals for this period in the late 1850s show Eggleston repeatedly and increasingly using illness as a respite from his pastoral duties and as time to contemplate and then pursue new interests. Rather than being engaged in his clerical work or the life of the Midwestern towns in which he found himself, Eggleston was developing a personal plan of study in literature and languages and ambitions beyond the church and the rural Midwest.[1]

He supplemented his salary with a variety of jobs which, taken together, sound more like copy for a twentieth-century common man, jack-of-all-trades author book jacket blurb than the resume of a nineteenth century clergyman. Such occupations as selling insurance, working as a subscription book agent, and booking and showing stereoptican displays were not, however, as permanent or as satisfying to Eggleston as his increasing involvement in literary endeavors. As chairman of the committees on Sunday Schools and periodical literature at the May, 1859 Methodist state convention, Eggleston had immediately focused on both the interest in children's education and the importance and impact of periodicals in America, even going so far as to suggest

---

[1] Biographical information for Edward Eggleston is based on the work of George Cary Eggleston, The First of the Hoosiers, Reminiscences of Edward Eggleston (Philadelphia: Drexel Biddle, 1903) and of William Pierce Randel, Edward Eggleston: Author of the Hoosier School-Master (Morningside Heights, N.Y.: King's Crown Press, 1946). In cases of conflict between these sources, I have relied on William Randel's second book on Eggleston, Edward Eggleston (New York: Twayne, 1963), for which Randel had access to the Eggleston letters now in the collections of the Cornell University Libraries. The latter book is especially detailed on Eggleston's early publishing, especially pp. 56-57, 66-76.

non-officially sponsored publications should be discouraged. He also moved from lecturing on literature for the YMCA to publishing the lecture and poetry in the Methodist The Ladies' Repository and contributing a series of travel letters to the Daily Minnesotan. A chance discussion with a friend also found him a publisher who encouraged Eggleston to begin a book on the Sioux.

In 1865, Eggleston became co-chairman of the Minnesota campaign for the Soldiers' Home and Sanitary Commission in Chicago. His visits to the city offered a congenial alternative to small town frontier society and produced the first of a series of contacts and contracts through which Eggleston became more and more a literary workman in the service of the century's proliferating periodicals. Alfred Sewell, chairman of a commission subcommittee, was founding The Little Corporal, a children's literary magazine. Eggleston became a regular contributor, reviving his earlier interest in Indian stories and writing some dozen in which he began his tendency to address the reader directly to clarify the difference between the reality of the information he presented and popular, sentimental, romantic conventions. By the spring of 1866, Eggleston moved to Chicago to become associate editor of The Little Corporal; he did not, however, resign from the church, but occasionally preached in Chicago as a substitute and edited a number of Sunday School publications. While his biographers generally see this as indicating both the difficulty of Eggleston's decision between the church and a literary career and his lack of confidence or surety of acceptance in the literary line, maintaining connections with the church also served Eggleston well in supplying publishing opportunities, sources of material, acceptance, and other business ventures. He returned to Minnesota for lecture tours, and in December of 1866, became editor of <u>The Sunday School Teacher</u> at one thousand dollars a year, writing the editorials and continuing a relationship based on his earlier piecework contributions of lessons. The publishers also produced a series of practical guidebooks for Eggleston; the first, <u>Sunday-School Conventions and Institutes</u> in 1867, indicates Eggleston's willingness and ability to use whatever material and contacts came his way to supplement his income and to diversify his publishing.

Eggleston wrote almost all the copy for <u>The Little Corporal</u>, using elements of a number of popular literature genres, including the comic, supernatural, and gothic. Despite the magazine's increasing subscriptions and growing national reputation, the publisher was slow in producing the increases in compensation he had led Eggleston to expect. When his Indian stories attracted the attention of J. W. Daughaday, editor of the <u>School Visitor</u>, Eggleston began to realize the potential for other opportunities. He submitted an article to Harper's, which was finally accepted though it remained unpublished for years. Harper's did offer to take expository sketches of interesting places at prices of twenty-five to thirty dollars. Eggleston developed contributions from the sites of his lectures and followed his predilections for emphasizing the factuality of his treatment in comments to his readers.

Eggleston also began to make full use of the publishing opportunities available in midwestern periodicals. The Ladies' Repository printed his literary lectures and translations from his program of self-education in literature and languages. The Chicago Tribune took a series of articles on conditions in midwestern prisons and poor-houses. The Chicago Evening Journal offered Eggleston a continuing column on life in Chicago. For The Independent, Eggleston wrote weekly letters, "Our Western Correspondence" and reports of various conventions. Eggleston was also making a name for himself with children's books, but his opportunity to make the eastward migration came through a meeting with Henry Bowen of The Independent while Eggleston was on a Sunday School convention and speaking tour to the East. Bowen spoke of a salaried position, and in 1870 offered Eggleston the post of literary editor of The Independent. The Midwest sent Eggleston off with an honorary doctorate in divinity from Indiana, and Doctor Eggleston went to New York with his sights more clearly set on literature. He sent his Hoosier word list to Lowell and began his confident assessments of contemporary literature in book reviews for The Independent. While initially his background interest in dialect and children's literature was evident in the reviews, Eggleston quickly moved to praising books which were elevating and used distinctive American language and characters. He criticized those with plots too exciting, atypical, or unrealistic. He found humor less significant and satisfying--and often more coarse--than his ideal, and he did not share in the contemporary acclaim of Mark Twain, claiming to prefer Irving and Lowell.

It was to this fellow editor and experienced writer that Richard Watson Gilder came to solicit contributions to the new Scribner's Monthly. The upgrading of the earlier Scribner publicity squib, Hours at Home, had been more than eighteen months in planning, and Scribner's Monthly was now to bow with fanfare in January, 1871, as a lushly illustrated competitor to the Harper magazines. Its editor, Josiah Holland, had been brought in above Gilder, the young editor of Hours at Home, because of the older man's reputation and wide popularity as the author of sentimental and pietistic advice to the young. Holland had, however, insisted that his magazine would not publish the sort of "pap" that he felt the Harpers specialized in. New contributors to Scribner's Monthly insured both interest and vitality, and Eggleston's stories were slated to appear alongside work like Stoddard's "Tartar Love Song."

Despite Eggleston's claims that he had no experience in the area of adult fiction, he responded promptly to Gilder's solicitation with "Huldah the Help: A Thanksgiving Story," which was very well received. He continued within the year with four more stories in Scribner's Monthly, each focusing, like "Huldah," on the kind of occasional and American pieces which for some years had found favor in the fiction of national magazines. His "The Story of a Valentine" appeared in Scribner's in February, 1871; "Ben: A Story for May-Day" in May; and "The Gunpowder Plot, The Story of a Fourth of July" in July. A letter from Eggleston to Gilder (in the Gilder Collection of the New York Public Library) dated June 26th indicates that

Eggleston's work was treated as an important feature in the magazine and publicly received in ways both flattering and annoying to the professional writer.

> I want to thank you for the excellent chance you gave my story. In placing Sehlig's striking illustration on the outside of the folio you have given it the best place in the magazine. I am greatly obliged . . . flattering notices . . . My best critics call it better than Huldah. I did want to beat Huldah, you know. I was jealous of my first born.--The Sunday Mercury copies the story without credit. . . . I am glad they did not use my name in such a way as to make me seem a contributor. . . . I see Huldah has been <u>butchered</u>. The story is emended & is going sourer <u>endlessly</u> as "John Harlow's Choice" without credit to you or me. It's bad enough to have it stolen, but to have the thieves disfigure it!

Eggleston went on to discuss writing a serial for <u>The Independent</u> and his plans to publish another story, "Priscilla." Gilder obtained "Priscilla" for <u>Scribner's</u>, possibly because it was written and ready for publication when Eggleston left his editorial position at <u>The Independent</u> later in the summer. Eggleston's ambitions in fiction were not limited to magazine publication alone or to what he had already written at the invitation of Gilder, to whom he confided his next larger plans: "When I get ten I want to put them into covers and see what the critics say. As a story writer, or rather as a love story writer, you are my god-father you know . . ."

The "love" stories Eggleston wrote at Gilder's solicitation added and developed dimensions in magazine romance. "Ben: A Story for May-Day" not only begins quite directly and modernly--"Ben stood pressing his face against the glass"--but also posits throughout the rather modern idea that marriage should be based on intellectual compatibility and personal attraction, rather than traditional beauty, money, social class, or family and community expectations. Eggleston had begun on this theme in his first "Huldah" story, but there he framed it in retrospect as a tale told by a respected judge who reveals only at the end that he was himself the family scion who married "the help." The immediate reception and long-standing popular preference for "Huldah" seem in part an audience perception of the charm of this treatment and the surprise ending. Eggleston, as he wrote to Gilder, was somewhat irritated by the preference given to the "first-born" Huldah, and in "Ben" he addressed his issue and his readers more directly.

> Of course you think, gentle reader, that the handsome poor boy got over his awkwardness, courted Mary, was shot at by her father, carried her off with a rope ladder, married her, begged old gentleman's pardon, made a fortune, &c., &c., &c. But you are wrong there; I know better. Mary's father was dead, and the story did not come out that way. Is not this my story, and can I not end it as I please? Could I not make Mary die and have Ben marry Sarah Little, who admires him so much? Couldn't I send Ben to sea and bring him back rich . . . ? And couldn't I have it discovered that Ben was the son of a Duke and heir to vast estates in the West Indies, and several castles in Spain? Of course I could, but what I shall do is to tell exactly the simple facts in the case, though they may not be half so interesting as any of the plots suggested above.

It was not so much that Eggleston was averse to the happy ending, but that he was using the Scribner's opportunity to work through alternatives to the kind of popular "love stories" he had been reading, reviewing, and criticizing as The Independent's literary editor. His overt insistence of countering his reader's romantic expectations, on telling the simple facts without sensational embellishment, and on ending the story as he pleased, meant in the case of "Ben" that the poor boy did study and work hard and win the rich girl of his dreams, but he had Ben then realize that the girl was not, after the achievement, so attractive to him any more--that she is shallow, dull, and pretty. Eggleston commented, "Of course Ben ought to have committed suicide; or at least he ought to have felt desolate," but instead Eggleston marries him off to the girl who has loved him all along, and whom he could have always had. Eggleston continues his ironic play with conventions, and plays with his reader until the very end of the story.

> I find it quite fashionable for disappointed heroes in novels to solace themselves with benevolence. That is what Ben has done for the rest of his life, up to this time; and I am glad, therefore, that my truthful story is in the style. In fact, Ben has founded a religious and charitable order.

Ben's "order" turns out to be a Harriet Beecher Stowe style consecration of marital love and family life. Eggleston's conclusion not only embraces the commonplace, but also encourages contrast with the dramatic religious alternatives other writers found preferable to a dull, happy ending marriage, e.g. Francis Marion Crawford with The White Sister, Henry James with The American, or William Dean Howells with Olivia's Protestant sisterhood in A Hazard of New Fortunes. But Eggleston also holds out on his romantic readers even in establishing Ben's marriage to the good and loyal alternative girl, for he insists "I am not going to give you a picture of Teetlet's agitation. That would be 'sentimental,' and there is nothing with which the market is so overstocked as sentimentalism."

Eggleston's success with such stories does not suggest that the very proper Josiah Holland's Scribner's Monthly was insisting on compliance to convention, even for its newest authors. Eggleston's stories continually reconsider the roles of women and the values of romance. "A Valentine" especially supports a somewhat liberated conception of American women. Like Eggleston's other first "love" stories, "Valentine" is marked by a great deal of framing, the first person author's explanations and instruction to his reader about the place of the story in terms of competing fiction. He addresses specifically "veteran magazine readers" who expect a "highly seasoned" feast:

> So, let me just honestly write over the gateway to this story a warning. I have no Cayenne pepper. . . . No cognac. No cigarettes. No murders. No suicides. No broken hearts. No lovers' quarrels. No angry father. No pistols and coffee. No arsenic. No laudanum. No shrewd detectives. No trial for murder. No "heartless coquette." No "deep-dyed villain with a curling mustache." Now if, after this warning, you have the courage to go on, I am not responsible.

Eggleston's appeal is to the honest American who can convince himself or herself to be beyond or above such ploys to facile interest, who will be flattered to be satisfied with a story in which reasonable people act reasonably and come to a happy end.

Interestingly enough, the "Valentine" list of literary stimulants actually predicts the techniques Eggleston would use in the novels he wrote while working as an editor and serially published in his own magazines. As Eggleston was completing his stories for the first volume of Scribner's Monthly, he left his job as superintending editor at the Independent to become literary editor of Hearth and Home. Hearth and Home had tried to promote its literary position in the late 1860s with Harriet Beecher Stowe's presence as literary editor, but she ended her limited involvement with the magazine when it failed to pay on time. Eggleston was given more work, more responsibility, more money, and a free hand to do what he would to make the magazine literary and to build its circulation. Practically, the new editor hired his brother, who supplied to Edward, as Calvin Stowe did for Harriet, reminiscences which were the material of local color fiction. Eggleston also began an editorial column, "The Leisurely Saunterer," parallel to Gilder's "Old Cabinetmaker" in Scribner's Monthly, and published a short serial of his own, "Uncle Sim's Boy," which shared and expanded many of the qualities, and even some of the plot elements, of his popular Scribner's stories. Eggleston's Hearth and Home audience seems, however, to have been less sophisticated, less the "veteran magazine readers," than the audience of Scribner's or the Independent, for Eggleston soon felt called upon to defend editorially the morality of fiction.

Eggleston began his first full-length novel, The Hoosier School-Master, as a feature for Hearth and Home. Working from his brother's oral stories of unshared experiences, Eggleston began writing and printing the School-Master episodes without much sense of how long he might continue or what the series' final shape would be (factors which would be evident from even purely textual scholarship). The editor found he had an enormous popular success. With each installment, the demand for more of The Hoosier School-Master and Eggleston's personal national reputation grew. Eggleston had never hesitated to pursue whatever genre increased his professional possibilities, and he now devoted much of his energies to making the School-Master boon into a perception of himself as a novelist. Either consciously or desperately in rushing continuations of the story, Eggleston began to use the mainstays of popular reading interest he had directly eschewed in his earlier Scribner's stories. The public interest continued, and Eggleston's writing quickly reflected a leavening of not only the elements in his "Valentine" list but also the elements of the supernatural he had used in his earlier work for children.

Eggleston did not personally profit greatly from the success of The Hoosier School-Master until its much later book publication in the Library Edition, and he always rather resented the public's preference for his first, and almost accidental, novel. Hearth and Home was, however, buoyed by public response to the serial, and Eggleston had found he could explore new literary directions without risk by running his novels in his own magazine. As long as Eggleston edited a literary magazine, it would serve as his vehicle of choice for publishing fiction. The magazine's relative lack of prestige meant that Eggleston, unlike other editors, need not feel he would be accused of pushing out other writers by publishing his own work. Eggleston's role as his own editor and his desire for profits from book publication made him more aware of and sensitive to the critical community than many of his contemporaries who felt their work certified by acceptance in the major magazines and revision by important editors. Whatever Eggleston could not use himself, he generally submitted to <u>Scribner's</u>, but increasingly, he looked for not only publication but also positive assessments from <u>Scribner's</u>, the <u>Atlantic</u>'s and newspapers' reviewers.

In rapid succession, Eggleston produced, published, and tested the reaction to a variety of serial novels. <u>The End of the World, A Love Story</u> was as much or as little a love story as <u>The Gilded Age</u> or <u>The Rise of Silas Lapham</u>, using its love interest as complement to an exposition of apocalyptic religion and the development of midwestern character types. Critics who had been taken by surprise by the success of <u>The Hoosier School-Master</u> met <u>The End of the World</u> with attention and generally positive judgments. <u>End</u> continues the overt authorial references to current literature, literary standards, and the lack of establishment recognition of midwestern traditions and language. Both in the commentary and in his treatment of individual characters and situation, Eggleston's writing was developing in relation to the warning Lowell had given him in replying to Eggleston's Hoosier word list: "Remember that it will soon be too late. Railways are mixing and the school-master rooting out." <u>End</u> consistently promoted the image of Eggleston as a midwestern chauvinist and Hoosier school-master, and it is in the novel that one finds his often quoted complaint about the absence of "shivaree" in Webster's Dictionary. Still, Eggleston was chagrined that neither the public nor the critics preferred End to School-Master.

His next full-length novel, The Mystery of Metropolisville, moved to Minnesota and the realm of Eggleston's own experience. The Mystery is a strangely hybrid book, begun while Eggleston was still editor of Hearth and Home but with the serial completed months after his departure from the post. The first third of the novel focuses on exposition as record or social history of American regional life and customs; the tone is much like the earlier Scribner's stories' emphasis on more quiet realism. The mystery of the title, such as it is, gets no attention or introduction. The reader is addressed directly with instructions on appropriate expectations and judgment of fiction. Functioning on every level as his own editor, Eggleston even wrote "Words Beforehand" and "Words Afterward" to accompany The Mystery of Metropolisville, further translating his fictional intention to the reality of such a town and such events in the real world.

And yet the last two-thirds of the novel are neither what we would consider realism nor consistent fictional convention. The overall effect is melodrama focused on the chicanery of small town land development and class conflict on a boom town frontier. The townspeople are even more bizarre and self-interested than those in The End of the World, though this time the motivation is love of Mammon and not of God. The characters are undeveloped—regional caricatures perhaps, but not sentimental fictional stereotypes. Plot and romantic subplot focus on the sensational and macabre. A mother frames her son and only saves him from a prison sentence after the intervention of a kindly minister. A strangely half-witted girl who fears most being bled to death by leeches drowns herself and is indeed sucked white. Mothers, however crude, are not loyal to their children, sacrificing them to pursuit of lovers and legacy. The sympathetic girl with a heart of gold meets her doom because her head is mush. Young people's romances are based on shared intellectual capacities or vaguely represented physical attraction. There is no longer a sympathetic author or narrator to hold the variants together or any supposed insider/observer to reveal to the reader the reality or romance in an unfamiliar region.

Looking to new avenues of publication and prestige on leaving his official position at Hearth and Home, Eggleston had spent more time on Mystery than on any of his previous writing, but the book required a great deal from its readers without supplying any of the assurances of realistic verisimilitude, fictional convention, or positive regional identification with the author or characters. Eggleston still depended on the novel to further his career, and he paid more explicit attention to its book publication, his compensation from royalties, and the critical notices than he ever had before. Critical opinion was not generally positive. Objections were made to the book's structure--or lack of it; the characters were seen as caricatures or types who wandered in and out of the story with no apparent functional, or fictional, purpose, and some felt the people and life pictured unnecessarily, or unrealistically, crude. But the criticism Eggleston took to heart, at least what he admitted publicly, was his failure to develop sustained plots.

Though he was disappointed in the reception of the *Mystery*, which marked the first real setback in his literary reputation, Eggleston put even more work into *The Circuit Rider*. The first of his novels preceded by extensive notes, the most directly out of his own experience, Eggleston claimed for the new novel a definite, positive purpose of honoring his former colleagues in the profession. Again based, like *The Hoosier School-Master*, on a positive identification of the author with his material, *The Circuit Rider* advertised itself in its preface as an appeal to sympathy with regional history and promotion of the unique western heritage in fiction. Eggleston told his reader he could not "treat the early religious life of the West otherwise than with the most cordial sympathy and admiration." Eggleston's choice of subject and treatment may be, and has been, seen as a reaction to the reception of *Mystery*, but *The Circuit Rider* was begun before the reviews of the earlier book were in. *The Circuit Rider* is more likely a grab for the audience and popularity of *The Hoosier School-Master* by a writer weighing his chances of success as an independent novelist.

Abandoning the disjunctions of sympathy and identification in *Mystery*, *The Circuit Rider* returned to a sympathetic authorial perspective and a positive featured character and regional profession. It returned also to some of the features of the 1871 *Scribner's*

Monthly "Ben" with a "high" lady brought to recognition of her true worth, but The Circuit Rider is more strident and specific than "Ben." As in The End of the World and Mystery, child turns against parent, and people are not as good as they might be. While Eggleston's preface focused on the story's veracity--opening with "Whatever is incredible in this story is true"--he later remarked that the difficulty of writing social history of the recent past would be the objections of those who had just themselves lived through it. Criticism of The Circuit Rider was primarily on artistic grounds, continued objection to the writer's use of undeveloped characters and faulty structure.

Though Eggleston had attempted to answer such repeated artistic criticism in plotting The Circuit Rider, he had followed his own judgment in deleting, between his preliminary notes and his draft of chapters, motives in physical sexual attraction. Eggleston later claimed he had decided the sexual element was inappropriate in a book dedicated to his colleagues on the circuit. Eggleston may also have fished out the sex he had considered including in The Circuit Rider for more timely considerations than respect for his subject and the sensibilities of his presumed religious audience.

The Circuit Rider was serialized in The Christian Union, a family magazine edited by Henry Ward Beecher and Lyman Abbott, which counted among its contributors Harriet Beecher Stowe. Eggleston knew Henry Ward Beecher as an editor of The Independent in 1861-63 and as the popular and well-compensated minister of such a large and liberal

New York congregation as Eggleston was soon to assume for himself. Henry Ward Beecher had also attracted a great deal of publicity in the newspapers, the courts, and religious and literary circles for the clerical sex scandal of his love affair with Libby Tilton during the writing of Beecher's famous novel, Norwood. While Ann Douglas has claimed that Beecher was "protected" by his success, one cannot help but think that 1874, the year a book was published on the Tilton-Beecher divorce trial, might not have seemed the opportune time to link sex and the clergy--especially for a writer trying to rebuild and extend his general popularity. Harriet Beecher Stowe's experience with Lady Byron Vindicated might also have suggested to Eggleston that even the most popular and successful of writers could suffer from linking sex with America's heroes.

Eggleston did not entirely stint the realistic, mundane hardships of a circuit rider's life or, for that matter, restrain himself from portraits of frontier rowdies or a romantic subplot. The Circuit Rider is, however, bereft of some of Mystery's excess excursions into deathbed confessions and suicidal leaps into rivers.

While some reviewers still found it a little far-fetched, Howells in the Atlantic and the Scribner's Monthly reviewer gave the novel high praise. Eggleston was rewarded for taking time and thought to put his critical cards together, factoring out the preposterous to concentrate on plot and stronger characterization.

What among his various alternatives seemed most interesting and productive to Eggleston in his developing profession as a writer would be clearer if Eggleston's next novel came soon after the decisions and receptions of *Mystery* and *The Circuit Rider*. But though the early novels had been produced regularly at nine month intervals, almost as reliably as his first child had followed his marriage, the succession was interrupted by an offer of the pastorate of a large, but faltering, Brooklyn church. Eggleston was apparently in a good bargaining position; he successfully negotiated a new name, an ecumenical orientation, and considerable freedom for himself as the new minister of the church. Though Eggleston bolstered both attendance and finances for his congregation, his tenure was not without controversy. He was abandoning not only Methodism, but also any vestiges of puritanical thinking--finding himself increasingly unable to see any conflict between being a Christian and having a good time. He was accused of everything controversial ministers are usually accused of, but he wrote articles, collected his children's stories, edited religious subscriptions books, and worked slowly on a new novel which was long enough in the planning and writing that Eggleston seemed more than usually confident of his performance and began to think of leaving his pastorate to devote himself solely to writing for a living.

The manuscript of the novel, *Roxy*, was submitted to *Scribner's Monthly* as Eggleston was about to leave on an extended European vacation sponsored by his congregation. Though he had established himself as a magazine writer of flexible abilities, *Roxy* was the first full-length work of Eggleston's subject to the standards of a major national family literary magazine. The reply Eggleston received from the Editorial Rooms of Scribner's Monthly on June 7, 1877 was prompt, but along with compliments and respect, Scribner's editor Josiah Holland offered Eggleston a short course in the realities and restrictions of the magazine's family audience and in the balancing act between editorial taste and literary ambition. The letter, now in the collections of the Cornell University Libraries, clearly establishes the problems of magazine publishing for a writer choosing to be realistic about the diversity of American life and sexual behavior. After assuring Eggleston that not only he, but also Mrs. Holland and Richard Watson Gilder, had laboriously read the handwritten manuscript, Holland plunged into the dilemma:

> I was anxious to be pleased, and I am. I have some queries about the Nancy business--not the character or the incident, but the way in which it is presented. I think it will give offence to a good many, but I don't see exactly how we are to dodge such matters, or how we are to present them as not to offend the squeamish. The question whether a disagreeable matter is so conveyed that a father would have no difficulty in reading it to his daughters is a good one, and a fair one to ask, under the circumstances.

While Holland found the character of Nancy Kirtley--the rough, sensual "animal" who provides Roxy's husband's extra-curricular interest--among those Eggleston had "drawn with great power," he pushed his anxiety on the writer with claims that "I shall have about as much personal responsibility in presenting this book to the public as you will, provided I publish it." Holland's dissatisfaction with the manuscript, however, extended beyond concern for the treatment of "a disagreeable matter." He objected to Eggleston's continual habit of slow and disparate beginnings in novels, claiming

> . . . the first quarter of the book is not well done.
> . . . It is patchy, and in laying in the "local color,"
> you have overdone many things. . . . While the work of
> the book is well done, as a whole, it was not well "laid
> out." . . . I am sure that every detail which hinders the
> progress of a story, for descriptions which seem less
> important, hurts it.

Eggleston had, of course, heard such objections to his narrative technique before from critical reviewers, but Holland also pushed new considerations of a strong editor's priority of taste. He, Mrs. Holland, and Gilder objected to the character of Bo-bo, the retarded boy to whom Roxy gives devoted attention. "For myself," Holland commented, "I am sure that idiocy cannot be made interesting. The story is weakened by the amount of Bobo." And "Roxy" was "a homely name for a girl who is sublime. It has no dignified associations in the popular mind." While Holland offered Eggleston the right to his own judgment in the matter of the title, he tried to make it clear to the novelist that advantage would lie in following the editor's wishes, offering to pass the burden of revisions and taste onto Gilder.

The conclusion of Holland's letter cajoled and enticed.

> We have come to no agreement, yet, in the matter of price,
> and nothing is decided, but in case I take the story,
> according to any agreement, I would like to ask you if
> you are willing to let Gilder "edit" the book. He has
> been so helpful to me and to others who have published in
> "Scribners" that I am sure he would do this book good by
> little tonings here and there of expression . . . You are
> very bold and free--a little overbold and free--and he is
> very cautious--perhaps overnice. The conjunction of the
> two will produce a wise result. . . .
>
> If the book is published in "Scribners," I want to have it
> do a great deal for "Scribners" and a great deal for you.
> I feel sure that if the book is modified to my wish it will

> be very popular, and bring you, not a very much wider
> recognition, perhaps, than you have now, but a higher
> one. It will give you a new audience--one of which any
> man may be proud--and the audience is so good, that I
> want not only to satisfy it morally but literarily. The
> book has the elements of a substantial success in it. The
> question is whether you are willing to listen to outside
> but warmly friendly suggestions in regard to its modification.

Despite Holland's blandishments and underlying threats, Eggleston was not particularly "willing to listen." In his own life, he practiced none of the nineteenth century father's superior hyperprotection of his daughter, and in Chapter XLVI of Roxy he had treated ironically the hypocrisy of claiming to protect young women from "matters" which were the subject of open and public gossip. By the time Eggleston returned from Europe, Holland had backed down on every substantive point, and Roxy began serialization in Scribner's Monthly in November in all essentials as Eggleston had originally written it. The serial was quite successful with Holland's good audience, and the subsequent book publication sold better than any Eggleston novel and better than almost any other novel which had been serialized in Scribner's Monthly.

Weary of his pastorate and heartened by the success of Roxy, Eggleston decided to become a full-time writer. Supplementing his work in fiction with more young people's books on Indiana, Eggleston worked slowly on his next novels. By the time his The Graysons--a story which placed Abraham Lincoln as the lawyer for the defense in a murder trial--was ready for publication, Scribner's Monthly had become the Century under Gilder's exclusive editorial charge. Gilder was slow in accepting *The Graysons*, but when it came to the *Century*'s actual editing and publishing the manuscript, Eggleston did not find the "god-father" of his love stories the "perhaps overnice" figure Holland had presented. The two men respected each other, and had a cordial--if not warm--social and professional relationship, and Gilder asked the writer for no major concessions or revisions.

Eggleston was generally able to choose his own direction both in fiction and in the historical writing to which he was increasingly attracted and to which he finally devoted his whole attentions. Roswell Smith encouraged Eggleston to follow his inclinations to history, assuring him that historical writing would be welcome in the *Century*. Eggleston pursued his interests and career, and promoted his daughter's, by co-authoring historical works for children with her. Among a generation conditioned to please editors and to follow their judgments of the popular tastes, Eggleston assumed his right to his own priorities. Though he wanted and was willing to coach his audience's tastes and though he continually met with resentment and disbelief the public's preference for *The Hoosier School-Master*, he knew the conditions of popularity and persona well enough to offer *The Circuit Rider* and *The Hoosier School-Boy* at crucial points in his career. In those books and others--including the late *The Faith Doctor*--however, Eggleston also allowed himself the pleasure of pointing without restraint to the self-interest, meanness, hypocrisy, and reality of those who set themselves up to control others' lives. Eggleston, at least, seems to have exercised and suffered primarily from controls he chose and imposed himself.

CHAPTER IX

BRET HARTE

For more than a century, discussion of California local color fiction has meant discussion of Bret Harte, and discussion of Bret Harte inevitably revolves around the phenomenon of his incredible popularity promoted through the <u>Overland Monthly</u> and subsequent failure as one of the highest paid writers for the <u>Atlantic Monthly</u> and <u>Scribner's Monthly</u>. If other new and outlander authors were supposedly held from receiving their due and writing their best by the dominance of magazines in the American literary market, Bret Harte is supposed to have been ruined by the rapid success, flamboyant praise, and big dollars from the eastern magazines which led him on his triumphal progress across the U.S. and away from the sources of his literary imagination. Harte's striking story shows the American literary magazines of the late 1860s and the 1870s following the tastes of the American mass audience, urgently seeking the new and the popular in a competitive battle of publisher/entrepreneurs. In promoting Harte, the literary establishment eagerly welcomed a newcomer and outsider. His unique literature was unbound by conventional restrictions of "gentility" in subject matter, sex, and depictions of women. Harte's biographers and critics have tended to concentrate on how Harte was affected by the publishing climate of his day, but the extraordinary rise and the debacle of Harte's career may well have had a larger effect on the publishing climate for those who followed him.

The Bret Harte of myth, the magnificent westerner who specialized in hearts of gold (though without personal knowledge of the condition), has now been variously discounted, but his was a name to conjure with throughout the midwestern and eastern United States in 1871. Newspapers throughout the country chronicled his triumphal progress eastward when he left California and the editorship of the Overland Monthly which had made him famous. Harte's "The Luck of Roaring Camp" in 1868 had awakened in the publishing establishment a vision of a new beginning for American literature. Despite the protests of Californians who found both author and story violated conventions of morality, respectability, and boostering portraiture of regional life, national audiences and prestigious publishers lavished unrestrained praise. Harte's narrative dialect poem, "Plain Language from Truthful James" (or "The Heathen Chinee"), printed as filler in the Overland in 1870, was reprinted in newspapers across the country. Its publicity and unprecedented appeal to the mass American audience had crowds gathered to read it through shop windows and brought them out again for a glimpse of the author. Samuel Clemens, a friend of Harte's in their early California days, realized the Harte boom was so encompassing that he decided Mark Twain would lie low for a while and wait until some of the furor passed.

But while contemporaries and latter day critics have considered

and reconsidered the phenomenon of a writer who garnered the best
financial terms in nineteenth century American magazine publishing
and who was treated like a prince of American literature by the
British audience for whom he recycled his early characters and effects
after his career was "played out" in the United States, relatively
little attention has been given to a continuous paradoxical factor
in the career of a writer whose fame was creating paradoxes. Harte's
work seldom sold well enough to return profits to his publishers.

  Harte had always been adept at finding people who would help
him without requiring much from Harte in return. His early adult
years in California show a young man of desultory occupations on the
edges of literature and culture. He occasionally supported himself,
tutoring and working for country printers, but generally returned
to living with relatives, preferring free time to develop friendships, read Dickens, and be "a writer." He placed some early
conventional love poetry in California's <u>Golden Era</u>.

  Harte's first salaried position as a writer was on the weekly
newspaper, the <u>Northern Californian</u>, which was owned and operated by
the father of a friend, who had joined the Harte family in looking
for something Bret could do to make a living for himself. The
<u>Northern Californian</u> carried Harte's poetic ventures, ranging from
whimsical humor through courtly exoticism not unlike the type made
popular by Bayard Taylor and the New York bohemian circle. His more
strictly journalistic endeavors tended to caustic observations on
the social and cultural doings of his provincial townsmen not unlike

the early work of fellow Californian Ambrose Bierce. Harte's career with the newspaper terminated abruptly, however, when he used this technique and his descriptive powers to headline a massacre of peaceful Indian families by the "Christian" whites of a neighboring village.[1]

Harte was exceptional among California journalists for his adaptability, for his ability to survive as a dandy and bohemian in the alternately rough and genteel societies of the San Francisco frontier, and for his incredible luck in procuring employment, patrons, patronesses, sinecures, and publishing contracts that benefited him personally without garnering much return to those who provided him opportunity and income.

After his hasty retreat from the Northern Californian, Harte returned to San Francisco and his literary ambitions, hooking up with the Golden Era, now under new ownership and attempting to become a higher class and more cosmopolitan journal. Though Harte's first official job with the Golden Era was as a printer, the lofty new directions exactly fit the tastes of a young dilletante who found

---

[1] Basic information on Harte's life comes from the major biographies: Henry W. Boynton, Bret Harte (New York: McLure, Phillips & Co., 1903); T. Edgar Pemberton, The Life of Bret Harte (New York: Dodd, Mead & Co., 1903); Henry Childs Merwyn, The Life of Bret Harte (Boston and New York: Houghton Mifflin Co., 1911; reprint ed., Detroit: Gale Research Company, 1967); George R. Stewart, Bret Harte, Argonaut and Exile (Boston: Houghton Mifflin Co., 1931); and Richard O'Connor, Bret Harte, A Biography (Boston: Little, Brown & Co., 1966). In cases of discrepancies, I have favored the less adulatory, later biographies and such comparative analyses as Margaret Duckett, Mark Twain and Bret Harte (Norman: University of Oklahoma Press, 1964).

most of California culture pedestrian and rustic. Harte styled himself the Golden Era's bohemian and society writer, began to write regularly for the periodical, and developed a relationship with another staff member, Charles Webb. From late 1860 through 1862, Harte wrote for the Golden Era; worked in its printing office; learned the delights of San Francisco's restaurants, saloons, and casinos; and attracted the attention and sponsorship of Mrs. Fremont and her literary and political salon. Mrs. Fremont is said to have helped Harte with his writing to the degree that she may have been virtually editing his work before it was submitted for publication. When Harte was no longer welcome at the Golden Era, for reasons which are unrecorded but which seem personal, Mrs. Fremont procured the first of Harte's patronage jobs for him.

Though Harte eventually was able to return to the Golden Era as a columnist and ascerbic observer of San Francisco's cultural pretensions--and to publish a collection of his Golden Era papers-- the journal had not done well since its transformation and could not supply its writers with the incomes or audiences to which they would have liked to become accustomed. Harte shared none of these effects with his fellow scribblers; his influential friends were able to get for him yet another government sinecure, at the U.S. Mint, with a higher salary and little to do. Harte was by then married and a father, but while he complained of his domestic responsibilities and restrictions, he seems still to have had time for the life of literary society.

Most interesting for his future development, in this period in 1863 when Harte worked at the Mint and was between extensive commitments to any periodical, he met Samuel Clemens, who worked in the Mint building and spent a substantial amount of time talking writing in Harte's office. Mrs. Fremont also managed to convince James Fields to publish the first of Harte's contributions to the Atlantic Monthly. Harte and his friends, for all of their distinctive western heritage, looked to traditional means of literary certification. For many, the goal was creation of their own magazine parallel in quality and literary perspective to the Atlantic Monthly. The first attempt at a California clone of an eastern literary magazine model came from the young California writers convincing Charles Webb to begin a weekly paper, the Californian.

The Californian was a sort of committee-edited enterprise which brought together the basic circle of the mid-nineteenth century California writers. Webb, Harte, Charles Stoddard, Ina Coolbrith and Samuel Clemens wrote most of the paper from its beginnings in 1864 through about 1866. Most of the time-consuming practical management and almost all of the financial resources of the magazine came out of Charles Webb. Harte used the Californian as a voice for free lance sarcasm on the pretensions and gaucheries of California's citizens. The group began to make names for themselves--and also a name for the group as a closed circle. Anton Roman, a California publisher and entrepreneur, thought to take advantage of what seemed a boom in California writing, and especially poetry of the frontier, by publishing an anthology of the state's poets. He asked Harte to add to and finish up a compilation of newspaper poetry. The collection, Outcroppings, was produced in 1865; the first edition sold out only because of the publicity and notoriety which came from the protests over Harte's selections and public persona.

Harte and Roman followed with another volume, seemingly to assuage their critics, but the interest did not hold enough to sell the second book. Roman was not especially delighted with the controversy, feuds between writers, or sales figures, but Harte continued to suggest further projects. He wrote to Roman as early as January, 1866, casually proposing volume publication of Harte's own work:

> I have some idea of publishing a little book of my California sketches and burlesques including the "Condensed Novels," which have been widely copied and seem to be popular in the East. Let me know what you think of it. Of course, I should depend entirely upon its sale in the East.[1]

Roman did not take Harte up on the offer of a collection of California sketches, but despite the growth in achievement and prominence of other western writers (Mark Twain published "The Jumping Frog of Calaveras County" in 1865, and the volume headlined by "The Jumping Frog" appeared in 1867) and the increasing ascerbity of the literary and journalistic community's view of Bret Harte, Harte had little difficulty in finding alternative publishers. The volume of Condensed

---

[1] The Letters of Bret Harte, assembled and ed. Geoffrey Bret Harte (Boston and New York: Houghton Mifflin Company, 1926), p. 4.

Novels appeared in 1867 and sold its initial small printing, in part perhaps from an affirmative Atlantic Monthly review. The Lost Galleon, a volume of poetry also published in 1867, did less well, and California reviewers accused Harte of plagiarism. Harte was fairly unconcerned with negative criticism. As a writer, he cared primarily whether he had an audience and whether he was well paid. Throughout his life, Harte held the attitude that all Harte disparagers were unfair and probably motivated by jealousy.

Harte had also received an increase in salary at the Mint and was gaining confidence from becoming a contributor to national papers. But with the Californian failing as Webb hit the outside of his financial limits, Harte was still looking for a publishing vehicle through which he could control the payment for his literary work and further his possibilities with an audience more sympathetic than his fellow Californians.

Anton Roman had conceived of starting a magazine for the promotion of western prosperity and development, the Overland Monthly, in 1868. Roman was initially hesitant about involving the cynical and controversial Harte in his new venture, but after Harte had proved sympathetic to Roman's idea of using native history as literary material, Roman engaged Harte as editor. Harte received a generous salary for overseeing the literary side of the Overland and was to be paid separately for contributing features using California's frontier traditions to make an attraction for the magazine. In less than a year, Roman sold the Overland as he realized Harte was taking it away from its original goal.

Harte's emphases an an editor go far to define an attitude toward literature and publishing relationships which might well account both for Harte's early success with the mass audience and for his failure in the eastern literary magazines. Harte saw literature, and especially the short story, as essentially a form of mass entertainment--unbound by the factuality of journalism or the direct authorial presence of the column or literary criticism. He saw success as a direct function of original and distinctive material. He denigrated those who felt they contributed to American literature but who offered no distinctive "characters" or unique subject matter. With full and exclusive charge of the Overland's literary selections and criticism, Harte also used his position to focus the magazine as a vehicle for promoting himself and his two close friends and colleagues: Charles Stoddard and Ina Coolbrith. These three, who came to be known as "The Golden Gate Trinity," filled the majority of the Overland's literary pages and alternatively occupied the magazine offices or Ina Coolbrith's apartment--plotting, planning, conversing, insuring that the circle did not expand.

Much as Harte's literary principles and personal success depended on the interest in something new and native, Harte's editorial largesse was no more available to new and radically different writers than opportunities in the established eastern magazines. Harte rejected Walt Whitman's "Passage to India." He rejected poetry submitted by Joaquin Miller, a California competitor for the mass audience interest in the romantic west, and denigrated Miller's request for an <u>Overland</u> review of a published volume with a withering letter not untypical of Harte's treatment of literary colleagues:

> My dear Sir,
> Although I shall not be able to use either of your poems, I think that I fairly appreciate the merit of their performance and promise. I cannot say that I greatly admire your choice of subjects, which seems to me to foster and develop a certain theatrical tendency and feverish exaltation, which would be better under restraint, just now. I see nothing in you worse than faults of excess, which you can easily check by selecting less emotional themes for your muse. You are on your way to become a poet, and will, by and by, learn how much strength as well as beauty lies in repose. The best thing in "Peccavi" is the quietest--the very felicitous and natural <u>lie</u> at its close. The rest is ecstasy, relieved by good phrasing, or a theme worn threadbare already, by the best poets of your kind.
> Yet I would not have you false to your dramatic tastes, but only suggest to you to develop your other faculties equally.
> I have to thank you for your volume. Let this informal and well-meaning attempt at criticism take the place of a notice in the "P.M."
> I should be glad to receive anything else from you. Try and condense something as long as "Sackcloth and Ashes" into thirty or forty lines.[1]

Harte's emphasis on subject, on the writer's finding a theme not already worn out by other hands, and his sense that an efficient use of talent meant mining the literary vein with which an author was uniquely identified in the public mind came through as clearly, if more kindly, in the editorial advice offered to members of the "Trinity" who were sure of publication in the <u>Overland Monthly</u>. Because he was unusually working at home in San Rafael, Harte wrote

---

[1] August 19, 1869, Geoffrey Bret Harte, ed., <u>Letters</u>, p. 8.

to Charles Stoddard April 24, 1870, about poems Stoddard had readied for the Overland:

> My Dear Charley,
> "The Albatross" is better, but not best, which is what I wanted. And then you know Coleridge has prior claims on the bird. But I'll use him unless you send me something else. You can, as you like, take this as a threat.
> In "Jason's Quest" you have made a mistake of subject. It is by no means suited to your best thought, and you're as much at sea in your mythology as Jason was.
> You can do, have done, and must do better. Don't waste your strength in experiments. Give me another South Sea Bubble, in prose, tropical picture--with the cannibal-- who is dead--left out. It's time, too, that you began to work with a long aim.[1]

Harte could afford to be more tolerant with Charles Stoddard, whose first volume of verse Harte had edited and whom--like the young Samuel Clemens--Harte had schooled and refined in the techniques of writing. Stoddard's directions were toward the "tropical picture" of his travels, and therefore, like Twain's Innocents Abroad, no competition for Harte's role of the writer as Californian.

Harte's own writing in the Overland was using this role to the hilt in the California romances which made his national fame and reputation. The first of these, in the second number of the new magazine, was "The Luck of Roaring Camp," based, as Wallace Stegner has pointed out, on an anecdote from a contemporary volume from a first hand observer, the Shirley Letters,[2] but developed in terms reminiscent of Charles Dickens, Harte's favorite author. "The Luck"

---

[1] Geoffrey Bret Harte, ed., Letters, p. 11.

[2] Wallace Stegner, "Introduction" to The Outcasts of Poker Flat and other tales by Bret Harte (New York: Signet, The New American Library of World Literature, 1961), p. viii.

had a reception in California which ranged from disinterest to charges of immorality through accusations that Harte's unrealistic and extreme character portraits would dissuade settlers and investors. Harte was more interested in the reception his story and the magazine he edited would have in the east, and this reaction was much more positive. The Atlantic Monthly wrote, asking for another story of the same kind, a letter addressed simply to the author of "The Luck of Roaring Camp," a salutation which seems to indicate that the editor had no idea that the author of "The Luck" was the same young Californian whose work Mrs. Fremont had pushed on him five years before. Bret Harte replied immediately--asking how much the Atlantic would pay.

Harte continued the tone and perspective of "The Luck" with "The Outcasts of Poker Flat," again in his Overland Monthly, and the eastern, midwestern, and even the British, audience and commentators seemed almost unable to contain their enthusiasm. The legend had even Charles Dickens himself moved to tears over Harte's stories. The Overland became well known through its promotion and association with Bret Harte, but his reported thousands and thousands of fans did not necessarily buy the magazine. Still, John Carmany, the Overland's new owner, felt Harte's growing reputation worth continuing his contract as editor on terms set by Harte.

Harte had long been looking for opportunities outside California, and such prospects seemed nearer as Harte was able to exploit consistently the interest in his novelty. After another story,

"Tennessee's Partner" appeared in the Overland and "The Heathen Chinee" had its surprise hundreds of reprints from the September, 1870, magazine, Harte became more than sanguine about the money he could make if he left California. Despite the failure of a sequel Harte wrote to "The Heathen Chinee" and perhaps because of increasing criticism of his personal and authorial morality and ethics from fellow Californians, Harte announced early in 1871 that he was leaving California and the Overland Monthly. Carmany claimed, seemingly with some relief, that he had spent a small fortune to make Bret Harte famous without any financial return to the magazine.

Though general histories often report that Harte left California to accept an unprecedented ten thousand dollar annual salary from the Atlantic Monthly, his only definite relationship with those publishers was as the author of the collected stories The Luck of Roaring Camp which Fields & Osgood had issued in 1870. The prestigious Boston firm was considered to have carried off a great publishing coup in getting the stories which were so popular across the nation, but the volume, as Howells later reported, was not selling well enough to bring significant profits to either the publisher or the author. Harte seems to have realized that his fame and fortune depended not on volume sales but on a relationship with a magazine, and though the Hartes had plans for visits in the publishing centers of New York and Boston (where the Howellses had offered to host the Hartes), the final destination of their eastward migration seems originally to have been Chicago and an attractive possibility for Harte to become editor and part owner of a projected new midwestern literary magazine, the <u>Lakeside Monthly</u>. This impetus and incident in Harte's eastward progress has often been ignored or dismissed with meagre analysis, perhaps because such a midwestern monthly never became of much importance in our national literary history, perhaps because Harte's pursuit and loss of the Chicago opportunity took little time out of the journey. Also, the story, while fully intriguing, is without the sort of substantive documentation out of which literary significance is generally made.

Chicago may, however, be important in explaining Harte's later career--or comparable lack of career--and in estimating the risks a writer as cultural hero ran with the popular audience met through the magazines. Chicago, most generally, is the chronological and geographical point of separation between Harte's productive literary and editorial work in San Francisco and his failure in the east. Both his contemporaries and almost all later observers have acknowledged that Harte's reputation in literature could have been better, and certainly would not have been worse, if he had died on the train from San Francisco. The obvious contrasts contemporaries saw between Harte's personalities in San Francisco and the east--the San Francisco Harte did not drink excessively, was loyal to his friends, had some reverence for eastern literary opinion, was prompt and efficacious in his editorial and literary duties--seem to indicate that the events of the journey may have had some significance.

Howells remembered Harte's saying in Boston that his terms to Carmany for staying on at the <u>Overland</u> had been a salary of ten thousand dollars, which Carmany was unable or unwilling to pay. Harte's account to his devoted editorial assistant, Josephine Clifford, and his own actions in Chicago indicate the terms were met, and perhaps exceeded, in the Lakeside Monthly offer. Harte spent a few days in Chicago, looked over the Lakeside establishment, and was to be feted at a banquet for the city's social, cultural, and business establishment where the editorship and partial ownership of the Lakeside were to be presented to him, along with a substantial token of esteem from Chicago's burghers and backers. Harte never arrived at the dinner.

Harte's later public explanation was that he had expected a carriage to be sent for him; when it was not, he sat down to dinner with his family. The carriage story achieved wide circulation in the press, perhaps as an addition to the Bret Harte legend. Howells reported having heard, though not entirely believing, it before Harte's arrival in Boston. Howells also claimed it was sufficient evidence for his feeling the Hartes' needs would only be satisfied by Howells's renting the finest--and only--carriage available in Cambridge to convey the couple from the Boston station on their arrival. To Josephine Clifford, however, Harte wrote,

> I presume you have read through the public press how nearly I became editor and part owner of the Lakeside, and how the childishness and provincial character of a few of the principal citizens of Chicago spoiled the project. For many reasons--some of which we discussed in San Francisco--I wanted the Chicago magazine, although,

> I have since found that financially, at least, I can do much better in New York or Boston . . .[1]

Ms. Clifford, always one of Harte's most valiant defenders, felt Anna Harte must have kept Bret from attending the dinner and so lost for Bret the opportunity he wanted most, but it seems unlikely that if Anna Harte could not keep Bret home and loyal in San Francisco, she had acquired such a degree of power on the train.

Bret Harte's reference to "the childishness and provincial character of a few of the principal citizens" as the spoiler seems more in keeping with a scenario in which some question was raised about Harte's adult and cosmopolitan habits and standard of character. There were certainly a number of factors which might have disturbed a middle American principal citizen's preferences in hiring a cultural leader for the city. Harte had a reputation as a man who didn't let his debts trouble him. (Howells pointed out, in the context of Mark Twain's repaying all the debts of his failed publishing venture, the importance, in a nation devoted to commerce, of the appearance of fiscal responsibility.) Perhaps especially since Harte was to be given partial ownership of the Chicago magazine, his freedom with other men's money might have occasioned some question from his backers--as it did later when Harte was to be given a German consulship by the federal government and Howells had to vouch for him to assure the appointment. Also, though all Harte's biographers suggest or insist on the platonic nature of all of Harte's

---

[1] Quoted by Josephine Clifford McCrackin in the Overland Monthly, September, 1902, quoted in O'Connor, Bret Harte, p. 130.

extra-marital liasons in San Francisco, the provincial curiosity might have been aroused by even the barest outlines of Harte's relationships with Mrs. Fremont, his wealthy patroness; with Ina Coolbrith, his confidante and literary companion, whose apartment offered solace from the interruptions of the office and the inconvenience of home; with Josephine Clifford, his devoted editorial assistant who leagued with Bret's mother in attacking Anna Harte; and with a number of other less literarily visible women.

Harte had and would always take umbrage at any questioning of his personal life or integrity, and one suspects that while the novelty and appeal of Harte's writing protected it from the constraints of gentility and respectability in middle America, the "genteel tradition" of combining respectability in public life with freedom in private life might have been required by the provincial midwesterners of a resident native hero.

Though critics frequently remark that Bret Harte seems singularly absent from his writing, many of the California stories which made his fame focus around romantic strong male figures. The continually repeated figures of the gambler and journalist show men who flaunt society's values because they are above them and better than them. With such characters, Harte restaged in the stories some of the archetypal actions of his own wandering California youth, often allowing them to speak in a voice reminiscent of Harte's own complaints about his dissatisfactions. Harte's characters are, however, always larger and more in control of life than Harte ever was of his own. The fictional young journalist doesn't leave town

and his job, but wipes the walls with the rough Californian. Unlike
Mark Twain, Harte was not willing even in his fiction to play the
buffoon himself. The male characters available for identification
are all heroes who either sacrifice themselves or are saved by a
strange sort of cynical optimism which is rewarded by ineffable luck.
And luck was what the hero Bret Harte had when he continued on from
Chicago to New York and Boston.

Though the many offers Harte anticipated did not eventuate,
and though James Osgood had not profited from the prior relationship
with Harte, the publisher of the <u>Atlantic Monthly</u> made good on the
promise of American literature and his goal of nationalizing the
magazine by offering Harte ten thousand dollars for a year's contributions. Such extraordinary compensation and opportunity was available
because of Harte's seeming mass popularity, but only a writer who
wanted something more than Harte already had would continue to write
under such a contract.

Once installed as the season's literary lion in Boston and
New York, Bret Harte set himself out to enjoy the advantages of his
fame in society broader than the increasingly few friends he had found
worthy and tolerant of him in San Francisco. While he appeared
differently to various groups and individuals (Howells remembered
him as not much of a talker, but Mrs. Aldrich, who disliked Clemens
and thought him a drunk, found Harte a delightful raconteur), it
seems whatever social life offered struck Harte as more interesting
and involving than continuing to write the sentimental romances of

old-time California. Alone in New York, without the sympathetic company of Ina Coolbrith and Charles Stoddard, with the time, financial ease, and freedom to write, Harte's production dropped to almost nothing. Samuel Clemens would later recall, in regard to their collaboration on Ah, Sin, that Harte would not write until the wolf had him by leg. It seems the situation of financial ease and artistic freedom long sought by writers--and which the magazines were often accused of denying to new talent--was exactly what would remove all impetus for Harte. He had what being a successful writer had always meant to him: fame, money, and freedom, and without a deadline or a direct editorial obligation, he postponed writing as long as possible-- and then delayed further by refusing to diminish his standards of craftsmanship. As the relationship with the Atlantic Monthly deteriorated after the contractual year, Harte found himself regularly in debt and a debtor to many of his colleagues.

In his dealings with the Atlantic, Harte proved himself incapable or unwilling to write when his income was assured in advance, and furiously resentful of any pressures to fulfill contractual obligations. The public interest remained strong enough, however, that publishers still considered Harte a potential popular draw. Osgood's magazine competitors looked for alternatives to salary arrangements as means to exclusive control over what Harte might yet produce. Roswell Smith, the business wizard of Scribner's Monthly, offered to serve as Harte's agent, guaranteeing to place all material in order to assure Scribner's the right of first refusal. When Harte announced work on his first novel, Gabriel Conroy, the American Publishing Co., the subscription house that had made such a good thing from Mark Twain's books, contracted for the volume publication, and Scribner's Monthly was eager to offer the magazine serial, though the editors had seen none of the manuscript.

Harte bragged to Osgood about the terms Roswell Smith was able to get for him, not only from Scribner's Monthly, but also fees in the thousands of pounds for British and other foreign rights. The American Publishing Co. paid out monthly advances for the book, which Harte was so slow to write that the novelty of a Harte novel had worn off long before the volume was ready. Gabriel Conroy was printed in serialization and subscription volume essentially as Harte wanted it, but it attracted no attention or critical approval comparable to the top-of-the-line prices which had been paid for rights. The book sales were phenomenally bad--so bad that Harte was convinced that the American Publishing Co. must be cheating him, since Gabriel Conroy was selling one to every twenty of Twain's Roughing It.

Even the publisher/entrepreneurs who had pursued Harte, perhaps against their editors' better knowledge or judgment, became disenchanted with the expensive prize who was not only personally unreliable but who could never seem to produce sales to match the scope of his popular fame. With the newspapers freely reprinting what they chose from the literary journals, Harte's mass audience was satisfied without buying the magazines which paid him income. The newspapers were not eager to pay Harte directly anything like the fees he demanded, and even the public reached by the subscription book agents did not feel Harte gave them enough to justify a purchase which would bring a return to his publishers. While the leaders of cultural standards had been willing to follow the general uncultured public in promoting Harte and had forsaken establishment literature's general restraints of morality, regional chauvinism, and female sexuality, no rewards came to compensate for the publishing adventure.

When Harte wrote to Howells proposing a series of New York poems for the *Atlantic*, he offered the inducement "I don't think anybody likely to follow me in this, and I know no one has preceded me,"[1] a judgment which didn't prove true for the never completed poetic series, but which effectively summarized the situation for popular writers who tried to follow Harte's use of the magazines. It seems that editors were more hesitant with other popular figures and other westerners and humorists, like Mark Twain, who had to be far more responsible and efficacious, more in keeping with the standards, when they came to the establishment magazines--because Bret Harte had been there before them.

In the opportunities offered to Harte, we can see parallels to the careers of Stowe and Eggleston. The publishing establishment showed its respect for writers who could capture the popular imagination with financial compensation, relative artistic freedom, and complimentary competition for publishing rights. In Harte's failure of production and professional irresponsibility, we can also

---

[1] Geoffrey Bret Harte, ed., *Letters*, p. 71.

see possible reasons why literary craftsmen and publishers had reservations about over-enthusiastic response to newcomers. The magazines often found that their reliable audiences marked a distinctive sector in the market for literature, and that the most generally popular writers did not make substantial additions to the magazines' readerships or fortunes.

As Harte looked back on his troubles and his associates in America's magazines, however, he tended to see the causes of his misfortunes in genteel restriction and literary fashion. When Stedman tried to help Harte by requesting a poem in 1888, Harte's reply of January 14th denigrated both the gesture and the kind of writing he assumed would be acceptable. He railed at Stedman,

> . . . the naive simplicity of your using a typewriter to ask me to copy out for you a whole sixty-line poem, in return!
> Be thankful that I have found time to copy the enclosed. It is, at once, chaste, non-committal, and brief--and lends itself beautifully to chirographical illustration. Be satisfied with it, my dear Stedman, and believe me yours always.[1]

Harte held himself superior to any of those former friends or colleagues who had found sustained success. Even Howells did not escape Harte's bitterness. When the wife of Harte's London illustrator asked for his opinion of Howells's A Traveler from Altruria, Harte's response indicated the contrast he felt between writing like his own and fashionable literature.

> There isn't a sensation of any kind in the book, nor an out-and-out laugh in its pages. You feel that it would

---

[1] Geoffrey Bret Harte, ed., Letters, p. 328.

> be vulgar, and this is perhaps the crowning satire on
> American fashionable literature--because quite
> unconscious, in when Howells speaks of himself, "the
> novelist," as a writer of romance! Fully a third of
> the book is made up of a lecture delivered by the
> Altrurian, chiefly to the farmers and labourers. And
> in such excellent and even scientific English![1]

When Harte did meet his former associates in London, his primary concern, however, was not for discussion of literary fashion but for the assurance that he had aged less and gained less weight than his contemporaries.

Bret Harte could not function in a cultural environment which demanded conventional respectability and business responsibility in the public lives of its writers, if not in the lives of the characters they created. He achieved the recognition, the fame, and the income he wanted by becoming a cultural hero and a representative of the romantic old West, but to sustain these prerogatives, he needed to participate in the business and fraternal cooperation of literature in a way which brought compensation to others as well as to himself. Harte was a climber in literature, but he never got past his first grand plateau. Establishment magazines and publishers encouraged and supported Harte since he had seemed to promise something new and to have captured the imagination of the great American public. Even the great public, however, then as now preferred popular writers who were prolific and reliable.

---

[1] Geoffrety Bret Harte, ed., Letters, pp. 382-83.

CHAPTER X

CHARLES W. CHESNUTT

Charles W. Chesnutt was the first black American professional writer and the first black writer who attempted to support a career in belles lettres by using the established literary channels of the national magazines and major eastern publishers. Chesnutt came to literature after a disparate career in which he had taken his eighth grade education from teaching in North Carolina through journalism in New York to his own legal transcription business in Cleveland and admission to the Ohio bar. Unlike many of his white counterparts, Chesnutt began to market his writing secure in an alternative source of income and professional reputation. His earliest published story was in the Cleveland News and Herald in December of 1885, but from the first Chesnutt wrote for the recognition of a wider sphere.[1] He seems to have both understood and subscribed to that maxim of publishing opportunity which Lowell handed down to Howells (". . . the barriers are very thin. . . . If a man has his conscience and one or two friends who can help him, it becomes very simple at last"), for Chesnutt petitioned George Washington Cable, who was then enjoying the grand popular success of The Grandissimes, for his friendship,

---

[1] General biographical background is based on Helen M. Chesnutt, Charles Waddell Chesnutt (Chapel Hill: The University of North Carolina Press, 1952).

interest, and support.

Cable and Thomas Nelson Page, in the late 1870s in Scribner's Monthly and in the early 1880s in the Century, represented the peak of editor Richard Watson Gilder's interest in southern fiction. Gilder had considered Cable as potentially one of America's greatest fiction writers, and had assiduously coached both his artistic sense and his understanding of the magazine market. Though Cable and Gilder had been in conflict over Cable's lush and indirect prose style and over the story "'Posson' Jone" which presented a rather rowdy view of a Southern preacher, Gilder maintained an avuncular interest in guiding the writer to whom he claimed, "I care more for your work than for any other writer of fiction who has written for the magazine."[1] Unfortunately for both Cable's own career and for Chesnutt's reliance on Cable to forward a relationship with Gilder, the editor had found Cable's second novel too obviously preaching and required three revisions, which took almost two years, before printing it, as Dr. Sevier, in the Century in 1883-84. Cable had moved the preaching into an article for the Century, "The Freedman's Case in Equity," a publishing event stunning in the abuse it provoked. Gilder defended Cable, allowing only a single commissioned reply to appear in the Century, and allowed Cable the last word of rebuttal. The controversy raged through 1885, and capped the only two years of sustained conflict in Gilder's long editorial career.

---

[1] Gilder to Cable, February 1, 1881, Gilder Collection.

Gilder was reluctant, then and later, to let Cable continue his use of the magazine for issues rather than art, and he found much of what Chesnutt offered even more objectionable. Cable moved to writing more objective history, and Chesnutt made his big splash in 1887 with the publication of "The Goophered Grapevine" in the Atlantic Monthly. "The Goophered Grapevine," while its base is a dialect plantation tale, is framed in the first person voice of a white narrator, a transplanted Northerner. Nothing in the story itself indicated the writer was black. "The Goophered Grapevine" and almost all the early stories which would be collected in The Conjure Woman, published by Houghton, Mifflin in 1899, use elaborately structured frames of narrators and interpreters around the familiar supernatural plantation stories. The initial "voice" is generally the white male narrator's, and his comments and his wife's surround the recorded oral stories of the archetypal shrewd old darkie, Uncle Julius. Even when the dialect tales are themselves uninterrupted, Chesnutt used his frames to teach and lead his audience to their significance. The practical narrator's emotionally sensitive wife speaks to her husband and to Uncle Julius, understanding and articulating the realities of slavery and black life implicit in the supernatural stories. The narrator, who alone is allowed to speak directly to the reader, suggests to his wife and to the audience that Julius's tales always have as their motive some point of advantage to himself--the sale of a horse, the saving of an old church--and generally deflects the strength of the woman's understanding and the appeal of Julius and his tales.

Knowing that his success depended on reaching a white audience and aware of the potential for reaction and difficulties through his friendship with Cable, Chesnutt used for some time the positive associations of the plantation tale and the established rhetoric of narrator/value center/character/wife framing to extend the supernatural from the tale in itself to the tale as symbol or analogy for the black experience. His elaboration on the plantation tale form and use of its familiar acceptability to condition his audience's emotional and intellectual recognition of slavery's realities made an immediate success.

Though publishers--and the public--would have been as willing for Chesnutt to write and rewrite his Uncle Julius dialect tales as they were for Bret Harte to continually recycle his mythical California, Chesnutt's range extended rapidly as soon as he began publishing regularly. Aside from the stories which were collected in two volumes issued by Houghton & Mifflin in 1899, Chesnutt published in the major national magazines enough additional stories to make a full volume, collected and edited by Sylvia Lyons Render, as The Short Fiction of Charles W. Chesnutt (Howard University Press, 1975). These eighty previously uncollected pieces plus the work which appeared in books in Chesnutt's lifetime indicate both currency and variety in the magazine writing, as well as a steady movement toward increasingly direct confrontation with the issues of race and genteel propriety.

Typical of Chesnutt's progress from Uncle Julius and the Conjure tales is the story, "The Wife of His Youth," which led

Chesnutt's second collection, The Wife of His Youth and Other Stories of the Color Line. "The Wife of His Youth" still centers on a black man past his prime, but considers seriously the emotional and social conflict in the character's loyalties to his black wife of slavery days vs. the sophisticated "blue vein" he has met later--and does it with a thoroughly ironic skepticism toward both minority and majority society which claims "character and culture" and not depth of pigmentation are entree to respectability. In some ways, it is surprising that "The Wife of His Youth" and Chesnutt's other magazine stories of the kind did not excite opposition. Though Chesnutt, in "The Wife," did not necessarily advocate the man's abandoning his wife--and thus did not run directly against middle American propriety--one almost suspects it was the intriguing local color of the color line that deflected the uproar that would have likely followed a white writer's presenting a similar situation.

Along with Chesnutt's first national magazine publication and success with his short stories, he remained interested in making a more direct address to the public on the racial issue. His friend Cable generally felt black writers should concentrate on universal, rather than racial, subjects--but when Chesnutt wished to make his own statement, "The Negro's Answer to the Negro Question," Cable not only sympathized but also engaged himself to interest Gilder in publishing the piece in the Century. Cable recommended Chesnutt's article to Gilder as a continuation of the discussion Cable had begun with his own earlier essays. Gilder was unwilling in 1889 to return to the controversy of 1885, and replied that "Mr. Chesnutt's . . . is a timely political paper. So timely and so political--in fact so partisan--that we cannot handle it. It should appear at once somewhere."[1]

The disagreement over the Century's printing Chesnutt's partisan paper was part of a larger movement of Cable and Chesnutt away from what Gilder considered "artistic" treatment of their Southern subjects. While Gilder was himself more of a liberal than not and defended the freedman's cause against unreconstructed Southerners, he continually opposed the polemic in fiction--and especially as motive in the novel. In 1889-90, Gilder rejected both Cable's third novel and Chesnutt's first novel. Chesnutt wrote to Cable of the disappointment and bitterness engendered by Gilder's criticisms:

> The kind of stuff I could write, if I were not all the time oppressed by the fear that this line or this sentiment would offend somebody's prejudices, jar on somebody's American-trained sense of propriety, would, I believe, find a ready sale in England . . .
> Pardon my earnestness. I write de plein coeur--as I feel. Mr. Gilder finds that I either lack humor or that my characters have a "brutality, a lack of mellowness, lack of spontaneous imaginative life, lack of outlook that makes them uninteresting." I fear, alas, that those are exactly the things that do characterize people of that kind, the only qualities which the government and society had for 300 years labored faithfully, zealously, and successfully to produce, the only qualities which would have rendered their life at all endurable in the 19th century. I suppose I shall have to drop the attempt at realism and try to make them like other folks.[2]

---

[1] Gilder to Cable, March 13, 1889, Cable Papers, Tulane University Library, quoted in Smith, Gilder, p. 71.

[2] Chesnutt to Cable, June 5, 1890, quoted in Robert M. Farnsworth, "Introduction" to The Marrow of Tradition (1901; reprint ed., Ann Arbor: The University of Michigan Press, Ann Arbor Paperbacks, 1969), p. v.

Chesnutt probably had good reason to believe a more ready reception than Gilder's might be available in England. He was likely aware of the British appreciation of other black American writers, ranging back to Phyllis Wheatley's 1773 reception in London which--while hardly attesting to British taste for black realism--provided her recognition and the opportunity to publish her first, and only, book. Likewise, the experience of Bret Harte, Ambrose Bierce, and others may have encouraged him to see the English audience as more accepting than the American. Chesnutt, however, continued to pursue American serial publishers, though his book was again rejected by Thomas Nelson Page, for the <u>Atlantic</u> and Houghton.

Chesnutt was attempting to move from the short story to the novel, from the periphery of dialect tales to the mainstream of critically-recognized fiction and authoritative statements on public issues, and from submitting separate short pieces to various magazines to serial publication of novels and book publication of all his work. At the same time, in the 1890s, Chesnutt's work became increasingly racially conscious and realistic about complex racial issues and identity, and Chesnutt was consciously estimating his opportunities to make a living by devoting himself solely to writing.

The book on which Chesnutt placed his hopes, but which initially found no favor with editors or publishers, was <u>The House Behind the Cedars</u>. This novel engaged directly that most usual plot of the nineteenth century, the love triangle in that period of engagement and marital choice which William Dean Howells often

lamented was disproportionately represented in the age's magazine
serials. Chesnutt's difference was that his heroine--a negro light
enough to pass for white, light as the author himself--was faced
with a choice between a life of comfort offered by a white man or
the marriage offered by a black. Chesnutt's vital characters were
now young, active, romantic--opening the possibility for comparison
to the white lovers of other novels, opening even, both in the
situation and presentation, the possibility for audience identification.
Consistent with almost all of Chesnutt's earlier work in that it
balances ends against means, rights against custom, House made a
clearer statement in removing the protections of and distractions
to the audience's understanding which had characterized the earlier
stories. Readers could laugh at or with the practical white male
narrator of the Conjure tales; they could see his difference from
and ignorance of black southern life as reinforcement of their own
sensibility or ironic humor. Even sympathizers with his wife's
affective understanding of the emotional truth behind the fables'
fantastic window dressing could be comfortable in the assurance that
she, like the Negro, was generally outside the power world and
unable to effect change except at the indulgence of her husband.
House at first seems more daring.

  John and Rena, the brighter than white mulattoes of House,
attempt to take the rightful place of their color, temperament,
inclination, and the majority of their ancestry. In their endeavor
to pass the color line, however, they get away with less than Uncle

Julius did in "The Goophered Grapevine." Both in itself and in terms of its observable difference from the majority of books of its day, House is remarkable less for its daring than for its retreat. John marries and fathers a child by a white wife of good family, but the woman is dead before Chesnutt's novel begins. Rena is not only jilted by her white fiance, but Chesnutt kills her off at the crucial moment through a relatively no-fault case of exposure, the result of her wandering distracted during a storm. Though there is certainly culpability available to be assigned, Chesnutt's willingness to plot in terms of early deaths can be seen as sentimental and safe as easily as realistic and risky.

Chesnutt's attempts to deal with the color line and the romantic and social dilemma of the bright quadroon were for an audience which had become familiar with the subject, and would hear far more of it, from the major white writers of the era. Chesnutt himself would later acknowledge Howells's 1891 novel on miscegenation, An Imperative Duty, as marking a direction for novels in which white characters "do not scorn dark blood."[1] Cable's many Creole stories deal with the romantic dilemma of the quadroon lady denied her love by society's insistence on a marital color line. Mark Twain's 1893 Pudd'nhead Wilson uses the theme in its switched twins, in a way not unlike Chesnutt's own emphasis on training and capacity or Chesnutt's

---

[1] "The Negro in Books," speech delivered by Chesnutt December 5, 1916, Ms. copy in Fisk University Library, quoted in William L. Andrews, "William Dean Howells and Charles W. Chesnutt: Criticism and Race Fiction in the Age of Booker T. Washington," American Literature 48 (November, 1976): 330.

use of half sisters in his next novel, The Marrow of Tradition. The white writers tend to avoid direct judgment of whether the white suitor and society are wrong in finding the quadroon an unfit wife, but Chesnutt's House did not go much further than was generally acceptable and saleable, and his problem may have been a function of trying to market a novel rather than stories. Even while House remained unpublished, he continued to find buyers for his other work.

Other, and younger, blacks were able to publish books in the mid-1890s. Howells's praise of Paul Laurence Dunbar's Majors and Minors for both its literary quality and its affirmation of the negro's place in the universal activity of art catapulted the young poet to national fame in 1896. While Howells, like Cable, publicly assessed the contribution of black writers by insisting on no difference or separation in their sensibility and art, Howells encouraged Dunbar to follow the early directions of his distinctive black dialect verse. Dunbar would later regret his willingness as a naive young boy to follow Howells's encouragement and direction, and moved from gratitude for Howells's help to feeling he had been done "irrevocable harm."[1] While Chesnutt had a few reviews of his magazine stories, nothing so highly encouraging or directed occurred in his own critical reception until Houghton Mifflin agreed to bring the best of his magazine stories out in the two volumes published in 1899.

---

[1] Benjamin Brawley, Paul Laurence Dunbar, Poet of His People (Chapel Hill: The University of North Carolina Press, 1936), p. 60.

With the issue of his first books, Chesnutt finally determined to leave his legal transcription business and commit his time entirely to professional authorship. Part of his reward came with Howells's first public attention to Chesnutt, a review in the May, 1900, Atlantic Monthly of the two books of collected stories: The Conjure Woman and The Wife of His Youth and Other Stories of the Color Line. Howells had met Chesnutt in New York while the review was in process, and their relationship and the review itself indicate a sense of respect, of two accomplished professionals dealing with writing and the profession on fairly equal terms--with none of the discovery and patronage which characterized Howells's early contacts with Dunbar or other beginning writers. Howells's review could hardly have been better; he assigned to Chesnutt all the dimensions of Howells's highest literary praise: comparison with the European and American masters, "seems to know quite as well what he wants to do in a given case as Maupassant, or Tourgenief, or Mr. James, or Miss Jewett, or Miss Wilkins"; certification of the realism and seriousness of Chesnutt's fiction, "the good school, the only school"; and establishment of the writer's persona and talent, "art of kindred quiet and force." Howells found Chesnutt a mature and conscious artist, and Chesnutt replied with a dignified letter of thanks.

Houghton Mifflin, pleased with the reception and sales of the volumes of stories, agreed to issue The House Behind the Cedars as a book in 1900. Chesnutt also received an offer to publish the novel from Doubleday, Page and a spectrum of lucrative opportunities for lectures and articles.

When Howells returned to the Harper's firm after the reorganization under Colonel Harvey, he was for a time actively involved in soliciting and reviewing manuscripts. One of his first official acts was to write to Chesnutt, inquiring after a novel manuscript Chesnutt had mentioned during their New York meeting. Chesnutt seems to have replied with an inquiry about serial publication in one of the magazines, probably especially desirable to him then for the sales and readership which might follow from the certification and exposure. At the time of their correspondence, all of the Harper magazines were losing money, and Colonel Harvey was continually reassigning editors and personally taking decision-making power for the magazines. The ambiguity of Howells's situation vis à vis the magazines and the backlog of novel manuscripts are evident in James's then finding resistance to having the firm decide whether they would use The Ambassadors and, even with Howells's solicitations on James's part, gaining no definite commitment until The Ambassadors was finally assigned as a serial in the North American Review in 1903. Whatever the specific reasons, Howells seems to have made a negative reply to Chesnutt's inquiry about a magazine serial. Howells offered Chesnutt instead the opportunity to use Harper's Monthly to make the kind of statement he had urged on Gilder the year before, suggesting "something about the color-line, and of as actual and immediate interest as possible--that is of American life in the present rather (than) the past, even the recent past"--and assured the writer that the firm "would not bar anything you thought good enough to offer for our consideration."[1]

Howells must have been aware that such an open-ended solicitation could produce just about anything from Chesnutt, especially since Chesnutt had replied to Howells's praise of the story volumes by stating his uncertainty about continuing their subject matter or realism. Still, Chesnutt did not make use of Howells's offer, perhaps because he was most interested in finding a publisher for his timely second novel, The Marrow of Tradition. Marrow was expressly an explication of the "recent past" of racial relations in the United States. There had been little of "kindred quiet" and much of force in the racial situation of the 1890s: Jim Crow laws, lynchings, and the Wilmington riot were fed in the popular literary imagination with such as Thomas Dixon's (the North Carolinian Baptist minister who was later to write The Clansman and Birth of a Nation) The Leopard's Spots and A. J. McKelway's (a Presbyterian minister and editor) defenses of southern terrorism in the Independent and Outlook,[2] an 1890s outgrowth of Henry Ward Beecher's Christian Union. Chesnutt's response was a novel which combined the themes and gimmicks of popular novels with a diverse, astute, and politically radical picture of black Americans' alternatives--all set in the horror of the Wilmington riot of 1898.

---

[1] Howells to Chesnutt, October 25, 1900, Fisk University Library, quoted in Andrews, "Howells and Chesnutt," pp. 331-32.

[2] Benjamin Brawley, A Social History of the American Negro (New York: The Macmillan Co., 1921), p. 312.

Chesnutt's *Marrow* centers around the lives and associations
of two half-sisters, essentially black and white "twins" with identical
looks and speech. The white sister is the wealthiest lady in town,
married to the archetypal powerful bigot, and mother of a pampered
child. She denies recognition, name, and inheritance to her black
sister, the cultivated, middle class wife of a brilliant black doctor
who represents all those gestures of education, accommodation, and
reason which Howells and other northern observers had found so
attractive in both Chesnutt and Booker T. Washington. The black
middle class professionals suffer from the disdaining and prideful
white aristocracy, the indignity and restriction of association of
Jim Crow laws, and the new generation blacks who speak the voice of
racial truth and have no use for the meliorism, accommodation, or
sympathy with the dominant white political and economic structure.
The black doctor is opposed for the leadership of the minority
community by an uncultured, but powerfully articulate, vital, virile
black who has lost a parent to the murdering Klan. The white liberal
observing figure is ineffectual in being properly "right."

Chesnutt hoped for a great deal, personally and politically,
from the publication of *Marrow* in 1901. Its stinging conclusion had
the black couple's child killed by a stray bullet in the riot fomented
by his white uncle and had the white sister pleading with her grieving
sibling, offering the name and inheritance denied so long, so that
the doctor brother-in-law would come to care for her own ill child.
All decency and dignity were assigned to the long-suffering black

characters who give the white aristocrat "her child's life," but reject the payment of her recognition. Some critics greeted *Marrow* as the successor to *Uncle Tom's Cabin*. Paul Elmer More, the new humanist whom Santayana would see as a decadent holdover of empty gentility, led the opposition in finding the final chapter intolerable. William Dean Howells, writing in December, 1901, in the small circulation *North American Review*, was shocked and grieved over the anger implicit in *Marrow*, but acknowledged the book's power and Chesnutt's strength as a spokesman for his people. The hope Howells had expressed in his first Chesnutt review the year before, that in the realm of literature there was no color line, had been corrected by events and the new novel. Howells found *Marrow* "with more of justice than of mercy," and while admitting the righteousness of Chesnutt's cause, thought "yet it would be better if it was not so bitter."

Better for whom? is the question at the base of most of the criticism and opinion which evaluates Howells's influence and Chesnutt's later career decisions. At the peak of his power and popularity, two years after he had decided to make a full-time commitment to writing and sixteen years after his first published story, Chesnutt had chosen to take the great risk of *Marrow*, a risk he hoped would pay off in recognition, influence, and sales. The book never caught fire with the buying public, and Chesnutt decided to return to his legal transcription business and to his role as the leading black businessman of his Ohio city. Chesnutt's abandoning his literary career has been seen as the inevitable rejection of the realistic and racially conscious writer by a public and critical establishment unwilling to hear what he had to say about American imperialism and racism. His daughter reported he turned from the fray with something like relief. Chesnutt's own assessment, in 1928 on accepting the Spingarn Medal of the NAACP, an organization of which both he and Howells were members, was that both his race and opinions ran before the fashion.

> My books were written, from one point of view, a generation too soon. There was no such demand then as there is now for books by and about colored people. And I was writing against the trend of public opinion on the race question at that particular time. And I had to sell my books chiefly to white readers. There were few colored book buyers. At that time the Negro was inarticulate, I think I was the first . . . who shared his blood, to write serious fiction about the Negro . . .[1]

Chesnutt's career clearly indicates the risk a writer ran in offering a message both powerful and difficult to avoid. When Chesnutt wrote fiction which cushioned his power in alternative points of view, he found only encouragement. When his mission was less problematical, unconditioned by humor and reinforced by the strong emotion of motherhood and brotherhood, he drew negative reviews and editorial criticism of polemic. His choices throughout were conscious ones, and he held some expectation the risk would be worth the prize. He sent his books, as Harriet Beecher Stowe had, to Congress and the President, hoping they would be a spur to action. His books were read

---

[1] Quoted in Farnsworth, "Introduction,' pp. xvi-xvii.

along with British classics and popular American contemporaries, and he had enough of assistance and publishing opportunity to continue writing and perhaps to make a living from it, had he chosen to continue.

Chesnutt wrote for wider recognition of his talents, for justice for his race, to make a difference and to make a reputation and living commensurate with what he had as the wealthiest black in Cleveland. Writing in the context of a southern literary tradition and market which had been conditioned by nostalgia and in the disrupted social and economic climate of the 1890s, he refused the "glories of the cheap success which awaits the charlatan in fiction" which Howells had warned against in his first Chesnutt review. Chesnutt found alternative success both expensive and slow, and so returned to his more reliable business. Chesnutt continued writing, however, until the end of his life, publishing a muckraking novel, The Colonel's Dream, in 1905 and continuing to supply stories to the prestigious national magazines, some furthering his exposition of racism and imperialism, some without racial or polemic imperatives.

While Chesnutt is less read today than those who, like Paul Laurence Dunbar, came younger to writing and publishing and who were grateful for their discoveries by white critics and then resentful of their limitations, Chesnutt was not only "the first . . . who shared his blood, to write serious fiction about the Negro," but also the first to come from so far outside any cultural establishment who approached writing and publishing as an equal and a professional. His decisions, if not his restrictions, were ultimately his own.

CONCLUSION

Rather than representing one pole in an opposition between art and practical business, between high and popular culture, and between feminine convention and masculine vitality, the national magazines of the nineteenth century brought together such disparities and provided the means to make authorship a viable profession in the United States. With few non-commercial opportunities for sponsorship or patronage and in the absence of International Copyright, creative writers could make a living from their work only if it could be made merchantable to consistent, large audiences. While subscription book publishing achieved this end for some individual writers and books, most Americans relied on periodicals which appealed to the American family by printing a diverse range of material. From publishers concerned primarily with profits through men of letters determined to raise the standards of American culture, the editors of these magazines balanced the interests of successive generations of American authors against the tastes of their subscribers and against the requirements of competition in the marketplace.

From their earliest success, the magazines were criticized by contributors competing for publication and by competitors for the attention of the American audience. Concentration of publishers in the oldest American urban centers in the northeast brought accusations that the East had taken over the British colonial role of promulgating values and writers on the nation. In the development of American magazines, however, aspiring writers throughout the United States saw the opportunity for personal recognition and escape from the limitations of less-rewarding careers and of life in provincial America. Many came to the magazines with great expectations of fortune, freedom, and continually expanding creative horizons. These new generation American litterateurs generally made their first appeal to magazine editors and the reading public through fresh subjects in the distinctive life of America's regions or the American traveler's observations of exotic life. Essays, sketches, and fiction tended to use actual or created authorial personas who provided a bridge between the values and language of the subculture and the generalized presumed standard of the nation.

The young magazine contributors soon found themselves learning the realities and limitations of publishing for a profit through America's family literary magazines. As the established Brahmin men of letters had realized earlier, both personal reputation and fortune depended on not grossly offending any of those who saw themselves as righteous critics or critical consumers of the literary product. In a country morally and socially dominated by organized religion and economically motivated by the prospect of upward mobility, large magazine subscriberships contained many who were strongly vested in protecting cherished beliefs and countering competing visions. Rather than finding that America did not take her writers seriously, the magazinists discovered that readers responded to the entertainment and information they offered with a determined belief in its influence. The most prevalent concern of the pulpit, the press, and the complaining subscriber was the potential effect on young people of reading heterodox religious opinion, representations of human sexuality, or association of liquor, profanity, or slang with characters otherwise presented as respectable or heroic.

Though much has been made of the specter of the termagant female reader, we find editors most often explaining the restrictions of magazine publishing in terms of deflecting the "warfare of the religious press" and of reminding contributors that a family magazine is a literary product for home consumption--and that the audience within that home is comprised of children and adolescents as well as adults. Young Americans of diverse social and educational backgrounds were seen as more fully participants in the cultural life of the nation than their European counterparts, and the magazines early engaged themselves as providers of a composite product which supplied good value in assuring quality reading for every member of the family. Within their own traditions and markets--and especially in terms of the conjunction of a rising new middle class, increasing literacy, and various evangelical movements which early embedded the "corruption of youth" as an essential, continuous, and to some degree uniquely American, ingredient in our laws--the magazine editors' exercise of prior restraint in literature available to children seemed a responsible alternative to risking the opportunities magazines offered or to the Comstock Leagues and litigation which later came to control the public morality and accessibility of literary products.

While many writers were bitterly frustrated by editorial suggestions that the sagacious reader could infer what convention deleted--and by what seemed the comparative freedom and even sensationalism of American newspapers and books bought by the large public--the prestige, publicity, and payments available through the magazines were strong impetus for compromise. Vigorous protests against "family" restrictions came generally from writers who were not themselves parents, and came when a writer felt he had little to gain--or lose-- from the magazines. Radically unconventional writers like Walt Whitman published only a small proportion of their work in the magazines, but few aspirants to literary success were willing to follow Whitman's bohemian path or to join Herman Melville in almost abandoning writing when his new books didn't sell as his early adventures had. Volume publishing, while free of many magazine restrictions, was generally unprofitable for writers, and those who looked to financial success from literature usually found means to accommodate the limitations of broad magazine audiences.

In the literary criticism, essays, and fiction of the magazines, the tension between audience expectations and artistic freedom or innovation developed into a pattern of writers' continually, though often slowly, expanding the perimeters of the admissable. In fiction, characters, narrators, and authors frequently commented on literary standards in general or the discrepancies between popular expectations of "stories" and the work at hand in specific. Problematical situations or language often came filtered through the perceptions of a character representing a less questionable standard. Beneficent intent and "a warning to young people" were arguments for presenting scenes and language beyond the pale of polite society. And increasingly, asserting the accuracy or veracity of a portrait of life came forward as a reason for expanding the scope of magazine literature.

Though there was much which would never appear in the popular magazines, the push for fresh American subjects brought a wide spectrum of regional life and authors before the national public. The gradual acceptance of "realistic" as exoneration or praise opened the way for a new school of native writing to reach the general audience. Whether one blames William Dean Howells as a "Miss Nancy" of compromise with restrictions or applauds him as the "Realist at War," the ability of a young man with little education and no connections to become--and the willingness of the magazines to accept him as--a major force for change through decades with the Atlantic Monthly, the Century, and Harper's Monthly indicates the extent of opportunity available to American writers through family periodicals.

In their attempt to make publishing literature economically profitable, the nineteenth century American magazines did not necessarily encourage writers to do the best and most innovative work they could. In broadening the audience for literature and broadening that audience's tolerance and taste, they fostered in American writers material and artistic expectations which were seldom entirely fulfilled. When the large magazines faltered at the turn of the century, even Howells would admit that in the popular magazines' search for commercial fiction to bastion their own fortunes, writers of quality were left behind. With the resurgence of literature and in revived and new magazines, the twentieth century saw clearly the magazines' commercial and artistic limitations. It took many years more for scholars to see the personal motivations, professionalism, compromise, and economic realities which conditioned the magazines' role in establishing authorship as a viable profession in the United States. The magazines brought a broader range of writers to literature than any previous or competing publishing vehicle. While some contributors felt themselves restricted by the magazines' audiences and editors, many parlayed self-interest and professionalism to increase freedom and innovation in American literature.

SELECTED BIBLIOGRAPHY

Books

Adams, John R. Harriet Beecher Stowe. New York: Twayne Publishers, 1963.

Alden, Henry Mills. Magazine Writing and the New Literature. New York and London: Harper & Bros., 1908.

Aldrich, Lilian (Mrs. Thomas Bailey). Crowding Memories. Boston and New York: Houghton Mifflin Co., 1920.

Aldrich, Thomas Bailey. An Old Town by the Sea. Boston: Houghton, Mifflin & Co., 1893.

―――――. Ponkapog Papers. Boston and New York: Houghton, Mifflin & Co., 1897.

Anderson, Frederick; Gibson, William M.; and Smith, Henry Nash, ed. Selected Mark Twain--Howells Letters, 1872-1910. Cambridge: Harvard University Press, Belknap Press, 1967.

Austin, James C. Fields of the Atlantic Monthly, Letters to an Editor, 1861-1870. San Marino, California: Huntington Library, 1953.

Ballou, Ellen. The Building of the House. Boston: Houghton Mifflin Co., 1970.

Beer, Thomas. The Mauve Decade. New York: A. A. Knopf, 1926.

―――――. Stephen Crane, A Study in American Letters. Introduction by Joseph Conrad. New York: A. A. Knopf, 1923.

Bikle, Lucy Leffingwell Cable. George W. Cable, His Life and Letters. New York and London: Charles Scribner's Sons, 1928.

Boynton, Henry W. Bret Harte. New York: McLure, Phillips & Co., 1903.

Brawley, Benjamin. Paul Laurence Dunbar, Poet of His People.
Chapel Hill: University of North Carolina Press, 1936.

_____. A Social History of the American Negro. New York:
Macmillan Co., 1921.

Bridgman, Richard. The Colloquial Style in America. London: Oxford
University Press, 1966.

Brooks, Van Wyck. Howells, His Life and World. New York: E. P.
Dutton & Co., 1959.

_____. The Ordeal of Mark Twain. New York: E. P. Dutton, 1920.

_____. Three Essays on America. New York: E. P. Dutton, 1934.

_____. The Wine of the Puritans; A Study of Present-Day America.
New York: Kennerley, 1909.

Cady, Edwin H. The Road to Realism; The Early Years, 1837-1885, of
William Dean Howells. Syracuse: Syracuse University Press,
1956.

_____. The Realist at War; The Mature Years, 1885-1920, of William
Dean Howells. Syracuse: Syracuse University Press, 1958.

Cary, Edward. George William Curtis. Boston and New York: Houghton,
Mifflin & Co., 1894.

Cary, Richard. The Genteel Circle: Bayard Taylor and His New York
Friends. Ithaca: Cornell University Press, 1952.

Cawelti, John G. Adventure, Mystery and Romance: Formula Stories
as Art and Popular Culture. Chicago: University of Chicago
Press, 1976.

Chesnutt, Helen M. Charles Waddell Chesnutt. Chapel Hill: University
of North Carolina Press, 1952.

Clemens, Samuel /Mark Twain7. The Autobiography of Mark Twain.
Edited by Charles Neider. New York: Harper & Bros., 1959.

Clifford, Deborah Pickman. Mine Eyes Have Seen the Glory, A Biography
of Julia Ward Howe. Boston and Toronto: Little, Brown & Co.,
Atlantic Monthly Press, 1978.

Cowley, Malcolm. After the Genteel Tradition; American Writers Since
1910. New York: W. W. Norton & Co., 1937.

Crane, Stephen. *New York City Sketches of Stephen Crane and Related Pieces*. Edited by R. W. Stallman and E. R. Hagemann. New York: New York University Press, 1966.

Curtis, George William. *The Duty of the American Scholar to Politics and the Times*. New York: Dix, Edwards & Co., 1856.

_____. *Literary and Social Essays*. New York and London: Harper & Bros., 1894.

_____. *Nile Notes*. New York: Harper & Bros., 1851.

_____. *Other Essays from the Easy Chair*. New York: Harper & Bros., 1893.

DeVoto, Bernard. *Mark Twain's America*. Boston: Houghton Mifflin Co., 1932.

Douglas, Ann. *The Feminization of American Culture*. New York: Alfred A. Knopf, 1977.

Duberman, Martin. *James Russell Lowell*. Boston: Houghton Mifflin Co., 1966.

Duckett, Margaret. *Mark Twain and Bret Harte*. Norman: University of Oklahoma Press, 1964.

Eggleston, George Cary. *The First of the Hoosiers, Reminiscences of Edward Eggleston*. Philadelphia: Drexel Biddle, 1903.

Exman, Eugene. *The Brothers Harper; A Unique Publishing Partnership and Its Impact upon the Cultural Life of America from 1817 to 1853*. New York: Harper & Row, 1965.

_____. *The House of Harper, One Hundred and Fifty Years of Publishing*. New York: Harper & Row, 1967.

Farnsworth, Robert M. Introduction to *The Marrow of Tradition*, by Charles W. Chesnutt. Ann Arbor: University of Michigan Press, Ann Arbor Paperbacks, 1969.

Fields, Annie Adams. *Authors and Friends*. Boston and New York: Houghton, Mifflin & Co., 1896.

_____, ed. *Life and Letters of Harriet Beecher Stowe*. Boston and New York: Houghton, Mifflin & Co., 1897.

Fields, James T. *Yesterdays with Authors*. Boston: J. R. Osgood & Co., 1872.

Flory, Claude Reherd. *Economic Criticism in American Fiction, 1792-1900*. New York: Russell & Russell, 1937.

Foster, Charles H. *The Rungless Ladder: Harriet Beecher Stowe and New England Puritanism*. Durham: Duke University Press, 1954.

Garland, Hamlin. *Hamlin Garland's Diaries*. Edited by Donald Pizer. San Marino, California: Huntington Library, 1968.

———. *Roadside Meetings*. New York: Macmillan Co., 1930.

———. *A Son of the Middle Border*. New York: Macmillan Co., 1923.

Geffen, Arthur Irving. "*Miss Ravenel's Conversion*, Sources, Composition, Publication, Reception, Reputation, and Influence." Ph.D. dissertation, University of Chicago, 1968.

Gibson, William M. and Arms, George. *A Bibliography of William Dean Howells*. New edition. New York: New York Public Library and Arno Press, 1971.

Gilder, Richard Watson. *Letters of Richard Watson Gilder*. Edited by Rosamund Gilder. Boston and New York: Houghton Mifflin Co., 1916.

Greenslet, Ferris. *The Life of Thomas Bailey Aldrich*. Boston and New York: Houghton, Mifflin & Co., 1908.

Gullason, Thomas A., ed. *Stephen Crane's Career: Perspectives and Evaluations*. New York: New York University Press, 1972.

Harper, J. Henry. *The House of Harper*. New York: Harper & Bros., 1912.

Hart, James D. *The Oxford Companion to American Literature*. 4th ed. New York: Oxford University Press, 1965.

———. *The Popular Book, A History of America's Literary Taste*. New York: Oxford University Press, 1950.

Harte, Bret. *The Letters of Bret Harte*. Edited by Geoffrey Bret Harte. Boston and New York: Houghton Mifflin Co., 1926.

Hawthorne, Julian. *Nathaniel Hawthorne and His Wife*. 2 vols. Boston and New York: Houghton, Mifflin & Co., 1884.

Higginson, Thomas Wentworth. *Cheerful Yesterdays*. Boston: Houghton, Mifflin & Co., 1898.

_____. *Margaret Fuller Ossoli*. Boston: Houghton, Mifflin & Co., 1890.

Hill, Hamlin. *Mark Twain, God's Fool*. New York: Harper & Row, 1973.

_____, ed. *Mark Twain's Letters to His Publishers, 1867-1894*. Introduction by Hamlin Hill. Berkeley: University of California Press, 1967.

Holmes, Oliver Wendell. *The Professor at the Breakfast-Table, with The Story of Iris*. Boston: Houghton, Mifflin & Co., 1890.

Howe, Mark Antony DeWolfe. *The Atlantic Monthly and Its Makers*. Boston: The Atlantic Monthly Press, 1919.

_____, ed. *Memories of a Hostess; A Chronicle of Eminent Friendships Drawn Chiefly from the Diaries of Mrs. James T. Fields*. Boston: The Atlantic Monthly Press, 1922.

Howells, Mildred. *Life in Letters of William Dean Howells*. 2 vols. Garden City, New York: Doubleday, Doran & Co., 1928.

Howells, William Dean. *Criticism and Fiction and Other Essays*. Edited by Clara Marburg Kirk and Rudolf Kirk. New York: New York University Press, 1959.

_____. *Heroines of Fiction*. New York and London: Harper & Bros., 1901.

_____. *Literary Friends and Acquaintance*. 2nd ed. New York and London: Harper & Bros., 1910.

_____. *Literature and Life*. New York and London: Harper & Bros., 1902.

_____. *My Literary Passions*. New York: Harper & Bros., 1895.

James, Henry. *The American Novels and Stories of Henry James*. Edited by F. O. Matthiessen. New York: Alfred A. Knopf, 1968.

_____. *The Art of the Novel*. Edited by Richard P. Blackmur. New York: Charles Scribner's Sons, 1934.

_____. *Henry James Letters*. Edited by Leon Edel. Cambridge: Harvard University Press, 1975-

James, Henry. *James Letters*. 2 vols. Edited by Percy Lubbock. New York: Scribner, 1920.

_____. *The Notebooks of Henry James*. Edited by F. O. Matthiessen and Kenneth B. Murdock. New York: Oxford University Press, 1947.

_____. *The Speech and Manners of American Women*. Edited by E. S. Riggs and introduction by Inez Martinez. Lancaster, Pennsylvania: Lancaster House Press, 1973.

Johnson, Robert Underwood. *Remembered Yesterdays*. Boston: Little, Brown & Co., 1923.

Kaplan, Justin. *Mr. Clemens and Mark Twain, A Biography*. New York: Simon and Schuster, 1966.

Lehmann-Haupt, Hellmut. *The Book in America, A History of the Making and Selling of Books in the United States*. 2nd ed. New York: R. R. Bowker Co., 1952.

Lewis, Felice Flanery. *Literature, Obscenity and Law*. Carbondale: Southern Illinois University Press, 1977.

Light, James F. *John William DeForest*. New York: Twayne Publishers, 1965.

Longfellow, Samuel. *Life of Henry Wadsworth Longfellow*. 3 vols. Boston: Houghton, Mifflin & Co., 1891.

Lowell, James Russell. *Letters of James Russell Lowell*. 2 vols. Edited by Charles Eliot Norton. New York: Harper & Bros., 1893.

_____. *New Letters of James Russell Lowell*. Edited by Mark Antony DeWolfe Howe. New York: Harper, 1932.

Lynn, Kenneth. *William Dean Howells, An American Life*. New York: Harcourt Brace Jovanovich, 1970.

McCullough, Joseph B. *Hamlin Garland*. New York: Twayne Publishers, 1978.

Mencken, H. L. *A Book of Prefaces*. New York: A. A. Knopf, 1917.

_____. *The Young Mencken*. Edited by Carl Bode. New York: Dial Press, 1973.

Merwin, Henry Childs. *The Life of Bret Harte, With Some Accounts of the California Pioneers.* Boston and New York: Houghton Mifflin Co., 1911.

Milne, Gordon. *George William Curtis and the Genteel Tradition.* Bloomington: Indiana University Press, 1956.

Morse, John T,, Jr., ed. *Life and Letters of Oliver Wendell Holmes.* 2 vols. Boston and New York: Houghton, Mifflin & Co., 1897.

Mott, Frank Luther. *A History of American Magazines.* 5 vols. Cambridge: Harvard University Press, 1938-68.

Nowell-Smith, Simon. *Letters to Macmillan.* New York: St. Martin's Press, 1967.

O'Connor, Richard. *Bret Harte, A Biography.* Boston: Little, Brown and Co., 1966.

Olsen, Tillie. A Biographical Interpretation with *Life in the Iron Mills,* by Rebecca Harding Davis. New York: Feminist Press, 1972.

Page, Walter Hines. *A Publisher's Confession.* New ed. Introduction by F. N. Doubleday. Garden City, New York: Doubleday, Page & Co., 1923.

Paine, Albert Bigelow. *Mark Twain: A Biography. The Personal and Literary Life of Samuel Langhorne Clemens.* 2 vols. New York: Harper & Bros., 1912.

Papashvily, Helen Waite. *All the Happy Endings: A Study of the Domestic Novel in America, the Women Who Wrote It, the Women Who Read It, in the Nineteenth Century.* New York: Harper, 1956.

Parrington, Vernon L. *The Beginnings of Critical Realism.* New York: Harcourt, Brace & Co., 1930.

Pemberton, Edgar T. *The Life of Bret Harte.* New York: Dodd, Mead & Co., 1903.

Putnam, G. H. *Memoirs of a Publisher, 1865-1915.* New York and London: G. P. Putnam's Sons, 1915.

Randel, William. *Edward Eggleston.* New York: Twayne Publishers, 1963.

Randel, William. _Edward Eggleston: Author of the Hoosier School-Master_. Morningside Heights, New York: King's Crown Press, 1946.

Render, Sylvia Lyons, ed. _The Short Fiction of Charles W. Chesnutt_. Washington, D. C.: Howard University Press, 1975.

Ross, Danforth. "The Genteel Tradition: Its Characteristics and Its Origins." Ph.D. dissertation, University of Minnesota, 1954.

Samuels, Charles E. _Thomas Bailey Aldrich_. New York: Twayne Publishers, 1965.

Santayana, George. _The Genteel Tradition: Nine Essays by George Santayana_. Edited and Introduction by Douglas L. Wilson. Cambridge: Harvard University Press, 1967.

Sedgwick, Ellery, ed. _Atlantic Harvest; Memoirs of the Atlantic_. Boston: Little, Brown & Co., Atlantic Monthly Press, 1947.

Simpson, Claude. Introduction to _Sister Carrie_, by Theodore Dreiser. Edited by Claude Simpson. Boston: Houghton Mifflin Co., Riverside Editions, 1959.

Smith, Henry Nash. _Democracy and the Novel, Popular Resistance to Classic American Writers_. New York: Oxford University Press, 1978.

Smith, Henry Nash and Gibson, William M., with the assistance of Anderson, Frederick, ed. _Mark Twain--Howells Letters, The Correspondence of Samuel L. Clemens and William D. Howells 1872-1910_. 2 vols. Cambridge: Harvard University Press, Belknap Press, 1960.

Smith, Herbert F. _Richard Watson Gilder_. New York: Twayne Publishers, 1970.

Stedman, Edmund Clarence. _Life and Letters of Edmund Clarence Stedman_. Edited by Laura Stedman and George M. Gould. New York: Moffat, Yard & Co., 1910.

Stegner, Wallace. Introduction to _The Outcasts of Poker Flat and Other Tales_, by Bret Harte. New York: The New American Library of World Literature, Signet Classics, 1961.

Stewart, George R. _Bret Harte, Argonaut and Exile_. Boston: Houghton Mifflin Co., 1931.

Stowe, Charles Edward. _Life of Harriet Beecher Stowe_. Boston: Houghton, Mifflin & Co., 1890.

Stowe, Charles Edward and Stowe, Lyman Beecher. Harriet Beecher
Stowe: The Story of Her Life. Boston: Houghton, Mifflin &
Co., 1911.

Stowe, Harriet Beecher. Lady Byron Vindicated; A History of the
Byron Controversy from Its Beginning in 1816 to the Present
Time. Boston: Fields, Osgood & Co., 1870.

Tomsich, John L. A Genteel Endeavor, American Culture and Politics
in the Gilded Age. Stanford: Stanford University Press, 1971.

Turner, Arlin. George W. Cable, A Biography. Durham: Duke
University Press, 1956.

Tuttle, Donald Rouel. "Thomas Bailey Aldrich's Editorship of the
Atlantic Monthly, A Chapter in the Belles Lettres Tradition."
Ph.D. dissertation, Western Reserve University, 1939.

Walker, Franklin. San Francisco's Literary Frontier. New York:
A. A. Knopf, 1939.

Webster, Noah. Dissertations on the English Language. Boston:
printed for the author by I. Thomas & Co., 1789.

Wilson, Forrest. Crusader in Crinoline: The Life of Harriet Beecher
Stowe. Philadelphia: J. B. Lippincott Co., 1941.

Winter, William. Old Friends: Being Literary Recollections of Other
Days. New York: Moffat, Tard, 1909.

Articles

Alden, Henry M. "Fifty Years of Harper's Magazine." Harper's New
Monthly Magazine, May 1900, pp. 947-62.

Andrews, William L. "William Dean Howells and Charles W. Chesnutt:
Criticism and Race Fiction in the Age of Booker T. Washington."
American Literature 48 (November 1976): 327-39.

Atherton, Gertrude. "Why is American Literature Bourgeois?" North
American Review, May 1904, pp. 771-81.

Austin, James C. "J. T. Fields and the Revision of Longfellow's
Poems: Unpublished Correspondence." New England Quarterly
24 (June 1951): 239-50.

Badger, G. H. "Howells as an Interpreter of American Life." International Review, May-June 1883, pp. 380-86.

Bishop, William Henry. "Authors at Home. T. B. Aldrich on Beacon Hill, and Round It." The Critic, 8 August 1885, pp. 61-63.

Carpenter, Frederic I. "The Genteel Tradition: A Reinterpretation." New England Quarterly 15 (September 1942): 427-43.

Donaldson, Gilbert. "Thomas Bailey Aldrich." The Reader, May 1907, 657-65.

Duffey, Bernard I. "Hamlin Garland's 'Decline' from Realism." American Literature 25 (March 1953): 69-74.

Garland, Hamlin. "Sanity in Fiction." North American Review, March 1903, pp. 336-48.

Gilder, Richard Watson. "An 'Open Letter' About Editing." The Independent, 10 December 1896, pp. 1669-70.

_____. "Journalism and American Literature." The Critic, 7 February 1891, p. 71.

_____. "The Newspaper, the Magazine, and the Public." Outlook, 4 February 1899, pp. 317-21.

Gordon, Clarence. "Mr DeForest's Novels." Atlantic Monthly, November 1873, pp. 611-21.

Higginson, T. W. "Letter to a Young Contributor." Atlantic Monthly, April 1862, pp. 401-11.

Howells, William Dean. "An Autobiographical View of the 'Weekly'." Harper's Weekly, 5 January 1907, pp. 19-20.

_____. "Diversions of the Higher Journalist." Harper's Weekly, 26 December 1903, p. 2090.

_____. "George William Curtis." Harper's Weekly, 10 September 1892, pp. 868-70.

_____. "Henry James, Jr." Century Illustrated Monthly Magazine, November 1882, pp. 25-29.

_____. "Mr. Charles W. Chesnutt's Stories." Atlantic Monthly, May 1900, pp. 699-701.

Howells, William Dean. "A Psychological Counter-Current in Recent Fiction." <u>North American Review</u>, December 1901, pp. 872-88.

_____. Review of <u>Kate Beaumont</u>, by John W. DeForest. <u>Atlantic Monthly</u>, March 1872, pp. 362-65.

_____. Review of <u>Majors and Minors</u>, by Paul Laurence Dunbar. "Life and Letters." <u>Harper's Weekly</u>, 27 June 1896, p. 630.

_____. Review of <u>Miss Ravenel's Conversion from Secession to Loyalty</u>, by John W. DeForest. <u>Atlantic Monthly</u>, July 1867, pp. 120-22.

_____. Review of <u>The Poems of Thomas Bailey Aldrich</u>. <u>Atlantic Monthly</u>, August 1866, pp. 250-52.

James, Henry. "A Letter to Mr. Howells." <u>North American Review</u>, April 1912, pp. 558-62.

Koerner, James D. "Comment on 'Hamlin Garland's "Decline" from Realism'." <u>American Literature</u> 26 (November 1954): 427-32.

Monteiro, George. "William Dean Howells and <u>The Breadwinners</u>." <u>Studies in Bibliography</u>. Edited by Fredson Bowers. Charlottesville: Bibliographical Society of the University of Virginia, 1962.

Wideman, John. "Charles W. Chesnutt: <u>The Marrow of Tradition</u>." <u>American Scholar</u> 42 (Winter 1972-73): 128-34.